THE 10 REALLY *dumb* MISTAKES THAT VERY SMART *Couples* MAKE

A TORAH BASED GUIDE TO A SUCCESSFUL MARRIAGE

RABBI BEN TZION SHAFIER

The 10 Really Dumb Mistakes That Very Smart Couples Make

Copyright © 2021 by Rabbi Ben Tzion Shafier

All rights reserved: This book is protected by the copyright laws of the United States of America. No part of this book may be reproduced in any form or by any means, electronic or mechanical, including photocopying, recording, informational storage or retrieval systems, without written permission by the author, except where permitted by law, for the purpose of review, or where otherwise noted ary *dumb* MISTAKES THAT VERY SMART *Couples* MAKE

Contents

Prologue vii

Introduction x

CHAPTER 1: No Marriage Should Work 1

CHAPTER 2: Love is the Glue 23

CHAPTER 3: Respect First 48

CHAPTER 4: Happy Wife, Happy Life 66

CHAPTER 5: For Women Only 81

CHAPTER 6: A Woman's Need To Talk 109

CHAPTER 7: Women are More Sensitive 145

CHAPTER 8: Learning to Live Together 157

CHAPTER 9: Mind Blind 163

CHAPTER 10: You Become an Expert at
What Your Spouse Does Wrong 187

CHAPTER 11: Tools that Bond 197

CHAPTER 12: Attraction 226

CHAPTER 13: Appreciation 235

CHAPTER 14: Best Friends Who Love Each Other 259

CHAPTER 15: Why Couples Fight 281

CHAPTER 16: I Hate Criticism 312

CHAPTER 17: Closing Thoughts 336

Sponsorships 341

Prologue

Mr. ADHD Marries Miss Anxiety

THIS IS THE TALE of Shayna and Bentzi Cohen. Shayna and Bentzi are your all-American couple, both bright, talented, and successful. Both brought up in good homes. Both confident and goal oriented. And both a bit surprised with what marriage has brought them.

Here's Shayna's version: "Dating Bentzi was exhilarating. He was filled with energy, always moving. It gave me a sense of excitement and adventure. But after three years of marriage, his ADHD is driving me crazy. He's always late. He never puts things away. And he's constantly forgetting things—he'd forget the baby at the store, if I didn't remind him. Why can't he just get it together?"

Bentzi has his own take. "When we were going out, I felt like her knight in shining armor. She would get nervous, and I would step in to smooth things over. If something happened between her and one of her friends, I would calm her down. I felt noble and gallant, rescuing the damsel in distress. But now I feel like her anxiety is over the top. Every *erev Shabbos* is high drama—and she's the queen. Why can't she just calm down?"

Shayna and Bentzi spend the next 20 years trying to change each other, but neither of them are successful. *Why not?* they each wonder. *If only he would change,* Shayna thinks, *our marriage would be so much better.* Bentzi feels the same way. *If only she would change, life would be much more peaceful.*

They nobly persevere. They try this and that and the other thing. They talk, they coach, they plead, they demand. Nothing helps.

Finally, after 20 years, they both give up. Suddenly, their relationship improves. "Not sure why," Shayna says, "but he's just so much nicer to me these days."

"Not sure why," Bentzi says, "but she's just much easier to live with now."

And *then,* finally, they live happily ever after.

I call it a tale because everyone thinks, *that would never happen to me,* and they're the all-American couple, because it seems to happen to everyone – he and she each spend an inordinate amount of time and energy attempting to change the other. It never works. Time after time, couple after couple, it fails. The only thing they achieve is a lot of frustration and bad feelings on both sides.

The worst part is that often, the traits they are trying to change can't really be changed. ADHD is part the makeup of an individual. Being high-strung is a disposition — not something they chose and not readily malleable. While there are certainly coping strategies and techniques that people can and should use to manage more effectively, the fact is that there are many core tendencies that are inborn and just aren't subject to change.

We all understand this—until we get married. When it comes to our spouse, we feel a moral imperative to correct them, straighten them out, and make them better. Not only doesn't it work, it creates friction between couples. He feels aggrieved because she just doesn't change, and she feels victimized because he demands that she become someone she's not. Each one feels frustrated that their spouse won't change and hurt that their partner doesn't accept them for who they are.

This particular tale has a happy ending, because while Shayna and Bentzi certainly made one of the 10 Really Dumb Mistakes that Very Smart Couples Make, eventually they got it right. But unfortunately, not every story ends as well.

Introduction

"Forty days before a child is born, a heavenly voice proclaims, the daughter of so-and-so to so-and-so."
—Sotah 2a

IN THIS WELL-KNOWN STATEMENT, Rav Yehudah describes the concept of *bashert* (preordained). Even before we were put into this world, Hashem preselected the perfect partner for each of us. Your bashert is perfect for you. Together, you become a complete unit.

There's only one problem…

Reality.

In 1901, the divorce rate in the United States was about 6%. The vast majority of marriages succeeded. Currently, the divorce rate in the United States is estimated at about 50%. Even though the rate in the Torah community is nowhere near that, the number of marriages that fail has skyrocketed. Based on my work with hundreds of couples over the years and my discussions with *rabbonim*, marriage therapists, and chosson and kallah teachers, I believe that the vast majority of divorces in our community could have been avoided.

The purpose of this book is to help you understand how to make your marriage succeed. It will introduce the concepts, perspectives, and skills that a couple needs in order to achieve a fulfilling, happy life together. Together we'll examine some of the most common pitfalls – the 10 Really Dumb Mistakes That Very Smart Couples Make.

But first, a word of introduction.

My introduction to the institution of marriage

How did I become a marriage guru?

I am a talmid of the Chofetz Chaim Yeshiva, and I was a high school rebbi for 15 years. About 20 years ago, the Rosh Yeshivah, Rabbi Henoch Leibowitz *zt"l*, asked me to start a program for young working men. These were guys who had been in yeshivah – some had learned a tremendous amount and others hadn't learned much – who now found themselves in the workplace. The Rosh Yeshivah felt that there was no support for them. No groups. No organizations. Some didn't even belong to a *shul*. That's how The Shmuz began.

The Shmuz is a cross between an old-fashioned mussar shmuz, an inspirational seminar, and an advanced science class, that focuses us on a Torah outlook on life. We started in Brooklyn, then expanded to Queens; pretty soon the Monsey group was formed. I would travel in and give a mussar Shmuz once a week. In short order we expanded by adding morning kollels, night programs, and social events. It grew into a beautiful program.

As we grew, my role remained the same – to give the Shmuz. But a funny thing happened. The Shmuz always addresses real life issues and concepts that we're all are supposed to know but somehow don't pay much attention to. Because the Shmuz was so relevant, many of the guys who attended connected to me personally as their rebbi. I became their go-to for all serious life issues.

In the early years, most of these guys were single and the questions they asked were innocent enough. But as time went on, many of them got married. In the initial stages of marriage their questions were still pretty innocuous – how to deal with a mother-in-law or what to do when you have a difference of opinion with your wife.

But as time went on, the questions became far more complex. I had guys who reported that they were experiencing a lot of squabbling, quarrelling, and outright fighting. I found myself spending more and more time counseling couples.

But here was the problem: I didn't know what to say. At this point I had been happily married for about 15 years. I had been learning mussar for decades, and my rebbi had taught me a lot about the inner workings of a person and the trappings of the human personality. I felt well-equipped to deal with most of the questions that were brought to me. But questions about marriage were different. It was rare that it was just one spouse who had a problem – that he was selfish, or she was spoiled. Usually, they were both great people with fine middos. If you were to meet either of them you would say, "Wow! They'll make a great husband (or wife)!" But when these two amazing people got married, something was going wrong.

The question was, why? And more importantly, what to do about it?

I would love to say that I davened sincerely and a sudden stroke of inspiration hit me. But that's not exactly what happened. I took couples to marriage therapists, to couple's therapy, to psychologists – nothing helped. In fact, many relationships turned from bad to worse. We lost a number of those initial couples. Their marriages failed, and that also meant that I had failed. They looked to me for answers and I had none. They looked at me as their guide to leading a Torah life and I didn't know what to say.

I began doing whatever I could to study and understand the institution of marriage. I read sefarim that dealt with marriage.

I read secular books – pretty much every popular, well-known, secular marriage book. I began consulting with chosson and kallah teachers and rabbonim. After a while, I started to see patterns. I started trying different things. Not all of the advice I gave in those early years was brilliant. Some things worked, and some things didn't. But slowly, I was putting the pieces together. And after many years and counseling many couples, I think that I have an understanding of what a marriage needs, how to develop a marriage, how to identify the issues that are challenging a couple, and what to do about it.

That's what I present to you here: a system for creating a successful marriage. We'll start with a basic understanding of the nature of the relationship. Then we'll explore the perspectives, understandings, and tools to create a vibrant, loving marriage.

Before we get started, I would like to give you a sense of what you will and won't get out of this book. To do that, let's look at the larger question: why is it that until about 100 years ago, the vast majority of marriages succeeded, but now they fail?

Why Marriages Fail

I WISH THAT I could tell you that there is one single reason that marriages fail, and one solution. Unfortunately, that's not the case. But there are a number of general reasons why marriages stopped succeeding.

Everything is disposable

In the past, divorce was simply not an option. It was considered such a great failure on a personal level, and such a great embarrassment to the family, that to the average couple it just wasn't something even to be considered. That is no longer the case.

Once divorce became a viable option, it became almost a self-fulfilling prophecy. Until then, couples were forced to work on their marriage. When the inevitable differences came up, they had no choice but to make their marriage work. She learned to compromise, and he learned to be tolerant. She realized she couldn't always get her way, and he saw that his attitude was causing her pain. The social pressure to be married and the stigma of divorce forced them to stay together long enough to make the accommodations that are needed for any marriage to succeed. It is true that there remained unhappy marriages, but many couples did the work needed to create a satisfying relationship.

Today, there is little social or economic pressure for a couple to stay together. Just as tablecloths, plates, cups, and spoons are now disposable, so is marriage. You try it; if it works, great. If not, get rid of it and move on to the next.

I saw an example of this when I was in a restaurant with my wife. It was a Manhattan restaurant, and the tables were way too close to each other. We couldn't help but overhear a young man at the next table say to his buddies, "I got married too late. I should have gotten married earlier, that way I could have gotten my first marriage over with and started my next marriage while I was still young." The shocking part was that he wasn't joking, and none of his friends found his statement outlandish.

The sad reality is that it has become normal and acceptable to get divorced. With the first bump in the road, they're both out the door.

This is the current social and economic reality. The fact that there's an open door can stop a couple from doing the work that is vital to a successful marriage. This book won't change that.

WII-FM

Another issue that affects marriages today is that society as a whole is tuned into WII-FM: What Is In It For Me. Everything about the society we live in seems to scream that message, *What about me? What's in it for me?* Me. Me. Me.

It's been that way since you were born. Since you were an infant, your parents have always focused on you. What is the best school for you? Who are the best friends for you? What is the best camp for you? In which high school will you flourish? Which yeshiva or seminary is best for you?

Then you got married. Suddenly, there's another human being here; it's no longer only about what's best for *you*, but rather, what's best for *us*. There's another half of *us* who doesn't necessarily share the same interests, desires, and inclinations as you. There's another half of *us* who has different needs and looks at things differently. Suddenly, for the first time in your life, you have to learn to say, "I'm not going to do it my way because my spouse wants it done otherwise."

What makes this even harder is that we're also spoiled. There has never been a time in history when so much materialism and luxury has been available to the common man. The average tax-paying citizen in our society lives with more luxury than did the kings of England 200 years ago. And while that clearly is a great blessing, it also comes with a cost. A young man and woman getting married today have lived an extremely pampered life. They have never experienced deprivation. They have never had to work hard to contribute to the needs of their family. They've been brought up like rich kids and suddenly they're cut loose, without Mommy and Daddy to fulfill their every whim and desire.

Part of the reason that Hashem gave us the institution of marriage is so that we would learn to be less self-centered and develop the ability to put others' needs before our own. It's a process that takes years and necessitates changing your very nature. This book will address many aspects of this challenge, and give you tools to become "other-centered" instead of self-centered. But simply reading this book is not going to suddenly change you; that takes years and years of giving.

An Unwholesome Generation

The third reason that divorce is far more common today is that our society includes a larger percentage of unwholesome or emotionally unhealthy people than existed in previous generations.

In terms of material possessions and luxuries, our generation is the wealthiest that has ever existed. But our generation is also more emotionally fragile than any generation before. (A little piece of advice: if you want to earn a good living today, do anything in the mental health field. You can become a social worker, therapist, psychologist, or psychiatrist—it doesn't matter—you will have an unending stream of people knocking at your door, because there are so many people who are suffering from psychological and emotional issues.) People who suffer from psychological or emotional difficulties may believe that marriage will solve all their problems and bring them everlasting bliss ("Once I'm married, everything will be different"). But that almost never works. In fact, generally the opposite occurs – their situation becomes *more* difficult. You still have to deal with your issues, and those issues are usually exacerbated and amplified by their impact on the relationship. Marriage doesn't cure depression, anxiety, poor self-image, or OCD. The only thing that marriage cures is being single. Nothing in this book will change that reality.

But before you give up hope (and ask yourself why you're reading this book), there are some things that *can* be changed—and those things can make a critical difference in the success of any marriage.

A Chutzpah!

Many years ago, a young man asked me if I would be *mesader kiddushin* at his wedding. I told him I'd be honored to officiate, but I charge for my services.

"What do you mean?" he asked.

"My price," I said, "is that you and your *kallah* have to meet with me for three counseling sessions before the wedding."

I thought it was cute way of saying it. I wasn't asking for money. I only asked for their time. I wanted to give them some perspective that would start them off on the right foot, but more importantly,

I wanted them both to feel comfortable coming back to talk to me when issues arose in the future.

Shortly after this conversation, I met the *chassan*'s father at a simcha. He introduced himself and then said, "I just want you to know that I think you have a lot of chutzpah! You think my son needs premarital counseling? You think something's wrong with him?" He kept ranting until he was actually red in the face.

I was not *mesader kiddushin* at that wedding, but I did learn an important lesson. That father assumed that if you bring together a *chassan* and *kallah* who have good *middos* and who come from good homes, they'll "figure it out." They don't need a road map and they certainly don't need coaching. That may have been true twenty or thirty years ago, but not today. I say this from firsthand experience based on my involvement with hundreds of couples. The fact is that the majority of couples getting married today don't understand the basics of marriage. The main reason that so many marriages fail today is that a successful marriage is a lot more complicated than it looks.

And that's what I offer in this book: a roadmap to a great marriage.

Why You Need This Book

Imagine you have a wealthy uncle and on your 16th birthday he wishes you a happy birthday and hands you the keys to a brand-new car. There's just one problem: you've never driven before. And to be honest, you never really paid much attention to how to drive. But you think, *listen, it's not a big deal; everybody drives, it can't be that complicated.* You get behind the wheel and start the car. You press on the gas – it makes a lot of noise but doesn't go anywhere. You think about it and remember that you've seen drivers moving the stick thing around, so you try that. You put it into gear, press on the gas and smash! You hit the garage wall. *What's wrong with this thing?!* You start it again, put it into gear and smash into the other wall. After crashing around for a while, you learn to steer a bit and you manage to get onto the road. You have to make a left turn, but you're going a little too fast, and you hit another car.

All day long you're crashing into things because no one taught you how to brake, how to slow down, or really, how to drive. Eventually you conclude that either this car is a lemon, or this whole thing called driving is just not what it's made out to be.

That's how most people get married. They get behind the wheel of this car called marriage and everything's good—for a while. But then you hit some rough spots. He said this. She said that. Before you know it, things aren't going so smoothly. Strong words are said. Feelings are hurt. No one can figure out what went wrong. They each try whatever comes to mind, but it doesn't help. So they conclude that either their spouse isn't who they believed them to be, or this whole thing called marriage isn't so great after all. But the problem is that they were never taught how to drive. They were never taught the basic skills necessary for a successful marriage.

Marriage is a complex, intricate weave of personalities, needs and circumstances. You could be highly intelligent, organized, and a very nice person, but if you don't understand the mechanics of this relationship, you're going to get into trouble. There will be hurt feelings, bruised egos and unmet needs. And often, trying to make things better will only make things worse. Because while everyone knows that a marriage requires work, not everyone knows what that means. Work on what? Change what? Do what differently?

If you've ever played competitive sports, you know that the adage "practice makes perfect" isn't exactly true. Practice makes you better at doing what you're doing. But if you're doing the wrong thing, practice is only going to make you better at doing the wrong thing. So when you make a mistake in your relationship but you don't understand what you did wrong, you're inevitably going to repeat the mistake . Pretty soon you and your spouse are in a toxic cycle as you each keep repeating your mistakes, triggering each other over and over again.

Eventually, things get so bad that you go for help. But often, the help is anything but helpful. To understand why, let's go back to our car parable.

Getting Unhelpful Advice

Imagine that you do finally learn how to drive your car properly. As you're driving one day, you hear a strange noise coming from the engine. You're not sure what to do. Bring it to the mechanic? Maybe it's nothing? You mention it to your mother, and she says, "Listen, I've been driving for 35 years. I'll take it for a drive, and I'll tell you right away what it needs."

Hopefully, you'll very politely change the subject, because the fact that your mother knows how to drive, and maybe even drives well, doesn't mean that she understands how a car functions. It certainly doesn't mean that she knows how to repair it when it's not working properly.

This is another error people make about marriage. Since it's all straightforward—you just get married and it goes—if you ever have any trouble, all you need do is ask someone who's been married for a bit and they can give you all the guidance you need.

But the vast majority of the world doesn't have a clue about how marriage works—and certainly not what to do when marriage stops working. Most couples who come to see me really don't know what went wrong and what they should change, and typically the advice they were given was either not helpful or downright harmful.

To responsibly advise a couple struggling in their relationship, one requires many things. First, a clear understanding of the role of husband and wife in marriage, and how that applies in our day. Then, great wisdom to discern personality types and temperaments as they play out against each other in a relationship. Of course, one needs to understand the fundamental differences between men and women. And finally, they need the ability to home in on the core issue and not get caught up in the emotional machinations of the individual parties.

All these skills take years of experience to develop, but not many people have that kind of experience. There are also lots of marriage books on the market, but most books don't offer much wisdom (I have read many popular marriage books – some are helpful, some are mediocre, and some are downright damaging). All these resources have one flaw: they are based on someone's conjecture, based on a theory that may or may not be true and relevant. There are many conflicting thoughts, approaches, and opinions about what a marriage really needs, and that itself makes building a strong marriage more complicated than it ever was before.

The Roadmap

A successful marriage has three components: commitment, love, and learning to live together.

The commitment to the marriage comes from the recognition that Hashem chose you for each other, and He doesn't make mistakes. Love is what holds the marriage together on a day-to-day basis. But the third component is what gives many couples the most trouble: they are committed to their marriage and do love each other, but they can't figure out how to live together harmoniously.

There is a roadmap. Hashem gave us the Torah as the guidebook to life. The Torah encompasses every aspect of life and guides us in every single thing that we do. The Torah instructs us how to get up in the morning, how to go to sleep at night, and how to handle every activity in between. It teaches us how to conduct ourselves in the home, in shul, and in business. The Torah directs us in all our dealings, and it also guides our most pivotal relationship – marriage. Hashem created us; He alone knows the nature of man and woman; and He gave us the system to create a harmonious marriage and live together in peace and happiness.

Life is about growth, and growth takes a lot of effort, time, and focus. Marriage demands its own unique work and that work isn't always easy or intuitive. But with the Torah as our guide, a couple can, with Hashem's help, create a vibrant, beautiful marriage.

In this book, I will present that roadmap to you, and help you avoid the 10 Really Dumb Mistakes That Very Smart Couples Make.

Chapter 1

No Marriage Should Work

> **מדרש רבה בראשית פרשה סח פסקה ד**
> מטרונה שאלה את ר' יוסי בר חלפתא אמרה לו לכמה ימים ברא הקב"ה את עולמו אמר לה לששת ימים כדכתיב (שמות כ) כי ששת ימים עשה ה' את השמים ואת הארץ אמרה לו מה הוא עושה מאותה שעה ועד עכשיו אמר לה הקב"ה יושב ומזווג זיווגים בתו של פלוני לפלוני אשתו של פלוני לפלוני ממונו של פלוני לפלוני אמרה לו ודא הוא אומנתיה אף אני יכולה לעשות כן כמה עבדים כמה שפחות יש לי לשעה קלה אני יכולה לזווגן אמר לה אם קלה היא בעיניך קשה היא לפני הקב"ה כקריעת ים סוף הלך לו ר' יוסי בר חלפתא מה עשתה נטלה אלף עבדים ואלף שפחות והעמידה אותן שורות שורות אמרה פלן יסב לפלונית ופלונית תיסב לפלוני וזיווגה אותן בלילה אחת למחר אתון לגבה דין מוחיה פציעא דין עינו שמיטא דין רגליה תבירא אמרה להון מה לכון דא אמרה לית אנא בעי לדין ודין אמר לית אנא בעי לדא מיד שלחה והביאה את ר' יוסי בר חלפתא אמרה לו לית אלוה כאלהכון אמת היא תורתכון נאה ומשובחת יפה אמרת אמר לא כך אמרתי לך אם קלה היא בעיניך קשה היא לפני הקב"ה כקריעת ים סוף

Hashem is the matchmaker

A Roman noblewoman once asked Rav Yosi bar Chalafta, "In how many days did G-d create the world?"

"Six," Rav Yosi bar Chalafta answered.

"And since that time, what does G-d do?"

"G-d arranges matches. The daughter of this one to this one, the daughter of this one to this one."

"What?" said the noblewoman. "Even I can do that! I have many maidservants and many slaves. I can match them up in a heartbeat. What is difficult about that?"

Rav Yosi bar Chalafta responded, "If that is insignificant in your eyes, you should know that to G-d it is like splitting the sea."

This woman took it as a challenge, and that night she matched up one thousand male slaves with one thousand female slaves. The next morning, she went to visit her slaves, and she saw that one had a black eye, one had a broken arm, and another had a broken leg. She said to the first one, "What happened?"

"What happened? You gave me that ugly woman! I can't stand her."

She asked the second one, "What happened?"

"You put me together with that horrible man. I hate him."

Each of her servants told a similar tale. She went running to Rav Yosi bar Chalafta and exclaimed, "Your G-d is true. Your Torah is great. What you have said is true."

Rav Yosi bar Chalafta said to her, "Is that not what I told you? If you think it is easy to make matches, you should know that to G-d it is like splitting the sea." **(Breishis Rabbah 68:4)**

Making matches isn't simple

While there is much for us to learn from this Midrash, one point is clear: matchmaking is far from simple. Finding a man and a woman who are suited to each other, where her strengths compensate for his weaknesses, and his gifts balance out her limitations, is a lot more difficult than it sounds.

The most obvious reason is that people are different. Each of us has different talents, aptitudes, and abilities. We also have different shortcomings, failings and imperfections. We have different likes and dislikes, and all of us have at least a couple of things that we just can't stand. In addition, people have different temperaments. Every human being has their own "right way" of doing things—which is never the way that you or I would do them. Other people are either too uptight or too laid back, too disorganized or too much of a neat freak, always late or punctual to a fault. When you think about it, finding two individuals who can be happy while operating so closely together sounds practically impossible.

We certainly see this in other areas of life. If you own a successful business, at some point, you will probably find that you cannot do everything on your own and you'll need to hire employees. It's a great idea to hire people who are good at the things you're bad at; it's unlikely that you possess all the skills and knowledge to do everything needed to run a thriving business. So if you need assistance with financial controls, or marketing strategies, there are plenty of skilled people you can employ. Bring people onto your team—but whatever you do, don't take in a partner.

Almost every partnership fails. It might be five years, it might be 10 years, but almost every partnership ends, and most end badly. The reason is simple: People have different ways of thinking, different ways of viewing things, and different approaches. One guy feels that the overseas market is *the* area for growth; his partner feels that the domestic opportunity is much greater. He wants to take the business this way; his partner wants to take it that way. No matter how alike they seemed to be when they started out, these differences eventually make them incompatible, and it's only a matter of time before the partnership dissolves. (In fact, the only thing worse than taking in a partner is taking in a family member as a partner, because then when it breaks up, your business *and* your family are a mess.) The point is that even when two people are very alike in nature and character, and share the same goals and aspirations, when you join them together in a long-time venture, inevitably the partnership eventually fails.

A marriage is a lot more than 9-5

Yet when a man and a woman get married, they aren't merely becoming business partners who share their 9-5. They are sharing life—*all* of it. The little things and the big things. From the time they get up in the morning until they go to sleep at night. They are partners in everything they do: Where they live, how they keep house, what kind of car they drive, how they bring up their children, where they vacation, who their friends are, how they spend their money… And they do these things together day after day, all day—for the rest of their lives.

In theory, it should never work. There are just too many differences, too many points that they will disagree on, and to expect them to live together forever in peace and harmony just seems unrealistic.

If that wasn't bad enough, there's another factor that should make marriage practically impossible: By the time a couple gets married, he and she are two fully developed people. They were brought up in different homes and are accustomed to different ways of doing things. In his family, being sharply dressed and making a good impression was highly valued. In her family, it wasn't. She values being close to family, and he wants to move far away. Since he was a little boy, he always dreamed of an open home, where people could just come by anytime—but she is way too private for that. And now they get married, and instantly, everything they do, they do together. If he's late, it reflects badly on her. If she overspends, he has to deal with the bounced checks. These two fully developed, opinionated, and just plain *different* individuals are expected to take their two very dissimilar lives and mold them into one.

And there's one more factor that should make marriage totally unworkable.

In most businesses, the partners are fairly similar. They may have differences in personality, or approach; one might be more outgoing and the other quieter; but in their attitudes, priorities, and values, they are usually the same. That isn't necessarily true about marriage. In fact, the partners in most business arrangements are far more similar to each other than the partners in any marriage.

That's because most business partnerships consist of two men opening an advertising agency, or two women establishing a retail store. Men are pretty similar to men. Women are pretty similar to women. The problem with marriage is that it's a union between a man and a woman—and men and women are a bit different from each other.

Well, maybe more than bit different.

Men and women are very different

Men and women aren't different marginally or incidentally. They're not different in regard to a few minor details. They are different in almost every imaginable way. They are different in their natures, outlooks, and values. They are different in the ways they approach life, objects, and relationships. They are different in the ways that they behave, relate to each other, and communicate. They care about different things and talk about different things. They enjoy different things and have different interests. They even have different ways of speaking, and often have trouble communicating because they mean totally different things even when they say the same things. In fact, men and women are so different that you would almost think that they belong to different cultures or come from different planets.

Since the 1960s there has been a strong movement in Western culture to ignore the differences between men and women and to attribute them to socialization. Experts claim that girls care more about their appearance than boys because that's how their mothers brought them up, or that boys don't show their emotions because they were taught that it's not masculine. A huge propaganda movement has tried to convince us that men and women are the same, and if boys and girls were brought up the same way, they would think and act identically.

The problem with this theory is that it's wrong. Dead wrong. In fact, it couldn't be further from the truth. Men and women aren't different because they are taught to be that way. They are different because Hashem created them to be different. They have different roles to play in life, and to allow them to flourish in those roles, Hashem formed the fabric of a woman and a man very differently. My rebbi, Rav Henoch Leibowitz, zt"l, would often quote the Gemara ((insert source)) that says, "Women are a nation unto themselves." Men are one nation; woman are a different nation. They are vastly different.

Boy and girls are different

In his book *Emotional Intelligence*, Daniel Goleman describes a study that was conducted to define gender differences. The study consisted of taking two groups of public-school children, boys and girls, and asking them at different ages to name their best friend.

When the children were three years old, about 50% of the boys named a girl as their best friend, and about 50% of the girls named a boy as their best friend. At that stage of development, mixed-gender friendships were common.

When the children were five years old, they were asked the same question. At that age only 20% of the boys named a girl as their best friend, and only about 20% of the girls named a boy as their best friend. By this point, it had become less common for boys and girls to spend much time playing together, and so it was rarer to find a best friend from the opposite gender.

By the time the children were seven years old, not a single boy named a girl as his best friend, and not a single girl named a boy as her best friend.

Why is that? Because at three years of age, children are in the infantile stage of maturity and their differences aren't significant. Boys and girls like the same games, have the same interests, and play together nicely. By the time children are five years old, boys and girls are very different. Boys are running around, playing rough and tumble games, and if they do sit down, it's to play with "boy toys"—trucks, action figures, and guns. Those things have little appeal to girls, who are very busy telling secrets or playing house, things the boys have no interest in. By the time boys and girls are seven years old, they have so little in common that the idea of a best friend of the other gender is almost unheard of.

Their worlds separate further as the children enter second and third grade. Watch children at the local public school: When teachers ask their students to form two lines, there is usually one line of boys and another of girls. Boys and girls naturally end up at separate tables in the lunchroom. If a boy were to sit at one of the "girls' tables," he would be laughed at or called a girl by other boys. When the children are in the school yard during recess, the girls will be off on one side of the yard playing jump rope or hopscotch while the boys will be off to the other side playing tag or touch football. Even though the classes are mixed, it is rare to find boys and girls playing together. The two groups have moved off into their own worlds.

These differences don't diminish with age – they increase dramatically. Consider children at 12 or 15 or 17 – the differences between genders becomes progressively greater. By the time they reach adulthood, their paths have completely diverged, and they are totally different species living in vastly different worlds.

Which brings us to the great complication of marriage.

You start with a man and a woman who are brought up in different homes and are accustomed to doing things in very different ways. Then, despite the fact that most business partnerships don't last more than 10 years, you ask them to join together for life. Although the reality is that men and women are different in almost every way, you put them together for a short courtship, break a glass, say mazel tov, and from that moment on, they live in closest proximity and share every aspect of life. You expect them to stay together happily ever after, but logically, it simply shouldn't work. Every marriage should fail miserably.

But Hashem wants marriages to succeed, so He created a number of unique tools to allow a man and woman to bond together. One is infatuation.

Infatuation

Infatuation is that strange state that many young men and women go through in the early stages of courtship and marriage. Its effects are powerful. He looked into her eyes. She looked into his. Bam! Suddenly, a mild-mannered, sober young man is singing from the rooftops. A mature, balanced young woman gets that faraway look in her eyes and can't concentrate on a word anyone says to her. They each feel differently, view the world differently, and act differently than they ever did before. They are in the throes of infatuation.

Infatuation Plays an Important Role

Hashem created infatuation to allow men and women to get married and create enduring, loving families. To take two individuals from different backgrounds, with diverse natures and upbringings, have them meet for a short time, and then ask them to live together for the rest of their lives in peace and harmony should be impossible. Infatuation is a tool that helps couples begin the transition.

The State of Infatuation

Infatuation works like a drug. It affects your senses and changes the way you think and feel. When you are infatuated, everything is wonderful. The whole world is filled with happiness and joy. Scientific studies show that infatuation significantly affects the brain chemistry. Dopamine, serotonin, and adrenaline (neurotransmitters, which regulate mood), are greatly increased. The infatuated couple experiences a rush of adrenaline which causes a sense of elation and rapture. They are high. In fact, studies show that infatuation changes the chemicals in the brain in a manner similar to cocaine use!

Under the influence of infatuation, a person experiences a mix of euphoria, coupled with delusion, tinted with hysteria, filtered through a lens of mania. A psychologist might define it as mild psychosis. While in that state, they are very forgiving and tolerant of each other. They are accepting and patient, they fully enjoy each other's company and would rather be with their spouse than anywhere else. Their usual sharp, critical eye, highly observant in any other situation, is dulled, and they see everything in rosy, beautiful colors.

"His bad habits will never bother me."

"It's so cute how she's always late."

One the most potent effects of infatuation is to blind a person to any real shortcomings or flaws in their spouse.

He's Perfect

My wife is one of the sharpest people I know. Many years ago, when we were engaged, I was a bit surprised when I overheard her talking on the phone. "Look," she told her friend, "I know no one's perfect. Everyone has flaws. But I'm telling you, he's *perfect!*"

Now, I wasn't going to be the one to burst her bubble, but I knew that she was in for a rude awakening.

In this state of infatuation, a couple can begin melding their lives together without the normal friction that would occur between two such different people. Infatuation functions as a tool to help a couple begin their marriage.

But infatuation was designed to be a temporary stage. It was created as an assist, to help a couple get started. The job of marriage is to go on to build a bond of real love. If they build that bond, their marriage flourishes and thrives. But if they don't, things begin to deteriorate very quickly, because infatuation is always short-lived.

Like a Kitchen Match

Infatuation works like the sulphur on a kitchen match. When you strike the sulfur tip against the phosphorous on the matchbox, it ignites a flame. The sulphur gets very hot, very quickly. For a second or two it will flare up, just long enough to light the wood of the match. That flare wasn't designed to last. It was designed to start the fire — not to keep it going. If the wood catches, the flame did its job. If not, it shone bright for a short while, but accomplished nothing.

Infatuation works the same way. It allows the couple to begin; it starts the process. But then they must do the difficult work of creating a true bond of love. They need to become attuned to each other's needs; and learn to actually care about each other. They have to discover who their spouse is and what they need. And they need to get accustomed to overlooking the shortcomings, flaws, and idiosyncrasies of their spouse.

Many couples experience a moment of revelation. It might be two weeks after the wedding or two months after, but one morning either he or she (or sometimes both) wakes up and says to themselves, "Oh my gosh, I can't believe it. I made the biggest mistake of my life. I married the wrong person!"

It's true that they made a mistake – but not the mistake they think. Their mistake wasn't marrying the wrong person. They made a far more fundamental mistake: mistaking infatuation for love.

Infatuation Blinds, Love Binds

One of the key differences between infatuation and love is that infatuation blinds you. When a person is in the infatuation stage, it's easy to overlook a spouse's flaws because their strong feelings of attraction and happiness make them literally blind to the other's faults. If they see the problem at all, it seems minimal and inconsequential.

But love is not at all blind. When a person is in love, they are fully aware that their spouse isn't perfect, but they love them anyway. They accept them for who they are.

Infatuation fools you into viewing the person as someone they're not. Love allows you to accept them for who they are. These are two very different states.

You Think You Know Him

Find a couple who has been happily married for many years and ask them the following question: "Did you know each other before you were married?" They will almost always answer, "Not at all. The person I'm married to is very different than the person I dated."

Why is that?

Most often, it's because we get to know someone by creating a composite picture of them based on our interactions with them. We take our experiences with the person, and (often subconsciously) we review the conversations and exchanges – what he said, how he said it, and when he said it. Then we create an image of who that person is. It may be an accurate representation of *some* aspects of that person, but it certainly isn't the *whole* person. It's the truth—but not the whole truth. And sometimes it's not even true at all.

In 12th century England there was a law that a bride must appear before her groom without makeup. It seems that women back then wore their makeup so thick and heavy that it wasn't uncommon for a suitor to meet a young woman, agree to marry her, and then discover after the wedding that his wife looked nothing like the woman he had courted. As a result, a law was passed obligating a young woman to appear before her prospective husband at least once without makeup.

In a sense this happens in every marriage. No matter how well a bride and groom think they know each other, they don't. They have each seen limited aspects of the other, under specific circumstances, all within the controlled environment of dating. Everyone is on their best behavior, putting their best foot forward. And while neither one was pretending to be someone they aren't, both were showing only part of who they really are.

At the same time, they were infatuated. When a person is under the influence of that drug called infatuation, they act in ways very different than they would otherwise.

It's easy to like someone who is nice to you all the time. When he says, "She's the first person who accepts me exactly as I am," and she says, "He is so sensitive and sweet. He never says a single unkind word to me," of course they like each other.

She was completely accepting of him because she was too infatuated to see a single flaw. And he was also infatuated, so naturally, all of his words were kind and sweet.

But after a while the drug wears off and the music stops. Both of them go back to being who they really are, and each is suddenly a whole lot less tolerant and accepting. While they certainly knew each other before, it was as *a person acting unlike themselves.* And it's at that point that many couples experience a rude awakening. *Wait. Who is this person? Is this the same guy that I dated?*

Love Takes Time

That's why most older couples say they didn't really know each other before they were married. Even more revealing, if you ask them if the feelings they have toward one another are similar to what they felt when they were "young and in love," the answer, again, is almost always no.

If they are happily married, the emotions they share now are far deeper and more significant than when they first met. But those deeper feelings don't just happen. They grow when you work on your marriage. As a couple, they had to learn to overlook each other's shortcomings and flaws. They had to learn to accept the other person in all their glory as well as with their quirks.

Unfortunately, many couples never find out how things work. They walk down the aisle thinking, *We are so in love. If this is the way we feel about each now, how much more so in five years! Our marriage is going to be perfect.*

Love Isn't Infatuation Grown Up

They're making a mistake. They assume that love is infatuation that grew and blossomed. It's not. Many very happy couples, deeply in love, will tell you that they hardly felt any infatuation in the beginning stages of their marriage. And many couples who were deeply infatuated have only a weak bond of love a few years later.

Infatuation is a temporary state. When it was there it felt like magic, but after six months or a year, it's gone. For many couples this becomes a critical moment. Yes, they still feel very strongly about each other, but it's different somehow. Now she says to herself, "He leaves his socks on the bedroom floor – and it bothers me." She mentions it to him repeatedly. He thinks, "She's really demanding, and it's annoying." Each of them wonder, "What happened to our love?"

The problem was that they weren't in love; they were infatuated. Infatuation was created to start things off, and then it fades away and is gone — never to return.

The First Really Dumb Mistake in Marriage

This is the first Really Dumb Mistake That Very Smart Couples Make: They mistake infatuation for love. Infatuation isn't love—it's magic, and the magic wears off. When it's gone, the real work on the marriage starts.

There is, however, another Really Dumb Mistake that closely follows this one.

I Could Have Done Better

After a while, most people come to the realization that their spouse isn't perfect. It might be their mannerisms, intelligence, moods, or disposition, but the initial sense of "my spouse is perfect" tends to fade.

And then begin the comparisons.

A man may notice that there are women who are more attractive than his wife. A woman might see that there are men who make more money than her husband. Or it might be a particular behavior that becomes the issue. *Why can't my wife be as organized as that woman? Why can't my husband be as responsible as that man?*

Sometimes a husband or a wife might think back to when they were single: *So-and-so was always so neat and organized. That other guy I went out with was so much kinder.* Doubts start to surface – did I choose the right one? Maybe I "settled"? They might reach the conclusion that they "could have done better." *Not that I'm complaining. Not that what I have is so bad. But I could have done better, and then I wouldn't have to go through what I'm going through now.*

The interesting thing is that they may be right. It could be that if they had pursued that "other person," they might have married him or her. Hashem doesn't take away a person's free will. But the question is, if they had in fact married that other person, would their life be any easier? Would they be happier now?

To answer this question, let's use a parable. Imagine your sister gets engaged, the wedding date is set, and you realize that this is going to be a big splash of a wedding. Everyone who's anyone is going to be there, and you want to look your best. You start shopping for a dress. You shop and shop, and finally you find the perfect outfit. It's affordable, it looks great — it's even modest. Fantastic. You buy it. There's only one thing missing: the right pair of shoes.

Not a problem, you think. *It's still four weeks till the wedding, plenty of time.* You start searching. This store. That store. But you just can't find the right pair. You shop and you shop. Nothing. Your try Marshalls, TJ Maxx, DSW. Nothing. You start to get desperate. It's now a week to the wedding and still nothing. Finally, two days before the wedding, you're running errands with your sister-in-law and you stop into Macy's, and in the clearance section you see the most exquisite pair of shoes. They're perfect! And the best part — they're on clearance, 50% off. Wow! *Chasdei Hashem!*

There's only one problem — the shoes are two sizes too small. "But look," you say, "I can't just leave them. They're stunning!" So you buy them, take them home, and wear them to the wedding. After the wedding (and after two hours of dancing) you come home and take them off. Your feet are killing you. And you come to the recognition that the shoe can be gorgeous and match perfectly, but if it doesn't fit, it's going to hurt.

This is analogous to marriage. Before you were born, Hashem chose the perfect counterpart for you, with his strengths balancing your weaknesses, and your strengths balancing his. But you don't know if he's tall or short, fat or skinny. You don't know if he's introverted or extroverted. He might have a great sense of humor or be sort of bland. There's only one thing that you know: that he is the one that Hashem chose as the right fit for you.

When you were dating, you might have met someone smarter, taller, kinder, or richer than your spouse. If you wanted to, you might have succeeded in marrying that other person. But you would have suffered, because the best qualities in the world all put together into one person doesn't mean that he's a fit for you. Just like the shoe has to fit for it to be comfortable, in order to have a happy marriage, you have to find the one that is the right fit—for you.

A marriage is a complex weave of needs, emotions, and temperaments. Some personalities mesh; some clash. Some things get on your nerves till you just can't stand them, and some things somehow don't bother you at all—but you'll never know which are which until you've lived with the person for five years or more. The two partners come from different homes, have different upbringings, and have vastly different natures and dispositions. To find the right match for all the components that must fit requires the wisdom of . . . well, the wisdom of our Creator. And that's the point. Hashem chose the right one for you. You fit together like a hand in a glove. And while he may not be the best *bochur* in Lakewood, he is the best one for you. She might not be perfect, but she is perfect for you. Your spouse is handpicked by the One Who knows your nature and the essence of your personality—*this is the ideal match for you.* Could you have done "better"? Maybe — but "better" doesn't mean a better marriage, and "better" certainly doesn't mean that you would be happy together.

The Second Really Dumb Mistake

This is the Second Really Dumb Mistake that Very Smart Couples Make. They look around and say, "I could have done better," and they might be right. They might have been able to snag a person who has more of a specific positive quality, or doesn't have the shortcomings that their spouse has. And they think, *if only I had married him, life would be so easy. I would be so happy.* (What they forget is that this other guy has his own constellation of issues, shortcomings, flaws, and idiosyncrasies that make *him* difficult to live with. Just ask *his* wife).

It boils down to a question of bitachon. Do I trust Hashem? Do I trust that Hashem has chosen the ideal life partner for me?

Bitachon is something that we often talk about but seldom understand. The Chovos Halevovos explains that in order to have bitachon, there are two concepts a person must fully embrace. The first is rather simple: that Hashem loves me more than I love me. As much as I want what's best for me, Hashem wants it even more. As much as I want everything to turn out well, Hashem wants it even more. As much as I want my success, Hashem wants it even more. As much as I love myself, Hashem loves me even more.

That concept isn't that difficult to accept. It is the second concept that gives us the most trouble in life. And that is, accepting that Hashem knows better than me what is for my best. As much as I think I know what I need, as much as I think I know how things should turn out—Hashem knows better.

This is something that trips us up all the time—the "I know what I need" game. *I need to marry that woman. I need to get that job. I need my child to get into that school.* And so I speak to my Creator, I beg, I beseech, I implore: *Please, Hashem, please! It's so important. I need it. Please.* But for some reason Hashem just doesn't listen. So I start making deals with Him. *Hashem, if you grant me this, I will... learn Daf Yomi/give money to tzedakah/work on not speaking lashon hara.* But Hashem still doesn't listen. You feel frustrated. *I don't get it! I need it. It's good for me. It' so important. Hashem, why aren't You giving me this? Are You angry with me? Do You have complaints about the way I'm acting? Hashem, why?!*

The thought that maybe, just maybe, this isn't what's best for you, never crosses your mind.

How many times has it happened that you hear someone claim that they absolutely, positively have to marry a certain woman? And they don't. She marries someone else. And then five years later he hears that the term *mentally unstable* is an understatement to describe her condition. *I have to get my kid into that class.* And six months later he finds out that there was another child in that class who would have been the worst possible influence on his child. "Trusting Hashem" doesn't mean trusting that Hashem will do my bidding. (In fact, that's a bit like saying, I'm the master and Hashem, You're my servant.) "Trusting Hashem" means trusting in His master plan, trusting that Hashem knows better than you do what is best for you.

The simple reality is that in so many of the choices that we make in life, we don't have an option other than to trust Hashem, because we simply don't know what's right. I have limited sight. I can see two weeks, maybe two months, into the future. But I have to make decisions that will impact things for years to come. When choosing a spouse, probably more than in any decision you will ever make, it's obvious that what's required is trusting Hashem, trusting that Hashem has chosen the ideal match for you as you are today, and for you as you will be throughout a lifetime of growth and change.

That should be a sobering thought, because I don't know where I'll be in twenty years. I don't know what type of person I'll become or how I'll feel about things then. People change. Circumstances change. Things happen. What was important to you when you were younger isn't what matters to you as an older person.

When you get married, you fully intend that it will be for life. But you are woefully ill-equipped to make that choice. You don't know the future. You don't know who you'll be then. And you certainly don't know who the person you're marrying will be. You are both works in progress, changing, growing and charting unknown waters. The decision of who to marry is something that any thinking person will quickly realize is above our capacity. You just don't have the ability to make such a choice. The only sane way to make that choice is by trusting Hashem. Trusting Hashem means trusting that Hashem knows exactly what you need now and for the future, and that Hashem chose the ideal partner for you.

The real challenge occurs when things aren't going smoothly. Every married person has to make adjustments to accommodate their spouse. (In fact, most people will constantly be adjusting and readjusting to their spouse's ever-changing way of doing things all throughout their lives.) And that's when the inevitable questions arise. *Did I choose the right one? Wouldn't I have done better with someone neater, or quieter, or more outgoing, or less confident, or not as showy, or more easygoing?* It's at this point that a person has to return over and over to this concept: Hashem knows what's best for me better than I do, and Hashem has handpicked this spouse for me –my ideal match.

The concept goes much further. When we think about "bashert," we usually interpret that to mean that before you were born Hashem searched through the millions and millions of possible matches and said, "Yes! This one. This the perfect match." And while it's true that you and your bashert are a perfect match, that isn't exactly what happened.

The Raishis Chachama, quoting the Zohar, explains that before you were born, you and your spouse were one unit—one neshama. Hashem split the neshama into two. Each of you were put into a body with a given temperament, nature, and inclinations. You were each assigned to different families and upbringings for your formative years. You were given the mission to find your other half, join together, and create a union. When you are each finished your jobs here on this earth, you will join together again as one unit to share in the World to Come forever. (Spoiler alert: if you think you spouse is going to gehonom, I have some bad news for you.)

The real work in marriage is to become whole. You were once one unit; you will again be one unit. Your job here is to learn to live in peace and harmony and overcome the obstacles that stand between you.

That is the Torah's concept of marriage. And I can think of no better illustration of this than the words I heard my rebbi, Rav Henoch Leibowitz, zt"l, say at the funeral of his wife.

The most romantic words that I ever heard

The Rosh Yeshiva was seven years older than the Rebbetzin and for much of his life he wasn't well. It was unspoken but expected that the Rosh Yeshiva would pass on before his wife, but that's not what happened.

The Rebbetzin took ill and passed away a short time later. At the funeral, the Rosh Yeshiva got up to speak. He began by saying, "Everything we did, we did together. We built the yeshiva together. We worried about the talmidim together. Everything we did, we did together. We went to Eretz Yisrael together. When I was sick, she worried about my health more than I did. I didn't have to worry about my diet or my medicine; she did everything for me. Everything we did, we did together." He must have repeated that expression more than a dozen times.

Then, in closing, the Rosh Yeshiva said, "I said a *hesped* (eulogy) for my father. I said a *hesped* for my mother. But I can't say a *hesped* for my wife. If I say a *hesped* for my wife, it is as if I were saying a *hesped* about myself. I can't do it." And he sat down.

With those words, he defined a Torah marriage. One unit. Together. Not an *I* and a *you*. Not *my needs* and *your needs*. One unit.

To make a marriage work, that commitment is the first key. It stems from an understanding that your spouse is the right one for you – part of you, perfectly formed for you.

Hashem knows what is best for you, and he brought the right person to you. Now you have to do the work to make your marriage as wonderful as it was meant to be.

There is, however, another mistake that many very smart couples make. It sounds similar to this one but is infinitely more damaging.

Chapter 2

Love is the Glue

> **ספר בראשית פרק יח**
>
> ט) וַיֹּאמְרוּ אֵלָיו אַיֵּה שָׂרָה אִשְׁתֶּךָ וַיֹּאמֶר הִנֵּה בָאֹהֶל:
>
> And the angels said to Avraham, "Where is your wife?" And he answered, "She is in the tent."
>
> **רש"י על בראשית פרק יח פסוק ט**
>
> בב"מ (דף פ"ז) אומרים יודעים היו מלאכי השרת שרה אמנו היכן היתה אלא להודיע שצנועה היתה כדי לחבבה על בעלה
>
> "These were ministering angels. They knew where Sarah Imeinu was. They asked the question to point out that she was modest, in order to make her more beloved to her husband."

Three angels come to visit

Parshas Vayeira opens with Avraham Avinu looking up and seeing three "men" standing on the horizon. He runs out to greet them, bows down in the sand, and says, "Please do not pass by your servant." He brings them back to his tent, gives them water, and runs to prepare an elaborate meal for them. He brings it to them and stands over them like a waiter as they eat.

At which point one of his guests says to him, "Where is Sarah, your wife?" Avraham answers, "She is in the tent."

An inappropriate question

The question sounds inappropriate. Here this man welcomes you into his house, graciously takes care of your every need, and while eating his food, you start probing about his personal life. "Where is your wife?" It sounds almost crude.

Rashi explains that these were *malachei hashareis*, the highest level of angels. They knew exactly where Sarah Imeinu was. Why did they ask this question? Because they wanted to make her more beloved in his eyes. They knew that Avraham would answer, "She's in the tent; she's not out in the public eye." By saying that, he would reinforce his recognition of her as a modest woman—and that would increase his appreciation for his wife, making her more beloved to him.

Why were the angels so concerned?

This is difficult to understand. We are not dealing with newlyweds. This isn't a couple of kids beginning their marriage. We are talking about Avraham Avinu and Sarah Imeinu at an advanced stage in their life—she is 90, and he is 99. At this point, they have been married for 74 years (*Yalkut Shimoni*). Why were the malachim so concerned with making Sarah more beloved in Avraham's eyes?

To make the question stronger, let me add an observation.

One of the biggest impediments to a happy marriage is self-centeredness. When every issue starts with me, ends with me and is about me, I am a difficult person to be married to.

Here we are dealing with two of the most other-centered people that ever lived. Avraham's life was focused on what he could do for others. Sarah's existed to support her husband. For both, there was no consideration of "what's it in for me." These were two incredibly refined and sensitive people – two perfect tzaddikim. Each one focused on the other's needs. Every expression was weighed and measured. Every interaction between them was guided by the question, *how will my spouse feel about this?* The peace, harmony, and love in that marriage is difficult to imagine. The Maharal writes that in the course of history there never was such a deep bond between husband and wife as there was between Avraham and Sarah.

That's why this Rashi is so difficult to understand. The malachim make an unusual comment just to make Sarah more beloved in Avraham's eyes; why was that needed? Why would they do something almost inappropriate just to make Avraham appreciate her a bit more?

And this problem becomes far more compounded when we focus on what followed.

A slip of the tongue

The angels tell Avraham that this time next year, Sarah will have a son. Inside the tent, Sarah overheard what they said and laughed in her heart, saying, "I can no longer have children, and my husband is too old."

Hashem then says to Avraham, "Why did Sarah laugh, saying 'I (Sarah) am too old'?"

Rashi points out that wasn't what Sarah said. She said, "I can no longer have children, and *my husband* is too old." When Hashem repeated Sarah's words, He changed them, saying that she said *she* was too old.

Rashi explains that Hashem changed her words for the sake of peace. Hashem didn't want Avraham to hear that his wife said that he was too old to have children. So Hashem changed her words to say that she called herself old.

Just so we are clear, "Hashem changed the words" is a polite way of saying, if such a thing could be, that Hashem lied. The halacha is that you are allowed to lie for *shalom bayis*. Hashem changed the truth so that Avraham shouldn't hear that his wife said he was old. Hashem lied for *shalom bayis*.

Avraham wasn't a fragile person

My Rebbe, Rabbi Leibowitz, zt"l, asked a question on this Rashi. When Chazal tell us that we may "lie for the sake of peace," they mean that in some instances we may lie to prevent hurting someone's feelings. Since people are sensitive, in some circumstances we are allowed to lie to protect their feelings and prevent strife.

Let's imagine that Hashem didn't change the story and told Avraham that his wife said, "My husband is too old." Do you think Avraham Avinu would have fallen to pieces? Do you think his reaction would have been, "Oy vey, my wife called me an old man! I can't bear it"?

Avraham didn't grow up in a juvenile-centered culture. He didn't live in a society in which youth was revered. Quite the opposite: in the world that he lived in, advanced age meant wisdom, sagacity, and life experience—things greatly respected. Every year of his life was another huge change in himself and in the world. His days were precious, and he invested them wisely. He is now standing at a point in his life where he is a gigantic human being and has lived every year of his life in perfection. He is not embarrassed about his age. (He also went on to live another 76 years;

clearly he wasn't *that* old.) So why did Hashem feel it necessary to change Sarah's words?

To answer this question and the question of why the angels wanted to make Sarah more beloved in Avraham's eyes, we need to understand the Torah's view of marriage.

What is the Leading Cause of Divorce Today?

What is the leading cause of divorce today? If you ask your friends, parents, neighbors, or coworkers this question, I suspect you will get a string of answers:

- Problems with the raising children
- Money problems
- Religion
- In-laws

I don't think any of those are true.

While all of these may be issues in a marriage, *none* of them are significant causes of divorce. There is only one major cause of divorce today – *fighting*.

Now, you may say, "Clearly, a couple that gets divorced is going to be fighting. But isn't it the issues that cause the fights? It's the question of how we discipline the children, or how we spend our money, or how we deal with your parents, that causes all the bickering."

But that is not correct. It's not the *issues* that cause fights. It's how the couple *deals* with the issues that defines their relationship. It's not the children or the money, or the religion, or the in-laws that cause the trouble. It's how the couple negotiates their differences over these issues that determines the success or the failure of the marriage.

In many very successful marriages, the couple has differences over major issues.

Irreconcilable differences

Studies show that 70 % of successful, longstanding marriages have *irreconcilable* differences. An irreconcilable difference is a major life issue where he needs one thing, she needs another, and there is no possible compromise. If he has a thriving business in New York City, and she has severe allergies and needs to live in San Diego, there is no middle ground. Chicago won't help either of them. If she wants to send the children to a *chassidishe* school, and he wants them brought up *litvish*, you can't compromise and have the kids running around with curly *payos* on one side. There is no solution that will satisfy both of them. And these issues never go away. They remain part of a couple's life throughout their marriage. Yet despite the existence of this kind of disparity, most happily married couples are able to create a longstanding, harmonious union.

Even more eye-opening, studies show that about a third of all the issues that couples fight about, big or small, have no compromise position. It's either your parents' house for the Seder or mine. We paint the living room green or blue, but mixing the two isn't an option. Yet despite these differences, many couples are able to maintain a loving, happy relationship.

Because two mature, reasonable people can figure out a way to deal with most anything that life throws at them. Sometimes my way, sometimes your way, but we're in this together and we'll work it out. And if we can't, there are always plenty of people who are older and wiser to guide us.

That's the key: as long as we're in this together. As long as we're partners, working together.

What's the secret to maintaining that sense of togetherness?

Predicting divorce

Dr. John Gottman, a leading marriage researcher, spent thirty years studying couples in depth. He has developed a method to predict whether a couple will divorce, and he is right 94% of the time.

His method is simple. He asks a couple to come his "lab" and he studies their interactions very carefully. He asks them to have a discussion about three issues in their marriage: one neutral, one mutually pleasing, and at least one flash point—something they find themselves often disagreeing about. While these discussions are happening, he monitors the emotional responses of the couple. To do that, he sits them down in two specially wired chairs facing each other. He monitors their blood pressure, pulse and respiration rate. He also videos the entire visit and reviews the recording afterward.

He's looking for a particular reaction: contempt.

Contempt is not quite hatred, not quite anger; it's the rolling of the eyes, that "what's wrong with you" look, that many couples exhibit. Dr. Gottman explains that if he sees a ratio of more than one reaction of contempt to five reactions of approval, the marriage is in danger. Unless they do something to change their relationship, it is almost certain to fail.

Contempt is such a clear indicator of a marriage in jeopardy because it's the opposite of love. And love is vital for a marriage. When there is love in a marriage, the couple is tolerant, accepting and forgiving of each other. Little things don't bother them. They know about each other's flaws, but it's okay. They are friends, so they look out for each other, and they compensate for the shortcomings of their spouse. That doesn't mean they won't have issues and struggles—they will—that's just a part of life. They will also disagree and maybe even fight. But they are one unit, together facing the challenges of life. They adjust to one another and somehow work out all of the challenges life sends their way.

If, however, the love in the marriage starts to weaken, things unravel quickly. The natural forgiveness and tolerance disappears. The couple begins to annoy each other and get on each other's nerves. Pretty soon each one feels they are being wronged, and they belittle each other (either aloud or just in their head). Under these circumstances, they see their spouse's flaws everywhere they look. Before long they start carping, complaining and criticizing, and become very difficult to live with. At this point everything is an issue, from who takes out the garbage, to who pays the bill, to what time we leave… Life will provide an endless stream of things to fight about, and fight they will.

The success or failure of a marriage pivots on this one issue—a bond of love. If the basic climate of the marriage is love, then even flaws are viewed in the context of love. *He's a good guy. Granted, he has flaws, he does things that I prefer he didn't—but he's still a good guy.* If the love in a marriage starts to wane, then you start hearing things like, *"He's a creep! He never does anything right. And the one time he did do something right, it was for the wrong reason and in the wrong way!"*

When a relationship hits that point, it doesn't matter how aligned the couple is in their thinking, goals and aspirations. It doesn't matter how much they love their kids and want to give them a wholesome upbringing. Squabbling and bickering is inevitable, they will grow further and further apart, the downward spiral will only worsen, and unless they correct their course, their marriage is doomed.

In short, the success or failure of a marriage depends on the love in the relationship. That doesn't mean that they will always be madly, passionately in love, and it doesn't mean they won't have ups and downs. It means that if the emotional connection is strong, they can weather all storms and manage whatever life throws at them. But if the love weakens, they are in trouble.

Hollywood got it right – but backwards

Hollywood got it right—love is the essence of a marriage, and a marriage without love is doomed. The only problem is that Hollywood got it 100 percent backwards.

In Hollywood, a man falls in love, so he gets married. After a while, he falls out of love – so he gets unmarried. Love comes. Love goes. Life goes on. On to the next one.

From a Torah perspective, we don't marry for love. We marry because Hashem has a master plan for Creation and each individual in it. Part of that plan is that a man and a woman belong together, sharing life, supporting each other, and working together as a complete unit.

In the Torah-based world, a man and woman are each incomplete. Half a car isn't very useful. Nor is half an oven or half a table. When a man and a woman are single, they are half a unit. When they marry, they are now complete and ready to take on their mission in this world. But it takes the right man matched to the right woman to complete each other.

Before you were born, Hashem chose the perfect match for you. You and your spouse fit together perfectly, and you are destined to share life together as one. When you are searching for your spouse, you are searching for the person that Hashem designed to be your match. Love is not part of the search process.

However, if you don't foster the love and keep it alive once you are married, the odds of your marriage succeeding are slim to none. In the heavy traffic of life, there are just too many issues, problems and difficulties for a marriage to survive without love.

In that sense Hollywood got it right – the lifeblood of a marriage is love. While we don't marry for love, it is the glue that keeps the marriage alive, and if there isn't a powerful bond of love in your marriage, it's unlikely that the marriage will last.

> *Love doesn't determine who I marry, but*
> *a marriage without love will fail.*

This seems to answer our questions about Avraham and the angels.

Why the angels asked

In a sense, the angels were repaying Avraham for his kindness. They asked the question, "Where is Sarah?" so that Avraham would answer, "She is in the tent." That would reinforce to him how modest she was, and that would make her more beloved in his eyes. They were giving him the gift of increased love in his marriage.

There are two key concepts here.

The first is that love in a marriage isn't static. It is either increasing or decreasing, but it never just maintains status quo. Because of their superior wisdom, the angels recognized the necessity of love in a marriage, and recognized that any increase is something worthy, holy and worth striving for—even if it meant that on some level they would overstep their bounds. Because the relationship between a husband and wife is based on love, and that relationship is one of the most precious entities in existence.

This is something that a couple has to be constantly aware of and focused on. The fact that things started well is nice, but the question is, how are things now? If you aren't actively working on maintaining the love in your marriage, it will naturally weaken.

But there is another concept that might be as significant, which explains why Hashem had to change what Sarah said.

If Avraham and Sarah were on this lofty level of love and bonding, what would have happened had Hashem repeated to Avraham exactly what Sarah said – "you are too old"? Why did Hashem change her words?

My Rebbe, Rabbi Leibowitz zt'l, explained that of course Avraham wouldn't have been broken by those words. But they might have made an ever-so-slight impression. They might have been felt by Avraham, and on some level, he might have been hurt. *My wife feels I'm too old to have a child.* And while it certainly wouldn't have led to anger or harsh words, it might have cooled, on even the smallest level, the powerful love that Avraham felt for his wife. Even this slightest degree of hurt and pain between spouses was significant enough for Hashem to change Sarah's words—to lie.

This is the second point: The relationship between husband and wife is very delicate and requires great care. Any increase is greatly valued, and any decrease can have grave effects. Anything that you do to increase the love in your marriage is good, right, proper, and holy. And anything that might damage it is worth avoiding even at great cost. We might think that cultivating love is frivolous or inconsequential—certainly not worth spending lots of time on. Yet Hashem Himself felt that even a tiny cooling of that love was significant enough for Him to change Sarah's words.

The second key to a successful marriage is working on increasing love and eliminating those things that damage that love. If a couple does this, they are well on their way to a happy home.

And, would be easy to have a beautiful, longstanding, successful marriage—if not for a few more *really* dumb mistakes that *very* smart couples make.

The 3rd Really Dumb Mistake

Imagine you meet an old friend you haven't seen in years. You barely recognize him—he's huge. When you were kids, he was a toothpick. Now he's 100 pounds overweight, chain-smokes, can barely move, and looks haggard.

"Shmiel," you say, "you look terrible!"

"I know, I know," he responds. "But what can I do? I love to eat. I hate exercise. And I'm so busy that I don't get more than three hours of sleep a night."

"But Shmiel, what about your health?"

"My health? My health?! It's lousy. I get sick all the time. I can barely walk up a flight of steps. I have zero energy. But what can I do? It's Hashem's will that I suffer. It's what Hashem wants. And if Hashem wants it, I accept it."

Shmiel is not the baal bitachon he thinks he is. His declining health is probably not what Hashem wants for him. While Hashem orchestrates everything in creation, He gave us a part in the equation—our *histadlus* (effort). In the simplest sense, *hishtadlus* means to live our lives in the ways of the world. To earn a living, we are supposed to get a job. To stay healthy, we are supposed to eat properly, exercise and keep our stress levels down.

Before a person is born, Hashem determines the perfect life setting for them: rich or poor, healthy or sick, and how many years they will live. Provided they do their part, Hashem arranges their life setting as it was intended to be. But Hashem doesn't take away *bechirah* (free will). If a person decides not to work for a living, he'll probably go hungry. If a person decides to jump off the Brooklyn Bridge, most likely he'll die That doesn't mean it was predestined to be—rather, it was a consequence of his choices. If someone chooses a lifestyle that includes extreme stress, obesity and chain-smoking, and suffers a heart attack at age 35—don't go blaming Hashem.

People in lousy marriages often blame Hashem. *I guess this is what Hashem wants for me. I was born to suffer.* What they fail to recognize is that just as good health depends on proper choices, so does a successful marriage. To stay physically fit, you have to do your part, and to have a good marriage you also have to do your part. "Your part," in this case, includes working on the marriage and keeping the relationship alive and vibrant.

Sadly, many couples find themselves in a stagnant relationship and can't figure out why. It started out so well. When he looked at her and she looked at him there was magic in the air. Now they find themselves wondering what happened to the passion, the fun, the love.

I have seen this over and over again.

The Courtship Must Continue
I respect my husband, but...

I got a phone call from a woman. She was very troubled. "Rabbi," she said, "thank you so much for taking my call. I have something very important that I need to speak to you about."

"Sure," I said. "How can I help?"

"I don't know how to say this… It's my husband. I mean… he's responsible. He's very involved with the children… He davens, he learns. I guess you could say he's everything I always dreamed of in a spouse…"

"So far it sounds pretty good." I said. "What's the problem?"

"The problem is I don't love him. I mean, I respect him, I recognize that he has many great qualities, but I just don't love him."

"I see. Tell me, how many years have you been married?"

"About ten."

"Do you have children?"

"Yes. Thank G-d, we have five children."

Having been down this road many times before, I had a hunch as to what the problem was, so I said, "Let me ask you, how many times did you and your husband go out last month?"

"How many times did we go out?"

"Yes. How many times did you go out? But I don't mean to a wedding or to a bar mitzvah or to a dinner. I mean, how many times last month did you and your husband go out alone, on a date—just the two of you."

"Um… I mean… I… We didn't."

"I see. What about the month before that?"

"Um…We didn't."

And the month before that?"

Silence.

"And the month before that?"

Silence.

"Okay. What about last year? How many times did you go out last year?"

Silence.

"What about the year before that?"

Silence.

I said, "If you were to ask me, it's obvious why you feel distant from your husband. It's because you're not spending much time together. To maintain a relationship with your husband, you need to spend time bonding and connecting. You need to be renewing that sense of love and affection in your marriage. And a big part of that is spending time together."

"But our goals are so alike," she said. "We both want the same things. And we do spend time together, we share our whole life.

Bringing up our children, taking care of all the things that go into keeping a Jewish home…"

"That's wonderful," I said. "But if you don't keep that bond of love in your marriage it's going to go from bad to worse, and pretty soon you won't be sharing much at all with your husband. If you want to improve your marriage, the first thing you have to do is to spend time together as a couple. What I want you to do is plan a time next week when you and your husband go out and just spend three hours together, just to talk, to connect."

She was quiet for a while and then said, "What would we talk about for three hours?"

From good to fair to bad

Unfortunately, this phone call is typical. A couple gets married and things go well for a while. As newlyweds, they only had each other, so there was plenty of time to talk and bond. Granted, they had things to work out, but they were both present and emotionally involved. Then along comes a baby, and now there's feeding and diapering, bathing and dressing. A few more years and a few more kids, and now add in homework and playdates, birthdays and simchas. Soon a whole new set of obligations crop up and there are also community responsibilities and board meetings, PTA and chesed committees. As the years pass they spend less and less time together, and before they even realize it, gone is the passion, gone is the sparkle. Their marriage goes into autopilot, just getting by, until they find themselves occupying the same house but living in different worlds.

Neither of them have changed. Their values or outlooks have not changed. They're just busy with life. And some five or ten years down the road, they find themselves wondering, "What happened to the passion? What happened to the love? What happened to our marriage?"

What happened was that they stopped spending time together as a couple, they stopped enjoying each other's company, and they stopped working on the romance in their relationship.

And this is the third of the Really Dumb Mistakes that Very Smart Couples make: They stop working on the love in their marriage. They forget that love is the glue that holds a marriage together.

The Role of Romantic Love

Hashem created a number of tools to help a husband and wife bond and view themselves as one. The first tool is infatuation. The second tool is romantic love. Romantic love is like infatuation in the sense that it involves the attraction between husband and wife, but it's very different.

Infatuation is instant. Romantic love takes time. Infatuation has a limited shelf life; it allows a couple to begin the process of marriage, then it vaporizes and is gone. Romantic love always functions as a catalyst for connection. Unlike infatuation, it doesn't expire. But the biggest distinction between infatuation and romantic love is that infatuation doesn't take work—it just happens. She looked into your eyes and you were smitten. Romantic love requires focus and intention. It's a little bit like exercise: you may enjoy it, but it takes discipline to keep doing it.

Most couples are pretty good at romance during the courtship stage – it's the love notes, the gestures, the compliments and the calls in the middle of the day. The problem is that once they're married for a while, they stop doing those things that brought them close to each other. Rav Pam, zt'l, Rosh Yeshiva of Torah V' Daas, used to say, "The courtship must continue."

Rekindling the spark

To maintain a marriage, a husband and wife need to keep the spark glowing. The only way to do this is by spending time together as a couple, talking, bonding, connecting, and enjoying each other's company. And part of that is going out together.

"Going out" means going out: Leaving the house, and the issues, and the problems, and the bills. It means getting a babysitter and going out as a couple.

To be clear, "going out as a couple" doesn't mean running errands, or doing chores, or going to see your in-laws. It means spending time alone. Without an agenda. Without talking about the kids, or finances, or any of the other thousands of issues that arise. And it doesn't mean going out to mark anniversaries and special occasions. It means a date night, every week.

As simple as it sounds, one of the most effective ways to improve the quality of your marriage is to make a religious ritual of going out once a week. *Religious* because it safeguards your *shalom bayis*, and *ritual* because otherwise it will fall by the wayside in the busyness of life, and two months or two years later, without understanding quite why, you'll find you and your spouse growing apart.

And there's one more thing.

I was working with a couple who were having serious problems in their relationship. After much cajoling, I got them to agree to go out, and because I knew their lifestyle, I added one proviso—no smartphones. If the babysitter must be able to reach you, take an old flip phone. They both agreed to this condition. Later I asked the husband how it went.

"It was okay."

"Okay?" I said. "What do you mean?"

"Well, she was texting her friends all night."

"Wait, I thought you guys agreed no smartphones."

"We did. She took an old Blackberry that she still had lying around." (I didn't even know you could still get service on those—apparently, you can.)

So let me say it clearly: "going out as a couple" means spending an evening with your spouse without answering the phone, texting, looking at your e-mail, checking WhatsApp, TikTok, or LinkedIn. It means spending an evening with your spouse and not "chatting" with other people; spending an evening with your spouse and just connecting.

We can't afford a babysitter

This one of the easiest steps in keeping a marriage on course, but often it's met with great resistance. A couple will come to speak to me because things between them aren't great, I'll make this simple suggestion, and I'll get a host of reasons why they can't possibly do this.

"We can't find anyone to babysit."

"My husband works crazy hours."

"We can barely afford to live. Who has extra money for going out?"

Even after I explain how vital this is for the health of the marriage, many times my words just don't penetrate. At that point, I'll look the couple in the eye and say, "Let's do a quick calculation. If you went out every week this year, and had to pay for a babysitter and whatever activity you guys did, what would the total cost be?"

Usually, the husband will give me a dollar amount.

"Good." I say. "Now how much does it cost for lawyer's fee, alimony, childcare and the cost of running two households? If you compare the two, its much less expensive to go out once a week. And a whole lot more pleasant!"

The strange thing is that it's so simple, yet so few people do it. And there's always a reason:

"What about my chavrusah?"

"I just started a new business."

"We simply don't have the time."

For each reason not to go out, the same answer applies: Just figure out how much time it takes for the custody battles and the legal fights over which school the children should attend, and then add in the time it takes to be a single parent shuttling kids back and forth between two households, and you'll quickly see that going out once a week is the most efficient use of your time.

Yet over and over, when I tell a couple that this is vital to their marriage, I get pushback.

I can't leave my children

One of the reasons that mothers give for not being able to go out is because it's not fair to the kids.

"My kids need me at night."

"If I'm not there, who's going to make sure that Ruchie does her homework?"

"No one else can get Shlomie to go to bed."

The sad part of this argument is that while it comes from a good place, it doesn't account for a basic fact of life: The single greatest gift you can give your children is a secure, happy home. And maybe the single greatest trauma to a child is to grow up in a home where the husband and wife are constantly fighting, or worse – they divorce. To a young child, Mommy and Daddy are the center of gravity. You are their source of identity. You are their world. If Mommy and Daddy separate, the very fabric of your child's existence crumbles. You might as well tell them that heavy objects will no longer fall, and the sun won't rise anymore.

People like to promote the idea that children are resilient and they'll adapt to the situation, but living through a divorce and the years-long custody issues following is traumatic. Being brought up in happy home is probably the single biggest ingredient in a child becoming a wholesome, well-developed person.

So if you are legitimately concerned for your children and want what is best for them, you should do everything in your power to make your marriage as vibrant as it can be. And if the cost is leaving them once a week, it's well worth it. Even if Ruchie doesn't know every Ramban in Chumash, she'll function very well in life. And even if Shlomie only gets a 70 on his math test, he'll be okay. But if their family comes apart—then all bets are off.

Rescuing Your Marriage from Your Children

Your marriage has to come first— before anything else. Before work, before social obligations, before learning and before community responsibilities. And before any other relationship. Your marriage comes before your parents and in-laws. The Torah says, "Therefore, a man leaves his father and mother, and clings to his wife." (Bereishi 2:24) When you got married, you left your family of origin. Your parents are no longer the center of your concern.

And not only does your spouse come before your parents, your obligation to your spouse comes before your children.

As strange as it sounds, you may have to rescue your marriage from your children. If you've just recently gotten married, you won't know what I'm talking about. But if you have children, you know that children are the single greatest obstruction to shalom bayis. They compete for your time. They complicate romance. They get in the way of everything that's going to bond you together as a couple. Obviously, they're a tremendous bracha, but their needs are great and will infringe on your marriage -- unless you learn, as a couple, to set boundaries. *Tuesday night is Mommy and Daddy's time to go out.*

If you cannot set boundaries, your marriage won't succeed. You have to take back your marriage from your children. You must dedicate time to your marriage, even at the expense of your children's homework. Even at the expense of them thinking it's not nice that you left them with a babysitter. (It also happens to be the greatest investment you can make toward their future.)

Does It Really Matter?

I've worked with countless couples who find themselves fighting constantly and aren't even sure why. They have the same life goals and ideals, they are both dedicated to their family, and both really want this marriage to work, but by the time they get to me they feel hopeless—ready to throw in the towel. Yet their differences aren't that great, and things used to be good between them. They once had a solid marriage, and they recall fondly their time together as a young couple in love. Oddly enough, nothing significant changed. He didn't start drinking. She didn't start gambling. Nobody went off the *derech*. The only thing that happened was that they stopped working on the relationship and they drifted apart.

That's when things started slipping. She said something. He took it the wrong way. She was hurt, so she replied in kind. One thing led to another. Voices were raised, things were said. Both walked away feeling betrayed and mistreated. This happens even in great marriages. The problem is when there isn't enough of a connection to mend the damage and get things back on track.

So the downward spiral begins.

Once it's him. Next it's her. Misunderstandings are met with sharp words. Retorts and barbs are exchanged, countered with accusations and complaints. Those complaints are refuted with counterclaims and allegations, on and on, until, over time, two people who were once lovers, confidants and the closest of friends, find themselves at war.

It should never have gotten to this point. Had their relationship been close, long ago they would have made amends and moved on. But they were distant. The usual tolerance and acceptance that carried them through the first stages of their marriage were gone. It's inevitable that in the course of daily life a husband and wife will hurt each other. They won't intend to, and they may not even realize it, but it's just too close a relationship, and there are just too many things going on, to always avoid hurt feelings. Being offended, or disappointed, or feeling that your spouse is insensitive to your needs, is just part of marriage – even the best marriages. The key is where you go from there. Are you able to repair the damage? Are you able to get back on track?

When a couple is close and there is respect and love in the marriage, there is tolerance and forgiveness. She knows you love her, and when you honestly explain that you didn't mean things the way she heard them, she can accept it. For your part, you can get past your hurt at being attacked for no reason, because you feel she really cares. As a couple, you can move on.

But if you are distant, then you don't feel you can trust her enough to be open and admit you were wrong. She feels too vulnerable to let it go, out of the fear that it might happen again. So each of you walk around hurt, with open wounds caused by your spouse.

Then, next time something comes up (and there's always a next time), you are even more distant from each other, and it's even more difficult to repair the damage. You start saying things like, "She's always picking fights."

"He's so insensitive."

"Nothing makes her happy."

"He couldn't care less."

"She's always looking for things to complain about."

"He's distant, cold, and uncaring."

Each of you have good reason (at least in your own mind) to be judgmental, intolerant and unforgiving of the other.

Soon, the relationship devolves further:

"After what she said to me, how can I ever forgive her?"

"He just proved that he's heartless. I don't think I can ever get past this."

The marriage is in deep trouble.

It didn't have to be this way. If there was a strong connection and bond between you, your feelings may have been hurt—but you would have been able to move on. Slowly, you'd be able to come together again, and your commitment, connection and love for each other would have been stronger.

I can't possibly stress this enough:

The success or the failure of your marriage is dependent on the love you feel for each other.

If there is a climate of love and affection in your marriage, you are friends who are understanding of each other and willing to overlook mistakes. The minute that climate of love slips, it's inevitable that each of you will feel wronged and taken advantage of, and it won't be long until both of you become smallminded, petty and vindictive. At that point, anything is enough to set the house on fire.

Love in marriage is vital; it's the grease of the wheels and the glue that keeps everything connected. But it isn't a constant. If you don't work on it, it will wither.

Love takes time. Love is the sweet notes and the e-mails, the texts and little gifts, the cards and the letters—all the things that a couple in love should be doing. You should be having an ongoing *love affair* with your spouse. It also means getting away—regularly. A couple should do their best to take a mini vacation every three months. It doesn't have to be for a week, and it doesn't have to be an exotic island destination. A simple hotel getaway for a few nights is enough. The idea is to make time for you as a couple. Make it the priority that it's supposed to be—not just during the first few years, but throughout your marriage. (Once there are kids in the picture you may have to adjust this, but vacations alone as a couple should always be part of your life.)

This is the easy part of working on marriage. It's enjoyable, it doesn't cause any emotional pain, and the results are dramatic. The only thing it requires is time and focus. *And more than any other single issue, this will likely determine the success of your marriage.*

Unfortunately, many otherwise smart couples make this grave mistake: they let the love dwindle and they suffer the consequences. And this is the **third Really Dumb Mistakes that Very Smart Couples Make**: they forget that love is the glue of a marriage. And real love takes work, commitment, time and dedication, and needs constant renewal.

So while the commitment to the marriage is the first pillar to a successful marriage, and provides the drive to keep working on the marriage, the love in the relationship is the second pillar and that is where much of the work needs to be focused—but it's not hard. The third pillar, learning to live together, is far more demanding. Many couples succeed at creating and even maintaining the bond and connection in their marriage. They truly love each other. The problem is that they can't live together.

To make it possible to live together, we need a system, a structure to deal with the multitude of issues that a couple will face throughout the course of life.

Chapter 3

Respect First

Two Not-So-Similar Scenes

I want you to imagine two not-so-similar scenarios.

The first one:

A young couple are walking down the street. He trips. Immediately, she says, "Oy! Are you okay? Are you hurt?"

That's scenario one. Here's scenario two:

The same young man and woman are walking down the street. Suddenly, he trips. This time her response is, "What's wrong with you, *klutz*?"

What's the difference between these scenarios?

The first one is when they were *chassan* and *kallah*. The second one is when they've been married for three years.

And she just committed the 4th really dumb mistake smart couples make.

The Formula for a Successful Marriage

> **רמב"ם יד החזקה הלכות אישות פרק טו**
>
> יט) וכן צוו חכמים שיהיה אדם מכבד את אשתו יתר מגופו ואוהבה כגופו
>
> *The Sages commanded a man to honor his wife more than himself and to love her as he does himself.*
>
> כ) וכן צוו חכמים על האשה שתהיה מכבדת את בעלה ביותר מדאי ויהיה לו עליה מורא ותעשה כל מעשיה על פיו ויהיה בעיניה כמו שר או מלך מהלכת בתאות לבו ומרחקת כל שישנא וזה הוא דרך בנות ישראל ובני ישראל הקדושים הטהורים בזיווגן ובדרכים אלו יהיה ישובן נאה ומשובח
>
> *The Sages commanded a woman to honor her husband exceedingly and to be in awe of him and all that he says, she does. And he should be in her eyes like a prince or king... This is the way of daughters of Israel and sons of Israel who are holy and pure, and in these ways it will be pleasant and praiseworthy.*

The Rambam gives us a formula for a successful marriage.

> "Our Sages commanded that a husband must respect his wife more than himself and he must love her as much as himself. Likewise, they commanded a wife to treat her husband with exceeding amounts of honor, treating him as if he were nobility. If a couple does this, their union will be beautiful and praiseworthy." (Rambam Hilchos Ishus 15:19)

In these short statements, the Rambam codifies the principles of marriage. Each partner has a part to play. He has his role. She has her role. Provided they each do their part, their marriage will flourish.

This Rambam is the foundation to a successful marriage.

Let's begin with the husband's role. He has to:

1. Respect his wife more than he respects himself, and
2. Love her as he does himself

Please note the order: Respect her more than himself and love her like himself. It sounds like respect comes first, as if it were more important than love. But didn't we just get through an entire chapter explaining that love is the glue of marriage? That without it the relationship would fall apart?

Why does the Rambam put respect first?

I'll love you for a thousand years—not

In the counterculture revolution of the 1960s the word "love" got bounced around like a ping-pong ball.

"Love. Love. Love. All you need is love."

I don't think that word means what they think it means.

"I met a beautiful girl and I fell in love. She didn't have to say a word. I just looked in her eyes and I felt love."

No, you didn't. You felt lust. You felt attraction. Your raging hormones were set off by a combination of novelty, desire, and infatuation that comes and goes like the wind.

"Her beauty outshines the sun. Oh, how deep is my love for her."

Till she gets a pimple and gone is your "love." (Or along comes someone younger and prettier, and you've found an even truer love.)

"I'll love you for a thousand years."

Right. In six months, he's going to leave her for someone else, because lust/infatuation has a shelf life and their "love" was based on it.

What's happening here is that people use the word love when they really mean lust, desire, or infatuation. They are mistaking the engine for the car. Desire and physical attraction are powerful driving forces that Hashem created to bring a husband and wife closer. But they are *tools*, not ends in themselves. The goal is a deep connection and attachment—love. Attraction may bring a man and woman toward each other, but it isn't love. Desire may bring a couple closer, but it isn't love. And even romantic love, which is so often confused with actual love, is anything but. Romantic love is possessive. *I want her and no one else can have her.* But real love is about giving, taking care of her. *I want the best for the one that l love.*

We have become so accustomed to misusing the word that it has lost all meaning.

When a 17-year-old says he loves his car, he doesn't love the car; he loves himself, and he loves what the car does for him. When someone says, *I love pizza, I love jogging, I love NY*, we don't even blink. But it's clear that the word has lost any significance.

The real issue is that the world doesn't understand what love is.

I love fish

Reb Leib Chasman once saw a talmid eating fish with a bit too much gusto. He said to the talmid, "I see you love fish." The talmid said, a bit sheepishly, "Yes, Rebbe. It's true, I love fish." To which Reb Leib Chasman replied, "You don't love fish. If you loved the fish, you would dress it up, take care of it, and make sure it was well-fed. You don't love fish—you love yourself."

Real Love

This illustrates a fundamental mistake people make about love.

When a young couple falls in "love," the man sees in the woman someone whom he thinks will meet all of his physical and emotional needs. The woman sees in the man someone whom she thinks will meet all of her physical and emotional needs. They are seeking gratification and they believe that this person will provide it to them. They're focused on what they're getting. But that's not love. Love is giving. Love is being concerned for the good of another.

Love means an actual bonding, connecting and caring. Being devoted to another person, not because I gain pleasure from it, and not because I desire her, but because I truly wish the best for her. I want what's good for her. I am here for her.

If you want to see real love, watch an older couple who are completely devoted to one another. Their children are all grown and out of the house, and they are alone—together. Their attachment is powerful. They care for each other. They look out for each other. They almost live for each other. Their connection is love. The youthful excitement of young lovers is a part of their past. Long gone are the moments of hot passion and lust. I assure you that at 85, she no longer looks like she did at 25. It doesn't matter—those tools are no longer needed. They served their purpose; they accomplished their goal. They helped a man and woman meld. Now they are one—dedicated, devoted, committed to each other.

I know a man who would go to the nursing home every day to visit his wife. Sadly, his wife had dementia and no longer recognized him. Nevertheless, he would go there every morning and spend the day with her, caring for her, helping her with her needs, being there for her. When someone asked him why he spent so much time there when she didn't even recognize him, he said, "How can I not be there for her? She spent a lifetime taking care of me." He continued doing this every day for five years until she died. That's love.

It's not a what's-in-it-for-me love. Not an am-I-getting-my-needs-and-desires-met love. It is a love of giving and caring, devotion and commitment. Real love.

That type of love doesn't just happen. It's not instant. It's not automatic. It requires focus, intention, and hard work. To understand how one achieves that lofty level of devotion to another, we need to understand "love" on a more fundamental level.

What is love?

To define love, let's look at the most instinctive type of love—the love of a parent for a child. When a mother holds her newborn child, we assume that she feels intense emotions. If we'd ask her, she would likely say, "I love my baby." But what is that feeling? What is it that she is experiencing? How would we know that she truly loves her baby?

One way of recognizing what she is feeling is by watching how she acts toward her baby. If her baby was crying and she callously looked on and didn't do anything, we would say, "That mother doesn't care! It's obvious that she doesn't love her baby."

That would be the first indicator we would look for. If a mother feeds, clothes, and fulfills all her baby's needs, it is clear that she cares about the baby.

But caring alone isn't enough to prove that she loves her baby.

Imagine that the mother was tired or had to go somewhere for a few hours. She puts the baby down and says, "I'm off duty now." Without assigning anyone to care for the baby in her absence, she simply leaves. We would conclude that this mother does not love her baby. A mother who loves her baby will take responsibility for the baby's welfare. It's not just a function she performs. It's her responsibility to ensure the baby's welfare at all times.

But even responsibility is still not proof of love.

The primary role of a parent is to provide what is the best for the child. A child is a diamond in the rough. The role of parent is to help polish that diamond. To do that, one has to respect the child as an individual.

Sadly, there are parents who do things, not for the good of the child, but for their own image. Instead of considering what is in the child's best interest, they make decisions based on what the neighbors will think, or how they'll feel facing their family. If we saw a mother shoehorning a child into the image of what was socially acceptable, without taking into account the welfare of the child, we would know the mother may love herself, but not the child.

So the final element we would look for, the behavior that would prove the mother's love, is *respect*. If we saw that a mother cared for the child, took responsibility for the child, and respected the child as an individual, then we would know conclusively that the mother loves the child.

Those are the three elements of love:

- A deep sense of *caring* about the other person
- A sense of *responsibility* to do whatever you can to help that person
- *Respecting* them as a person, not relating to them simply as someone to serve your needs and desires

That's a pretty good working definition of love.

But not all love is the same.

A man may be a son, brother, father, uncle, nephew, and friend. A woman may be a daughter, sister, mother, aunt, friend, and niece.

In each relationship, the degree and expression of love will be different. In each, the amount of care, the type of responsibility, and the extent of respect will vary.

But marriage is a unique relationship.

First, it is the closest. The Torah says, "He shall leave his parents' house, cling to his wife, and be one flesh." (Bereishis 2:24…) The Ramban explains that this means that in marriage, a man and woman view each other as one body—one entity. As close as you may be to your parents or siblings, those relationships are eclipsed by the sense of attachment, bonding and commitment that you have toward your spouse. My father, a"h, would regularly refer to my mother as "my better half." Much more than a cliché, it defines the relationship – two halves of one unit.

With any other person, you share a part of your life—with your spouse, you share your whole life. You may enjoy spending time with your brother, but when you're done, you go back to your own life. You still spend time with your parents, but your time with them is limited, it's just one part of your day.

By contrast, a husband and wife join their existence together. Their dreams and aspirations. Their goals and hopes. Their home, their possessions, their food, their money. It is by far the most inclusive relationship—no other relationship even comes close. Chazal tell us that a woman only dies to her husband. He is the one who is most affected by the loss, because with her death he loses a part of himself.

However, the greatest distinction between marriage and other relationships is that the love is not guaranteed. You will always love your parents. You will always love your child. You will always feel attached to your siblings. But when it comes to your spouse, you have to actively protect that love. Otherwise, it can disappear.

And while marriage is the closest connection between two people, it is also the most delicate.

In all other relationships, love just happens, and it remains. As great as a mother's love is for her child, it isn't something that she works on. It just occurs. Hashem wants children to be brought up with care, so He created a maternal instinct in women. Granted, it is a huge undertaking to bring up a child. Some children have very difficult personalities and they seem to do everything possible to make you dislike them, but despite that, you will still love them. You may have a tough time living with them, but that sense of devotion will always be there. It is *your* son. It is *your* daughter. A mother will give up her life for her baby. There is nothing the child did to deserve that devotion. And there is nothing the mother thought about or decided that made her feel that way. A mother's love is natural and instinctive.

All family relationships work this way. The love you feel toward your sister wasn't something that you planned. You didn't wake up one day and say, "I think it would make life sweet if I felt a sense of affinity toward my siblings." You grew up together. You shared life together. You just feel connected. You might work to make that relationship better, but that love wasn't something you chose.

Same for the love that a child has toward his parents. A young child identifies himself as the son of Mr. and Mrs. Goldstein; it's who he is, how he walks into the world. As he matures and forms his own sense of identity, his parents are his roots. They are a part of who he is and he is part of them. The love is inborn.

But marriage is very different. First, you only met your husband once you were both mature, fully-developed individuals. A year before the wedding, you didn't even know who he was. You'd never met him, never saw him, knew nothing about him. You certainly weren't connected to him. He wasn't part of your family. And now you're supposed to join with him and become one unit. This bond has to be actively created—it won't just happen. *We fell in love, and then forever and ever we remained in eternal bliss.* That might work in fairy tales, but not in real life. In real life, learning to love another person takes real commitment, devotion, and hard work.

In marriage, the love is not automatically there, like it is between parents and child, or between siblings. In marriage, love waxes and wanes and is dependent on how the couple interacts. If the relationship is good, the love is strong. If the relationship falters, the love withers.

And the relationship is very sensitive. A husband and wife each have expectations, wishes, and desires. When their expectations aren't met, the reaction is, "My spouse doesn't care about my needs. She doesn't care about me." Because you are so connected, you are also so vulnerable. When you're feeling exposed and your spouse isn't there for you, it's your best friend who is letting you down, and that hurts. When you unthinkingly make a hurtful comment, it cuts her to the core. With a wrong word, or the smallest expression, feelings are hurt. Not just hurt – deeply wounded. How could you, my lover, friend and confidant, do that to me? Because the relationship is so delicate, the passage from bliss to agony happens in the blink of an eye. If a couple doesn't repair the damage, the relationship can spiral downward. No longer do they feel attached, no longer do they feel bonded. They become antagonists, each battling for their needs—and the love vaporizes.

Respect is a Tool

Hashem gave us tools that create love. We've discussed infatuation and romantic love; there is also friendship, appreciation, physical touch and intimacy. All of these bring a couple closer—none are a goal in themselves. These are simply tools that help a husband

and wife care for each other and feel a sense of responsibility for each other's welfare. The end goal is love.

Respect is another tool. It doesn't always get top billing. Respect doesn't sound as interesting as love or as exciting as romance. Yet in some ways, it's more important.

If I don't respect you, I can't be dedicated toward your welfare. I can be attracted to you, I can use you, I can get what I want out of you, but to dedicate myself to the betterment of another I have to fundamentally respect that person for who they are—not what they can do for me.

I believe that is why the Rambam listed respect first.

Love is the glue in marriage. It's a necessity. But *first* you have to respect your spouse. The minute the respect starts to decay, the love does as well. Love can't exist without respect.

Full-Time Shmuz?

Rabbi Alter Chaim Henoch Leibowitz, zt"l, and his first Rebbetzin did not have children. Their *talmidim* were their children. As a result, I spent a lot of time in their home and got to see their marriage up close. I don't think anyone treated the Rosh Yeshivah with more reverence than the Rebbetzin did. I never heard her call him by his first name. She always addressed him in third person, "the Rosh Yeshivah." She would wait on him hand and foot. When he wasn't feeling well, she watched over him like a hawk. Her life was the Rosh Yeshiva.

When I was about 40, I came to a crossroads in my life. I had begun the Shmuz, under the Rosh Yeshivah's direction, as a side project. As the Shmuz grew in popularity, I was still a high school Rebbi, and between spending time with the talmidim, preparing shiur and my new responsibilities with the Shmuz, it was difficult to balance everything. I made an appointment with the Rosh Yeshivah to ask for guidance.

When I arrived at their apartment, the Rebbetzin greeted me and led me to the dining room. As the Rosh Yeshivah and I sat down to discuss the issue, I could hear the Rebbetzin washing dishes in the kitchen. After explaining my dilemma, I asked the Rosh Yeshivah what he felt I should do. He thought a moment and said, "I think you should stop teaching. I think you should leave the classroom and devote yourself full-time to the Shmuz."

At that point, I heard the water in the kitchen stop. With a towel over her arm, the Rebbetzin walked in, looked at the Rosh Yeshivah and said, "Is the Rosh Yeshivah sure?"

The Rosh Yeshivah put his hand on his beard, thought a moment, and said, "Yes. Yes. I think so."

I want you to appreciate what had just transpired. The Rosh Yeshivah was a bastion of *daas* Torah. He was one of the *gedolei Yisrael*. His *talmid*, a *rebbi* in his own right, comes to ask a life-altering question. The Rosh Yeshiva thinks and then states his opinion. Then, without invitation, his Rebbetzin walks in and questions his judgment. In some circles that would be considered mutiny! He's the Rosh Yeshivah. He's a *gadol*. Question his judgment? Chutzpah!

But that wasn't the way Rosh Yeshivah viewed it. He heard her opinion, thought about it, and calmly said, "Hmm. Let me think… Yes, I think so." At that moment, I understood their marriage. As much reverence as the Rebbetzin had for the Rosh Yeshivah, he had for the Rebbetzin.

Unfortunately, that level of respect isn't the norm.

Child vs. Spousal Disrespect

Did you ever notice that children are very polite outside the house? When they're home, you can't get them to lift a finger. When they visit friends or relatives, they're quick to help. The neighbors tell you how helpful they are, and you wonder whose kids they're talking about. At home, you can't get them off the couch.

At home, kids feel relaxed — maybe too relaxed. That's why they often don't put forth their best. Outside, in public, they know that people are watching, so they act very differently. As adults in marriage, we are much the same. After a few months, or a few years, our common courtesy and basic respect toward each other starts to weaken. While we remain courteous to others, within our own homes we act very differently.

I once heard a *badchan* say: The best tool for *shalom bayis* is a telephone. A couple could be fighting and screaming, but when the phone rings, she picks up the phone and everything changes. "Hello? Oh, yes. Sure, dear. Oh. Absolutely. No trouble. Thanks so much for calling."

Maybe her husband should call her on the phone!

Familiarity Breeds Disrespect

John Gottman, whose study predicts the success or failure of a marriage based on the degree of contempt in the relationship, conducted another fascinating study. He invites couples into his lab, asks them to discuss a series of issues, and closely monitors their responses. Then, he asks them to discuss the same issues with people they've never met before. His goal is to see if the way the husband and wife speak to each other is different than the way they speak to strangers.

Here's what he found:

When a stranger offered a different opinion, that opinion was more readily accepted than when their spouse offered a different opinion. Additionally, if they didn't agree with the stranger's opinion, both spouses would argue less and were more polite to the stranger than when they disagreed with each other. Gottman says that this holds true for marriages of all lengths – from newlyweds to couples married decades. It seems to be a rule that we treat strangers with more respect than we do our spouse.

I've seen this in my own work with couples. A man can be a serious *talmid chacham*, someone whose opinion is respected far and wide, but at home everything is different. If he says something to his wife, she acts like she didn't hear it. When someone else tells her the exact same thing, she exclaims, "Oh, that's a great idea. I never thought of it that way."

That's a relatively benign example. Sadly, I've witnessed exchanges between spouses that are anything but benign.

"Ruchie, that's the stupidest thing I ever heard in my life!"

"Stop, Dovid, that's ridiculous!"

If you heard these words in a vacuum, you might assume these two people hate each other. But then you find out they don't. In fact, they're quite fond of each other. But without realizing it, they're eroding the fabric of their relationship.

When a husband offers an opinion and his wife shoots it down, she is telling him, *I don't respect your opinion. I don't respect your perspective. I don't respect you.* When a husband dismissively disregards his wife's opinions, he is telling her, *I don't care what you think. I don't cherish you.* If disrespect grows unchecked, the marriage can start unraveling. Once respect goes, love follows shortly thereafter.

And this is the 4th of the Really Dumb Mistakes that Very Smart Couples Make—they stop treating each other with respect.

That's Just the Way I Talk

"Oh, come on, rabbi," people tell me. "We're very close. You can't expect us to be so formal. You can't expect us to always respond calmly, *Oh yes dear, I think that's a good idea, however...* Our marriage is good, but this is how we talk."

I agree that you can't be "so formal." The Chazon Ish says that such formality has no place in a marriage. But you still need to talk with respect. Otherwise, your relationship is going to suffer.

People react differently to disrespect. Some people simmer. Others react quickly. Either way, there will be a reaction. It may take a day, a week, or longer, but eventually something seemingly insignificant will trigger a blow-up that appears like an overreaction. The spouse who is overreacting may not even be aware of the root cause. The root is feeling disrespected. If the disrespect happens often enough, the feelings can reach critical mass.

The Culture of Disrespect

This is especially true today. It seems that America is now the land of disrespect. It comes out in many ways. One is dad jokes. "Oh, that's dad. He's a goofball." "That's just dad being dad." In the not-so-distant past, the father was seen as the wise leader of the family. That reputation has eroded to the point that that he's treated as a bungling fool or irrelevant sideshow. "Oh, there goes dad again."

It's especially sad because while respect is critical for all relationships, it is doubly significant in your role as parents. From the time my kids were little, I made it a point that any time my wife called me, I'd run to respond immediately. Not because I was so makpid on shalom bayis, but because I wanted my children to see that when Mommy calls, Abba runs. I wanted them to know that Mommy is treated with respect. As parents, you create the culture of your home. If you act with respect to each other, that is what your children see as regular, normal and expected. If you act with disrespect toward each other, that is what they see as regular, normal and expected. And it won't be long until they model your behavior.

Sadly, what passes for normal civility in our culture is neither civil nor normal. It seems that human beings have forgotten how to act like human beings, and it surfaces in our marriages. Spouses treat each other with appalling disregard. It's so common and "normal" that we forget how wrong it is. Yet it's not only rude and uncouth, it damages the relationship. It destroys the family unit. It's not the way Jewish people treat each other.

As much as I hate to have to spell it out, let me lay out some basic rules of conduct:

- Don't make fun of each other
- Don't mock each other
- Don't make jokes at each other's expense

Even if it's funny. Even if your spouse doesn't mind, and even if she laughs. (If you do want to make fun of people, a great target is yourself. There are few things quite as humbling, and no one gets hurt when the humor is self-deprecating.)

Included in this is being polite—using expressions like "please" and "thank you." I think it's worthwhile to record a few conversations that you have at home and listen to the way you speak to your spouse. Then compare that to the way you speak to friends or neighbors. You might find it eye-opening (if not jaw-dropping).

We are all brought up well, and certainly outside the home we are polite, courteous, and proper. The problem is that not long into a marriage, the niceties start to slip. Before you know it, gone are the civilities and courtesies, and people who supposedly love each other speak to each other in manner that is gruff, curt, and I dare say, downright rude.

"Impressive"

Many years ago, I brought a young couple to the Rosh Yeshivah. They had been married less than a year, but their relationship was deteriorating rapidly. The Rosh Yeshivah asked both of them to come into his office and spoke to them briefly. Then he asked the husband to step outside while he spoke to the wife. He then asked the wife to step outside while he spoke to her husband. The entire session lasted less than an hour, yet that little meeting changed the direction of their marriage.

If you're wondering what mystical secret the Rosh Yeshiva used, it was actually just a bit of old-fashioned wisdom (maybe a lot of wisdom). The Rosh Yeshiva knew this fellow well and suspected what the problem was. When he spoke to the couple, he listened closely, and he heard what he expected.

This young man was very successful in yeshivah. He was a *masmid* and a *talmid chacham*. He also thought highly of himself—perhaps a tad too highly. Even though he married a fine young woman, he felt that she wasn't on his level. After the Rosh Yeshiva spoke to the young woman, he called her husband back in and said, "What a *chashuv* young woman. I'm very impressed. Very impressed." Then he asked the man a few questions. In the course of the conversation he repeated his assessment several times: "I'm very impressed with her. A very impressive young woman."

When this fellow heard his Rebbe say the words: "What a *chashuv* young woman. I'm very impressed," that changed his image of her. That little change made all the difference in the world. They are now happily married over 20 years later.

Respect First

This is the great insight of the Rambam. Respect comes first.

You have to work on the love in your marriage. You have to spend time together, and use romantic love as well as the other tools that bond, like appreciation, touch, and physical intimacy. But before any of them, there has to be respect. If there isn't mutual respect in the marriage, nothing else will work. Respect is the foundation for a successful marriage.

But there are other elements needed for a successful marriage.

Chapter 4

Happy Wife, Happy Life

> **רמב"ם יד החזקה הלכות אישות פרק טו**
>
> יט) וכן צוו חכמים שיהיה אדם מכבד את אשתו יתר מגופו ואוהבה כגופו
>
> *The Sages commanded a man to honor his wife more than himself and to love her as he does himself.*
>
> כ) וכן צוו חכמים על האשה שתהיה מכבדת את בעלה ביותר מדאי ויהיה לו עליה מורא ותעשה כל מעשיה על פיו ויהיה בעיניה כמו שר או מלך מהלכת בתאות לבו ומרחקת כל שישנא וזה הוא דרך בנות ישראל ובני ישראל הקדושים הטהורים בזיווגן ובדרכים אלו יהיה ישובן נאה ומשובח
>
> *The Sages commanded a woman to honor her husband exceedingly and to be in awe of him, and all that he says she does. And he should be in her eyes like a prince or king... This is the way of daughters of Israel and sons of Israel who are holy and pure, and in these ways it will be pleasant and praiseworthy.*

THE RAMBAM GIVES US the formula for a successful marriage: The Sages commanded a man to honor his wife more than himself and to love her as he does himself. Likewise, they commanded a wife to treat her husband with exceeding amounts of honor, treating him as if he were nobility. If a couple does this, their union will be beautiful and praiseworthy (Rambam Hilchos Ishus 15:19).

Each spouse has their role to play. If he does his part and she does her part, the Rambam tells us that their lives will be pleasant, life will be beautiful.

But if you read this Rambam carefully you might notice that it's not quite balanced.

His role is to:

1. Respect his wife more than himself
2. Love his wife like himself

Her role is to:

1. Respect her husband exceedingly as if he were nobility

ספר בראשית פרק ב

יח) וַיֹּאמֶר יְדֹוָד אֱלֹהִים לֹא טוֹב הֱיוֹת הָאָדָם לְבַדּוֹ אֶעֱשֶׂה לּוֹ עֵזֶר כְּנֶגְדּוֹ

Hashem said, "It is not good for man to be alone, I will make for him a helpmate opposite him."

You don't have to be very good at math to notice a discrepancy here. He has two jobs. She has one. He has to respect her and love her, but all that she has to do is respect him. Isn't that curious? Does that mean that she doesn't have to love her husband? Didn't we just spend two chapters discussing that love is the glue that keeps a marriage together? Is he condemned to a loveless marriage?

To understand this, we need to take a short tour of this creature called the human being.

A Helpmate Opposite Him

Before Hashem created Chava, Hashem said, "It is not good for man to be alone. I will make for him an *ezer kenegdo*—a helpmate opposite him."

A young fellow preparing for marriage may read this with great joy. "Wow! A helpmate! This is great. A Polynesian maidservant at my beck and call. My every wish will be her command. Marriage is going to be wonderful!"

Then he gets married and discovers that it isn't quite like that. But why? Didn't the Torah define her role as his assistant? Isn't she supposed to serve him? The problem is that he missed the second half of the definition—a helpmate *opposite him*. And it's not just guys; many women also completely misunderstand what *ezer kenegdo* means.

Ezer kenegdo: A helpmate opposite him

"*Ezer*" translates simply as *helper* or *helpmate*. But *kenegdo* isn't as straightforward. While the word *kenegdo* translates as "opposite," the Maharal explains that "opposite" has two meanings. It can mean *antithesis* – the inverse, completely unalike; male is the opposite of female. But *kenegdo* can also mean "opposite" as in "facing" – "The Jewish Nation camped opposite (facing) the mountain" (*Shemos* 19:2).

The Torah uses the expression *kenegdo* to teach us that in marriage, both meanings are valid. She will be a helpmate opposite to him in nature, and a helpmate facing him on his level. She's not subservient, not submissive, and not second-rate. She's an equal. They are two *equal partners* in this marriage.

Historically, this isn't the way the secular world viewed marriage. For thousands of years, women were treated as second class citizens—at best. In Western Civilization for the past 150 years there has been a movement toward women's equality. From a Torah perspective, there never was a need for a women's equality movement because in a Torah marriage, the woman has always been an equal partner. She is an *ezer kenegdo,* a helpmate that is on his level, his equal, to join together with him.

The word *kenegdo* also means "antithesis" or "different." Since man and woman are opposites, they do things differently. In fact, they do everything differently. They have different approaches. They have different perspectives. They have different feelings. It's not just a few things that they will disagree on—rather, they will disagree on most things. They are opposite in nature.

To appreciate just how different men and women are, let's try a little experiment.

As soon as you see the word below, I want you to think of its opposite.

What is the opposite of black?

I'm sure you answered "white."

Now let's try some more:

What is the opposite of up?

Down.

Hot?

Cold.

In?

Out.

Male?

Female.

That's right – men and women are opposites. They are completely and totally different. Not in *some* ways. Not in *some* areas. Rather, by nature, they are absolutely, completely opposite.

The Maharal explains that this is what makes marriage different from any other relationship. If man and woman were similar, getting along would be easy. They would agree on everything and life would be simple. Or, if man and woman weren't equal, again, marriage would be simple. In most relationships there is a clear hierarchy, like between a parent and child, boss and employee, or rebbe and talmid. In those relationships, whenever a difference in opinion surfaces, it's apparent who's in charge, and they get to decide what to do.

In marriage, however, there are two equal partners. No one is the boss. No one is in charge. And since man and woman are opposites, they will have different opinions, and when the differences surface, finding a solution isn't easy.

Selective Amnesia

Men and women are different in temperament, nature and disposition. They are different in what interests them and what they talk about. They are different in emotional priorities and sensitivities. They have different aspirations, goals and ambitions. In short, they are different in almost every imaginable way. The only thing they seem to have in common is selective amnesia.

Both men and women get married and then completely forget how different they are. It's a bit odd, because everyone seems to know that boys and girls are different. But then they get married and amnesia sets in. Men treat their wives as if they were men and women treat their husbands as if they were women. This is a major obstacle for marital happiness, because if you don't understand that your spouse is different, you can't meet their emotional needs, and it's almost impossible not to hurt their feelings.

To see how this plays out in marriage, let's begin with an observation.

When did you start thinking about your marriage?

When do women start thinking about marriage?

While I've never done a formal study, it's my belief that by the time a girl is 12 years old, she has a pretty good sense of what her marriage will look like. She's observed others, formed opinions, and has a good idea of the way she intends her marriage to be.

When does the average man start thinking about his marriage?

Again, while I haven't formally studied the issue, I would say a man starts thinking about his marriage about five years after his wedding.

While this may be tongue in cheek, it does illustrate how men and women view marriage, and the needs that each have.

DMCs

One Friday night when my oldest daughter was in eleventh grade, she told me that two of her friends hadn't come to school that day.

"Why not?" I asked.

"They were up late last night having a DMC."

I had never heard of a DMC before, but it sure didn't sound good. So I asked, "What's a DMC?"

"Oh, come on, Abba. You know – a deep, meaningful conversation. They were up until three in the morning talking. It got so late that they were too tired to come to school the next day."

At the time of this conversation, I had taught high school boys for 15 years and never once did I hear of two guys not coming to shiur because they were up late sharing their feelings and revealing their inner secrets to each other, hour after hour deep into the night. Not once.

Friends vs. Buddies

Generally speaking, women form connections with each other

that are strong, close, and very real. That's not necessarily true of men. Certainly, men are sociable. They have buddies. They slap each other on the back. But the type of emotional friendships and deep connections that women have is typically not found by men.

This difference begins at a very young age.

Every six-year-old girl has a *best friend*. And they remain BFFs until, heaven forfend, her best friend betrays her by revealing her secret, and then it's on to someone else. Throughout childhood, women crave close relationships and learn how to create and maintain them. They seek out friendships. They value friendships. They even rate themselves according to how many good friends they have.

Guys have friends. But typically, these are friends they do things with and hang out with. Naturally they talk, but the nature of what they talk about is vastly different. They talk about stuff: Things they do, things they wish they did. But the idea of sharing their inner world isn't naturally a part of a guy's nature. And the connections that they form with other guys are much less involved than the connections women form.

If you speak to a high school principal, you'll see this difference clearly. In many girl's high schools, a big part of the role of principal is to be part social director, part social worker, helping the girls work through issues surrounding their cliques and social lives. Ask a boy's menahel how he handles these issues and he won't even know what you're talking about.

Throughout her life, a woman will seek out close friends to confide in and share her life with. It's something that is a part of her essence and something she needs. Guy have friends, but their relationships aren't anywhere near as close and connected.

When I was about 20, I approached Rav Dovid Harris, shlita, who was then one of the roshei yeshiva in Rochester, NY. I said, "I don't feel I have a best friend in yeshiva. I'm friendly with many guys, we're buddies—but I just don't feel like I have a best friend." Rabbi Harris looked at me and said, "Who does?"

It's typical for a guy to have many friends that he hangs out and does stuff with, and he may even have a best friend, by which he means the guy he hangs out and does stuff with most frequently. But men rarely have the deep, intense connection that women typically have with each other.

Try this: ask a woman to name her best friend, and she'll answer right away. Then ask her when she last spoke to her best friend. If it wasn't this morning, it was yesterday or the day before.

Ask a man if he has a best friend and he'll answer, "Absolutely. Sure."

"When was the last time you spoke to him?"

"Oh, about five years ago."

The craving to be connected to another human being is much stronger, much more real, for women. This is one of her basic needs in marriage. To understand this, let's look at how the Torah tells a man to act toward his wife during their first year of marriage.

> ספר דברים פרק כד
>
> ה) כִּי יִקַּח אִישׁ אִשָּׁה חֲדָשָׁה לֹא יֵצֵא בַּצָּבָא וְלֹא יַעֲבֹר עָלָיו לְכָל דָּבָר נָקִי יִהְיֶה לְבֵיתוֹ שָׁנָה אֶחָת וְשִׂמַּח אֶת אִשְׁתּוֹ אֲשֶׁר לָקָח:
>
> *When a man takes a new woman, he should not go out to war... and he should make happy the woman whom he took.*

The Torah directs us that during the first year of marriage, a couple should try to spend as much time together as possible. But spending time together isn't enough. There is a particular focus that a husband has to have during this time: *He should make happy the woman whom he took* (Devarim 24:5).

A man is commanded not to engage in some normal activities during this year (such as going out to war) so that he should be free to focus on one thing – making his wife happy. Rashi makes this even more clear by noting that it doesn't mean they should be happy together, celebrating their union. Rather, he should make his wife happy.

This is a rather perplexing mitzvah. Why is making his wife happy so vital? If you're using the first year, *shanah rishonah*, to build *shalom bayis,* there are many things to work on. Happiness is only one feature of life. It's nice, but why does the Torah specify happiness in particular and make it a commandment? And why is the focus on *him* making *her* happy? As if that's the only thing that matters?

Happy Wife, Happy Life

One of the deepest needs a woman has is to feel connected to others. As an adult, that translates into a need for bonding with and affection from her husband. Being cherished by her husband fulfills one of her most basic, essential needs—the need to be loved.

When a man focuses on making his wife happy, he will find himself constantly thinking, *What does she need? What will please her?* By doing that, he is showering her with attention, letting her know that she is special in his eyes. That sets the foundation of their entire marriage. Once she knows that she is precious to him, she will be happy in the marriage.

One of the great principles of marriage is: *A happy wife is a happy life.* If a woman feels cherished, if she feels loved, the marriage will succeed. If she doesn't, it is very unlikely that the marriage will work. This element is so important that the Torah directs men to focus on it for the entire first year of marriage. If done correctly, it will set the foundation of their marriage.

Pikuach Nefesh for a Woman

In an *iggeres,* the Steipler Gaon writes a powerful statement:

> "The main hope of a woman is to have a husband who loves her. If she sees this isn't so, it crushes her spirit and can be close to *pikuach nefesh.*"

The Steipler explains that this is a core need in a woman. She needs to be cherished, appreciated, and esteemed. She needs to be looked at with eyes that say, "You're the only one, you're special to me." When this need is met, she feels fulfilled and happy in the marriage. If it isn't met, she's miserable.

This is exactly why the Torah says, "Make your wife happy." A husband was given that obligation because by doing so he demonstrates his love for her, and she *needs* his love.

Answer for the Rambam

I believe that this is why the Rambam doesn't specify that a wife must love her husband—she doesn't need the commandment. If she knows that she is cherished, she will love her husband automatically. She craves the relationship, she deeply needs it, and provided that her needs are met, she will love her husband as a matter of course. As long as he shows her in word, deed, and action that she is beloved, she will love him, as she wishes for nothing other than bonding with her husband.

Men typically don't have that deep need for close attachments. For a man, that level of bonding is not as natural. He has to be given a specific mitzvah to love his wife. He has to work on it—it's not instinctive, it's something he has to learn. For that reason, Chazal commanded him to respect *and* love his wife.

The need to be loved is one of the central distinctions between men and women, and surfaces often.

How's your marriage?

When a couple comes to my office, I'll often ask the husband, "How's your marriage?"

"Baruch Hashem," he says. "Good."

Then I'll ask his wife, "How's your marriage?"

"Terrible. It's horrible."

Wait a minute, I want to ask. *Aren't you guys married? To each other?*

The answer is yes, they are married to each other, but there are two marriages – his marriage and her marriage. And they are very different.

A woman needs to know she's loved and cherished. At the core of her essence is a profound need for attachment to her husband. She needs constant reassurance of his love. If that's present, she will feel satisfied and happy in her marriage. A man typically doesn't have that need. It's not vital to him. He's not focused on it. Even if they aren't connecting all the time, he can still feel happily married. He can love his wife, know it, but not need to share and connect. Because he doesn't feel the same need, he may not shower her with the attention that she craves.

Most *shalom bayis* problems start at this point: the wife doesn't feel loved. Statistics show that two-thirds of divorces are initiated by women. It's typically the woman who first expresses deep dissatisfaction. It's the woman who feels her needs aren't being met. She might not have any other complaint. She might not feel criticized, or unappreciated, or that her feelings are negated. But if she doesn't feel that he showers her with attention, that he loves her—she won't be happy.

This is a fundamental difference between men and women. Little girls dream of marriage but boys don't — it's not part of the essence of a man. The essence of a man is achievement. Little boys rate themselves by their accomplishments, how they measure up, how good they are at what they do. Girls rate themselves with a different set of criteria: Am I special? Am I lovable? Am I worthy of being loved?

He Love Me, He Loves Me Not

Do you remember the image of a little girl plucking a daisy and pulling out the petals one by one, saying, "He loves me, he loves me not, he loves me, he loves me not"?

I believe that every woman goes through that stage in the beginning of her marriage, always wondering if her husband really loves her. (And when I say the "beginning," I mean the first 30 or 40 years.)

This is one of the most difficult concepts for us guys to get: that a woman can be emotionally and psychologically healthy, but when it comes to her husband's love, she's isn't secure. She needs constant reassurance that her husband really cares about her.

A Wise Man Pursues His Wife

Chazal tell us that it is the man who pursues the woman (Kiddushin 2b). This isn't just during courtship. A husband should pursue his wife long *after* they are married, letting her know again and again that he cherishes her, that he is there for her, and that she is number one in his eyes.

Many guys don't get that. If his wife needs constant reassurance about the relationship, he assumes he is married to an insecure person, or a very needy person. "Why do you need me to constantly say these things?"

There's an old joke where a kid asks his grandpa, married over 60 years, for the secret to marriage. To which his grandfather responds, "When I first married your grandma, I said to her, 'Dear, I'm telling you now that I love you. If I ever change my mind, I'll let you know.' Since that time, I never changed my mind."

I don't know if that trick worked back then, but I can tell you that if you try it today, you are going to suffer the consequences.

Who initiates the Date?

Which brings us to a very important point. Many guys take the attitude that since the relationship is so important to her, let her be the one who pursues it. They tell their wives, "If you want to go out, I'm available. Just tell me the night, darling, book the restaurant and I'll be there." Oddly enough, not only doesn't she plan the date, she gets upset, and the poor guy can't figure out why.

I'll tell you why: by telling her to plan the date, he's telling her that he doesn't care. His wife thinks, *if I have to actually plan the date, then what's the point. He doesn't care anyway. Forget the whole thing.* While I hate to be formulaic, the formula for success is: It's the man's job to plan the date, it's the woman's job to find a babysitter.

But the weekly date isn't enough. There are a many ways for a man to make his wife happy: gifts, notes, talks, having fun and spending time together. But the main thing a man has to know is that his job is to give her the sense that he loves her. The way to do that is to focus on making her happy. The key is not really the externals, important as they may be; it's sending her the message over and over again that "You are precious to me, you are important to me, you are number one." When a woman feels that, she's happy, she's fulfilled, and her natural ability to love flows forth.

This brings us to a corollary point: A woman has to learn to be tolerant of the fact that her husband doesn't have the same emotional needs as she does. He may never be as good at fulfilling those needs as her girlfriends. It doesn't mean he doesn't love her, just that he feels that love in a different manner, and expresses it differently.

A Wise Woman Builds her House, a Foolish Woman Destroys it

If a woman feels unloved, that's a problem and it has to be addressed. However, it's important to understand that it's the obligation of both partners to deal with the issue. Obviously, her husband has to do what he can to make her feel cherished and special. But she needs to explain to her husband what it is that she needs.

This is when "A wise woman builds her house, and a foolish woman destroys it" (*Mishlei* 14:1). If you recognize that your needs are not being met, deal with the issue. Don't overreact, don't explode; that will make you uglier and destroy your *shalom bayis*. Sometimes, you just have to be *mevater* (give in) and the next day, when things are calm, explain to your husband what you're feeling. If you're dealing with two reasonable people, which is almost always the case, then it just boils down to misunderstandings.

The 5th really dumb mistake

This is the 5th Really Dumb Mistake that Very Smart Couples Make: Not understanding that women are from Venus—they need constant connection and constant reassurance of love, and it's a husband's job to provide that.

This is one of the keys to success in marriage. If a woman feels she's cherished, the marriage has the foundation to succeed. I would say that 90% percent of shalom bayis problems are solved when a woman feels that her husband cherishes her.

But before you go assuming that it's all the guys' fault, I'll share one more point: There are many women who make it difficult for their husbands to like them, let alone love them.

Chapter 5

For Women Only

IMAGINE THAT BEFORE YOU were born, a *malach* said to you, "Your lot in life is to suffer, but you have a choice. You can either live a life without love or a life without respect. It's your choice to make."

Which would you choose – a life without love, or a life without respect?

Interestingly, the choice you make is likely dependent on whether you are male or female.

Most women would choose the second option. Respect is important, but who could bear a life without love? Most men, however, would choose the first. "I mean, being without love isn't great, but I could bear it. To live a life where I'm constantly not enough, not making the grade—that's unbearable."

This is not guesswork. In a book called *For Women Only*, Shaunti Feldhahn tells women about the inner lives of men. She's a novelist who tried to make her fiction as true to life as possible so she would interview people to see how they would react to given situations. She discovered that men kept answering her questions "wrong." Being curious by nature, she began investigating. She conducted surveys, and then follow-up surveys, finally hiring a polling company to frame questions in ways that would be unbiased. Over and over, men seemed to answer her questions in a manner she never expected.

One question they asked was: If you had a choice between living your life without love or without respect, which would you choose? 74% of the men said they couldn't live without respect. It's nice to be loved, but respect is a requirement. Yet most women would say the exact opposite: I could endure a life without respect, but to live without love—that's impossible.

This illustrates a basic difference between men and women that has a huge impact on marriage.

Gender Differences

There was a book published several years ago that became a bestseller. It was called, "Everything Men Know About Women." The book sold over a million copies. Women all over the world bought it because they felt it did a great job describing the way men understand women's emotions.

The book was blank.

Nothing in it. Two hundred empty pages with nothing printed on them. Women would pick it up, see nothing inside, and start laughing. "See, that's what I've been saying all along, what does my husband know about me? Nothing."

It seems to be an accepted fact among women that men don't know much about their inner world. And while that may be true, women don't know a whole lot about men either. The vast majority of us make fundamental errors in dealing with the opposite gender because we don't understand why they do things, what matters to them, and how they see things.

But once you understand the differences between how men and women think, feel and view things, you can adjust your attitude toward those differences. And that will be a game changer for your marriage.

Let's begin with one of the most basic differences.

Boys Will Be Boys

When my youngest son was born, he had five mothers – my wife and his four older sisters. With his birth their dreams came true – here was a real, live baby doll. They could dress him up. They could feed him. They could play mommy to him. He was catered to and waited upon. He was the prince.

His older brother was already a teenager and living away from home. We no longer had any "boy" toys around, so the girls had a field day. They would put ribbons in his hair and dress him up and give him dolls to play with. I was starting to get a little uncomfortable with the situation, but then he turned two. He discovered toy trucks. He abandoned the dolls, bows and ribbons. He was a boy and boys don't do those things. He never let them dress him like a girl again.

The differences between boys and girls surface at a young age and are almost universal.

Back to the Schoolyard

In a schoolyard, boys and girls play different types of games. But even when they play the same games, they are played for different reasons and with different goals.

Girls typically play as a group; their games are interdependent. The goal and focus, the "fun of it," is being part of the crowd. Because the games are all about connection, when a girl falls, the game stops, and all the girls surround her and ask if she's okay.

Boys play games that are independent. The purpose of the game is to show how good they are. When boys play on teams, their focus is on who is the star of the team. When a boy falls during game, it's expected that he get out of the way so the game can go on.

Studies show that girls take turns twenty times more often than boys, and their pretend play is usually about interactions in nurturing or caregiving relationships. They prefer to avoid conflict because it interferes with their goal of staying connected, gaining approval, and nurturing. In a boy's world, the games are typically competitive. There are winners and losers—and losing is a big deal. From the age of about eight until eighteen, a boy's social status is largely determined by how well he plays.

I was once invited to speak in another city and an *askan* in that community told me that he had gone to a particular yeshiva. My brother-in-law had attended that yeshiva around the same time, so I asked the *askan* if the name Rabbi Meir Kramer sounded familiar.

"Oh, Meir! Of course I know him. What a great ballplayer!"

My brother-in-law was 53 at the time. He had been a rebbi for over 25 years and probably hadn't touched a basketball in a decade. But this fellow remembered him as "a great ballplayer." To him, it was clearly a big deal.

A big part of this is because male relationships are not symmetrical. They're hierarchal. Boys play to win, to dominate. In a boy's game there are always winners and losers, status achieved or not achieved. That's because a boy's world revolves around honor and respect. It's what drives him.

Women are driven by connection to others. Girls don't play to win. They play games like jump rope – holding the rope so their friend can jump as many times as she can. When girls do play competitive sports, their motivation is to be a part of the team.

It's a bit ironic that the most popular girl in the class is often the least liked. Many girls want to be friends with her, but she can only have so many good friends and invariably there will be girls who feel snubbed by her and they will be resentful.

The male typically doesn't need many connections. The male needs respect. That's not to say that women don't consider social standing important and men have no concern about social connections. But in terms of primacy and centrality to their very essence, generally, women need friendships and men need respect.

He Needs Respect

This explains the Rambam's description of the roles that spouses play toward each other. A woman's primary need in marriage is to feel that she's loved. A man's primary need is to feel respected. He needs to feel admired, or at least accepted. It's an innate need. It's a need when he's young and it doesn't go away when he matures. He no longer needs to be the best ballplayer, but he still has a need for respect. And more than the need for respect, he is all but allergic to *disrespect*. Treat a man with disrespect and he will bristle and writhe, and one thing's for sure—he won't like you. This is a foundational principle in the Rambam.

At her core, a woman needs to feel loved. If she doesn't feel cherished, she can't be happily married. At his core, a man needs to be respected. He might like to be loved, but in his world, respect takes precedence. If a woman shows great love to her husband but no respect, they will have a very difficult marriage.

This is something Western society seems to have forgotten. Go to a drugstore and you'll find aisles and aisles of "I love you" cards. This reflects a societal view that love is *the* most important ingredient in relationships. Don't misunderstand me. Love is vital in marriage. But there are differences in the way it's expressed, nurtured and received. When he feels that his wife respects him for who he is, he's happy. If he knows that his wife doesn't respect him – even though she may love him – it destroys him. If a woman doesn't understand this, she'll often damage her husband without even knowing it. But if she understands this basic need, she can be the greatest support to him.

A young man I knew well asked if he could bring his kallah to meet me. When they arrived, I spoke with them for a few minutes, and then I asked him to wait in another room while I spoke to his kallah.

After a few minutes, I called him back into the room. When he walked in, I saw something that made me gasp.

His kallah stood up, waited until he sat down, and then took her seat.

The kallah stands up when the chosson walks in?! I had never seen that before.

I asked her about it later. She said, "I was taught that you're supposed to stand up when a *talmid chacham* walks into the room."

I can't describe the joy I felt when I heard that. Her chosson was brilliant, and was a talmid chacham, but he sure didn't think that of himself. In fact, he didn't think much of himself at all. He had a poor self-image, and that was his greatest challenge. He was very hard on himself and often felt depressed because of his perceived failings.

But his kallah held him in such high regard that she stood up when he walked in!

This was the greatest gift she could give him. *My wife respects me so much that she stands up for me.*

As long as she continued treating him that way, he'd always be a kind, generous, giving and sensitive husband. If she stopped treating him with respect, that would destroy him and their relationship.

While this idea may sound simple, it becomes a major sticking point in marriage—without either party knowing why. Let me illustrate with an observation.

Why do mothers-in-law have a bad reputation?

When I finished writing the first book in the *Shmuz on the Parsha* series, it needed a final copy review. The book had been edited, but mistakes tend to creep in; a missing period here, a misplaced comma there. My mother-in-law has a very good eye for detail, and I asked her if she would do it. She graciously agreed and checked through the manuscript.

When I was writing the acknowledgements that would appear at the beginning of the book, I wanted to thank her. I was tempted to write, "I would thank my mother-in-law for her contribution to this book, but nothing gives a mother-in-law more joy than correcting her son-in-law, so I don't have to thank her." (Of course, I didn't write that. But years later my wife told her mother about it, and my mother-in-law said, "Oh, he should have written it, it's cute.")

While I meant it as a joke, it seems that mothers-in-law have a bad reputation. I think that one of the reasons for that actually stems from a good trait. By nature, women are nurturers. They are caregivers. While that's a beautiful attribute, sometimes it works against them.

As an example: a young woman gets engaged and brings her future husband to meet her family. Her mother is very impressed with him. "Great guy! So many good qualities." She thinks it's a source of pride and honor to have such a fine young man join the family.

But even a great guy can be improved. And so, being the nurturing caregiver that she is, she quickly notices a number of ways to improve him. "I mean, he's a very fine person, but he would be even better if..." In her quest to help him be even better, she points these things out to her future son-in-law. Very quickly, she becomes very unpopular. Because while her words were only meant with the best of intentions, not many young men enjoy being "improved."

Men don't take kindly to being corrected by their mother-in-law, and they don't take kindly to being corrected by their wife, either.

The 10-Point Home Improvement Program

I believe that most women, before they get married, have already identified a number of items that, when "corrected," will greatly improve their husband. The average *kallah* walks down the aisle with a ten-point home improvement policy, the focus of which is that fellow standing under the canopy—her husband-to-be. *Look, he's a great guy, but... First off, those shoes have got to go. And those ties, forget about them... Then there's this coming-late business...*

To her credit, she's patient, and she doesn't begin implementing her program until a week or so after the wedding, when he can't find the checkbook. She then innocently and very politely points out that if he were more organized it would save him a lot of time. She even offers to help him rearrange his desk. Yet for some reason, which she can't quite figure out, he doesn't get all warm and fuzzy. *Strange*, she thinks to herself. *Here I am, showing him how much I love him by offering to help him improve, and he doesn't even acknowledge it, let alone thank me.*

But she is resolute. The next week when he's looking for a bill, she again lovingly points out, "You see, dear, that's what I was saying. If you would be more orderly, it would save you time."

And again, oddly enough, he doesn't well up with appreciation and gratitude.

This goes on for a while until one day she notices the strangest thing. *It's almost like the more I help him, the worse he gets. It's like he's working against me. It's like he's some obstinate two-year-old, who needs to get his way!*

But she is determined not to let his childlike behavior ruin their marriage. So she now makes it a point, every time she can, to show him how much his bad habits are hurting him. "Dear," she says to him one day, "your desk is such a mess, it's a wonder you can even find yourself there. Ha, ha, ha." Oddly, he doesn't laugh. *What is wrong with this guy?* she thinks to herself. *What is his problem?*

His problem is that he's a guy, and guys work differently. In a woman's world, being connected to others is one of the highest priorities, and caring for others builds that connection. One way a woman shows that she cares is by helping. She'll offer advice. She'll express her opinion about how her friend can do things better. It's a sign of love that she looks out for the betterment of her friend. She means it that way, and her girlfriend understands it that way. If she didn't try to help, she would actually feel bad. *If I really cared, I would help her.* A woman's interdependence and connections to others make her feel good.

But that's not the way it works in a guy's world.

Guys value independence. Self-reliance is a great source of pride: *I got this—it's under control.* Needing others is a sign of weakness. It's a sign that he can't make it on his own.

To go over to another man and offer him advice on how to do things better implies that he isn't good enough. He can't get the job done. In a man's world, he would only ask for advice if he really needed help, and then he would find an expert to guide him. For another man to come over and offer his opinion about how he could do it better would be an affront. Try going over to a guy changing a tire and say, "You know, if you were to hold the tire *this* way, it would be a lot easier." You're almost asking for a fistfight. The natural male tendency is to feel, *Who does he think he is? I'm quite capable of taking care of this myself. If I needed his help I would ask. Otherwise, keep your opinion to yourself!*

A woman needs to realize that when she offers *unsolicited advice,* she might well be insulting her husband. To her husband, her well-intended words are heard as: "You're not capable. You need my help. You're only half a man." He's likely to think, *Why can't she just let things be? Why does she feel this constant need to improve me?*

This female drive to help surfaces all the time in day to day activities.

Turn on your blinker

Imagine we get to be a fly on the rearview mirror as a couple drives down the highway. The husband is driving. He's 38, he's been driving since he's 18, and he travels more than 15,000 miles a year. By now he's logged over 250,000 miles – without a single accident, not even a fender bender. He's an excellent driver.

His wife, on the other hand… Well, let's just say that she's not the best driver. Even though she doesn't drive a fraction as much as he does, she's been involved in a few collisions. What's interesting, though, is that whenever he gets behind the wheel, she feels this incessant need to help him drive. "Dear, don't forget your blinker. Be careful, there's a stop sign there. Watch out for that red car in the next lane."

It's not that hard to imagine what he's thinking. *Here I am, a mature adult, I've driven almost a quarter of a million miles without a single accident, and she thinks I can't take care of myself?*

What makes this difficult is that she can't understand him. *Why does he have to get so huffy? I'm just trying to help!* And he can't understand her. *Why does she feel this constant need to criticize and correct me? Why can't she just leave me alone?*

The reason they can't understand each other is because they each view things from their world. In a woman's world, helping a friend is a sign of love. But a man will experience it as a sign of disrespect.

When you direct, guide, or try to change your husband, he doesn't think, *look how much she loves me.* He thinks, *she believes I'm not good enough.*

It might be true that women aren't insulted when they're offered advice. But men sure are. When you try to change, mold, shape, improve, or help your husband, you're insulting him.

To be fair, many men also have this nasty habit and go to great effort to change their wives. When a man tries to change his wife, what she hears is, *I'm not acceptable as I am. He doesn't cherish me. He doesn't love me. If he loved me, he wouldn't be trying to change me. If he is trying to change me, it means that I'm not worthy of his love. I need to be different from what I am to be loved.*

Trying to change your spouse erodes the relationship. It says to a spouse you're just not good enough—you need to change. No one, of either gender, responds well to that message.

The reason this chapter is focused more on women is because when a man tries to change his wife, the damage usually isn't as great—women seem to be more accustomed to it, and it isn't as insulting. (It's still a bad habit and very unwise.) And most men, once they recognize the damage they're causing, can stop. Women, on the other hand, seem to have an inborn need to change their husbands. They often can't even understand why it's insulting.

When someone tries to get them to recognize the damage it does to the relationship, there is a huge amount of resistance.

"Why is he so immature? He knows I mean it for his good. He even agrees with me. Why is he being such a baby? Why can't he just grow up?"

The reason you feel that way is because you are you. When you offer this kind of help to your sisters or your aunt, it's probably well received. But in the male world, it is anything but well received.

For women who have difficulty grasping this, here's a simple example.

You were so thin back then

Picture a couple sitting on a couch together. They're married for five years. She turns to him in a romantic moment and says, "Do you remember our third date? We walked around the lake."

He smiles sweetly at her and says, "I sure do. Wow, you were so thin back then."

What do you think her reaction is going to be? I highly doubt it will be a sense of nostalgia. Most likely there are going to be tears—maybe even some sharp words. But why? He didn't intend to hurt her. He didn't say she's unattractive now. He was just reminiscing. Nevertheless, when you tell a woman she used to look better, it's not very complimentary. She's not going to take it well. Anyone – male or female – can understand why that's insulting.

Just as men have to be sensitive to things that are insulting to their wives, a woman has to be sensitive to the male nature and what's insulting to her husband.

This might be the single biggest thing a woman does that makes it difficult for her husband to be happily married to her: she tries to change him. Although it comes from good intentions, and it's probably true that she only means it for his good, it makes it difficult for him to like her, let alone love her.

This is the 6th Really Dumb Mistake That Very Smart Couples Make: women forget that men come from Mars and their need for respect is very deep, and very different, than a woman's need.

Socks on the Floor

A couple came to me. They had been married for many years. Their marriage was okay, the wife reported, but he has an annoying habit that drives her crazy—he doesn't clean up after himself. He leaves his dishes on the table after eating. He leaves wrappers on the counter. He leaves his clothing wherever they may be. And no matter how many times she asks him to improve, no matter how many times he promises that he will change, he still leaves his socks on the bedroom floor.

I asked her to describe what happens. She explained that she mentions it to him. And she mentions it again. And again. And again. And again. And again—all to no avail. Finally, one day she loses it. She screams, "CHAIM, WHAT'S WRONG WITH YOU? YOU'RE 40 YEARS OLD! WHY DO YOU STILL LEAVE YOUR SOCKS ON THE FLOOR?!"

I said to her, "As you mentioned, this isn't the first time that you asked your husband to pick up his socks. In the past, when you asked, did it help?"

"No," she said. "The very next day he did it again."

"I see," I said. "And I would imagine that you might have mentioned it a few times after that."

"I sure did!"

"And a few times after that?"

"You bet!"

"And still he didn't change his ways?"

"No. That's the most frustrating part. He just won't change."

"I understand. You asked time after time after time and it hasn't done any good. So here's my question, and I want you to think long and hard before you answer it. Is he a nice guy?"

"Is he a nice guy?" she repeated.

"Yes, is he a nice guy?"

"Yes," she said in a low voice.

"Okay. Is he considerate?"

"Yes."

"Does he help you around the house?"

"Yes."

"So why doesn't he pick up his socks?"

I let the silence hang there for a while and then I said, "I'm sorry to be the bearer of bad news, but he may never change. Some people have great skills in one area, but they're sloppy. Other people are very neat, but they're incompetent in other areas. If you have been trying and trying to get him to change and you're not getting anywhere, this might be one of those situations where you have to face the fact that he's not going to change. And then the question becomes, what do you do?"

I have a simple answer to that.

The Overweight Wife

A man once asked me for advice. He's happily married, loves his wife, but when she had their first child, she put on a little weight. Not long after that she had their second child. Again, she put on some weight. She never got back to her pre-birth weight after the first child, so these extra few pounds were in addition to the extra pounds after the first child. Then she had a third child. They are now married seven years and his wife is 40 pounds heavier than when they met. She's not obese—but it bothers him.

"Rabbi, you have to understand," he explained. "I'm a doctor. I work in a hospital, I'm around young nurses all the time, and they are trim and fit. I don't want to look at them, but it's very hard. I offered my wife anything she wants to help her lose the weight. I offered to pay for a private trainer. I offered to pay for a dietician. She's just not willing. What should I do?"

"Young man," I replied, "you have a choice to make. Either embrace her as she is or suffer."

He was stunned.

"Believe me," I said, "I'm sure she would like to lose that weight. I don't know of a woman who looks in the mirror, sees that she is 40 pounds overweight and says, 'That's great! Just what I always wished for.' You can be sure that it bothers her. But right now, she can't do anything about it. Do you know why? Because change is very difficult."

You might think, *What's so hard? She can join Weight Watchers and stick to the diet. She can learn to eat nutritionally-balanced meals and snacks, she won't go hungry. What's so difficult?*

The answer is that change is difficult. Changing your eating habits is hard. Sticking to a diet is hard. And many times there are just too many things going on in life for a person to take on a new set of obligations. One of the basic realities of life is that that while your spouse has many strengths and talents, they also have weaknesses and shortcomings.

To women I say, just as changing *your* issues isn't simple, it's the same for your husband. If a husband imposes on his wife to be skinnier, neater, or whatever, he's going to pay the price. His words aren't going to be received as words of love. Every time he points it out, he's damaging the relationship. The same thing happens when women try to change men.

Women, it's not your job to change your husband. Men, it's not your job to change your wife. It's the worst thing you can do. The minute you embrace them for who they are is the minute you can begin to be happily married.

But I'm right. He does need to change.

Yes, you are right. But you have a choice to make. You can be right, or you can be happily married—you're not going to get both. If you've tried and tried and it hasn't helped until now, then this issue is unlikely to change. It's up to you whether you accept that reality or pay the bitter price of damaging your relationship.

Are you at your ideal weight?

Next time you find yourself with an insatiable urge to correct your husband, try this simple solution. Before you say anything, go over to a mirror and look at your reflection very carefully. Then answer one question: are you at your ideal weight? (If you are, wait until you hit 40.)

Why aren't you at your ideal weight? There are many exercise classes available. There are many diets out there. Why don't you just stick to the diet and remain at your ideal weight? When you're brutally honest with yourself, you'll acknowledge the answer: Change is hard. And just as change is difficult for you, it is also difficult for your spouse.

You might protest that your weight doesn't bother him. Firstly, who says it doesn't? But even if it doesn't, I'm sure that there are plenty of things that you do that *do* bother him. And I don't think you would be very appreciative if he pointed them out to you, even if he only had your best interests in mind. (And if weight isn't your challenge right now, how about your losing patience with the kids? Or not being able to keep up with housework? Or being jealous of your sister? Or coming late, overspending, or being lazy… We all have stuff. It's very easy for you to see how his "stuff" is preventing him from being as great as he can be; he can see the same for your "stuff.")

This is one of the most fundamental concepts in any relationship: all human beings are flawed. Some things can change. Some can't. But if you insist on trying to change your husband, you're going to pay for it. He's not going to say, "Yes dear, I love you so much for helping me change." He's going to feel hurt. He's going to feel disrespected.

While this is but one small example, it is reflective of a much larger issue that affects both women and men: accepting that some things just aren't going to change. Even though they should. Even though they are basic. Even though they are so easy for you; your spouse isn't you.

Jackets on the Chair

When I speak about this topic, I often use the socks-on-the-floor example. Once, when I was speaking in Chicago, a woman raised her hand and said, "Rabbi Shafier, do you remember you were here two years ago, and you gave that example about the socks on the floor?" Actually, I didn't. But she continued, "It changed my marriage."

"What do you mean?" I asked.

"Well, my husband would come home at the end of the day, take off his jacket and put it on a dining room chair. Sunday night he put a jacket on one chair. Monday night he put a second jacket on the second chair. Tuesday night and Wednesday night, the same. By Thursday, his entire wardrobe was in the dining room."

You could hear the audience trying to restrain themselves.

"What happened?" I asked.

She continued. "I used to scream at him."

"Did it work?"

"No."

"What do you do now?" I asked.

"You told me to embrace him for who he is. So now, on Sunday night, when he leaves his jacket on the chair, I take it upstairs and hang it up. Monday night the same. Tuesday night, the same..."

"How's your *shalom bayis* now?" I asked.

"Wonderful."

I asked all the women in the room stand up and clap.

Of course, it's still his responsibility to put away his jacket. We should all be better. Everybody should be perfect. But we're not. It's his responsibility to get his act together, and one day he might, but he also might not. This woman finally accepted that, and it changed her marriage. Even though it's obvious, I can't say it enough times: You can either be right, or you can be happily married—not both. Because marriage isn't about being right. It's about working together as friends and lovers to find the best possible outcome for everybody.

Just to be clear, this doesn't mean you have to be a doormat and forever keep your mouth closed. If your partner is doing something that really bothers you, there is nothing wrong with communicating that. Doing that is normal, natural and certainly part of a good marriage. But that means communicating effectively (which we'll get to in chapter...). It means that you mention it to your spouse in a tactful way once or twice. But when you did that already, and you did it again, and you did it again, and the same annoying habit hasn't gone away, then you need to make a difficult decision: Do you keep up this futile attempt to make your spouse into something they aren't going to become, or do you accept the reality that your spouse is different than you?

The most difficult part about this approach is that if it's something that truly bothers you, likely it's an area that you are strong in. You're going to keep wondering, "Why is it such a big deal? Why doesn't he just stop doing it? Why doesn't he just change?"

That's when you have to say to yourself, *he's not being passive-aggressive* or *she's not doing it because she doesn't care about my feelings*. They do it because they have a different temperament and a different nature, and just because this area comes easily to me, doesn't mean it's easy for my spouse. You simply have to come to terms with the fact that this point is difficult for them to change.

Should he work on his bad habit? Absolutely. Should she work on what's annoying him? No question about it. He shouldn't leave his socks lying around. She shouldn't write a check without telling her husband. That's 100% correct. But *you* also have things to work on. And just as you have great difficulty changing the things *you* do, so does your spouse.

Whenever his annoying habit surfaces, say to yourself, *my job is to change me. My job is to accept my spouse for who they are.*

Making a Mench Out of Him

Both men and women fall into this trap of trying to change their spouses, but in general women are more affected than men. Worse, sometimes the woman does it *b'shitah*. She thinks, *If not for me, who's going to teach him to be a mentch?*

When I hear this I have only one answer – "Madam, I guarantee you're not going to teach him. Has it worked until now? Or is it destroying your marriage?"

But who's going to teach him to be a mentch?

Maybe nobody. He may never be a *mentch*. Yet one thing is certain – your complaining is not helping. It's not changing him.

It's harming your relationship. Your choice is simple: Either be happily married to a flawed individual or have a miserable marriage to a flawed individual. There is nothing you can do to eradicate the flaw.

(Don't think things would be different if you were married to someone else. You will have this exact problem no matter who you are married to. The specific annoying habit might be different, but it will be there. We all have stuff.)

Bad Advice

Once, I was giving a shiur on shalom bayis in Queens, NY, and Torahanytime was streaming it live. I spent a lot of time on this subject, repeatedly saying, "Don't try to change your husband."

After the shiur, a man came over to show me the string of texts that his wife – who was watching the shiur at home – sent him during the shiur. The basic gist was something like this:

> *My rebbetzin said that that if you see your husband doing something wrong and you don't correct him, you're not accomplishing your mission in life. Hashem put you here to be an ezer knegdo. If you don't correct him, you're not doing your job.*

I said to him, "First, I sincerely doubt the rebbetzin said that or anything like it. And if she did, believe me, her husband doesn't know about it, because that certainly isn't what the Torah means by *ezer kenegdo,* and it's about the worst advice you can give a woman, unless you're a divorce attorney looking to drum up business."

So I would like to say this as clearly as I can:

Don't correct your husband.

Don't try to improve him.

Don't try to make him better. He's fine.

The more accepting you are of him, the happier he'll be, the more he'll love you and the happier you'll be. But the more you try to correct him, change him, or improve him, the more you're sabotaging your relationship, because you're treating him with lack of respect. It's hard for a man to love a woman who's constantly poking him in the eye, constantly jabbing at him. It makes him reactive and angry. He's reactive and angry not because he's immature, but because in the male world, in the male psyche, to be on the receiving end of such behavior is downright insulting.

Why is he being so sensitive?

"But it's for his good."

"And he knows it."

"Why can't he just grow up?"

"He just has an overblown male ego!"

All your girlfriends may agree with you. Maybe even your rebbetzin will agree. But you are headed for trouble, because what you and they don't understand is that by trying to change him, you're demeaning him. Just as he has to learn how to be sensitive to things that hurt *you*, you have to understand his inner world and what matters to him.

At the core of their essence, men need to feel respected. When his wife tries to change him, it's wrong, destructive, and damaging.

"But he's acting like a child!"

If that's your opinion, keep it locked in your heart. Don't treat him like a child. If your husband thinks that you treat him like a child, he's going to treat you like his mother. There are going to be things your spouse does that bother you. That's just part of living with another human being. It's your spouse's responsibility to change, but you have to recognize that change is very difficult.

You can't even change yourself. Just as you accept yourself, you have to learn to accept your spouse.

I think this is clear and we can move on to the next topic. But...

But... But... But...

I once delivered a five-part marriage seminar in Brooklyn. Because it was a large crowed, it was arranged that after the *shiur*, the audience would write down their questions. The papers would be collected and handed up to me to read and answer.

In one session, I repeatedly stressed the point that your job is not to change your spouse. I said it over and over (and over and over). I thought I made it pretty clear. But when the questions came up after I was done, one woman after another asked the same question.

Question #1: Rabbi, what if I try to change him nicely?
No. Madam, it is not your job to change your husband, even if you do it nicely.

Question #2: What if I use positive reinforcement?
No. Not even if you use positive reinforcement.

Question #3: What if I use humor?
No. Don't do it.

Question #4: What if I use consequences?
This was more than I could handle, and I jokingly (although not so jokingly) responded, "Let me play that out for a moment. 'Shloime, if you don't pick up your socks, you're not getting lunch tomorrow.' Yeah, that will do it, that will really help your marriage... Please don't do it. It's not your job to change your spouse. It doesn't work. It damages the relationship. Don't do it."

I thought the women in the audience got the point, but then I got emails after the *shiur*.

> *Rabbi, I enjoyed the shiur very much and I'm not arguing with your point. I'm just asking so I can better understand: If I can't change my husband nicely, or with humor, or with positive reinforcement, or with consequences, how am I going to change him?*

I'm not kidding. I actually received that email.

The clincher, though, was this one:

> *Maybe so many women are commenting on this, despite all the time you spent on this topic, not because we're not understanding you, but maybe because we don't agree with you.*

Of course you don't agree with me—you're a nurturing caregiver and you want to help. You want to shower your husband with everything good and you know that you can make him even better. In fact, you're going to keep trying to make him better even if it kills you, him, and your marriage. Which it will.

As much as your attempts to change him are well-intentioned, as much as it's only coming from your love for him, it's destructive. It's rude. It's damaging. It's not your job. Don't do it.

Your Side of the Mechitzah

The following rule applies to both men and women: Keep your eyes on your side of the *mechitzah*. Gentlemen, you have a job in life. Hashem put you on this planet to grow and accomplish — to work on who *you* are. Keep your eyes on your side of the *mechitzah*. Change yourself.

Ladies, Hashem put you on the planet to grow and accomplish — to work on who *you* are. Keep your eyes on your side of the *mechitzah*. Change yourself.

The One Way to Change Your Spouse

Because this is such a hot issue, and seems to be so ingrained, I will share with you a secret. There actually is a way (and it's the only way known to man) to get your spouse to change.

Let me illustrate with a *mashal*.

A man finds himself locked in room. He looks around and sees cement walls and no windows. There is only one way out—a door. He pushes, but it won't open. He pushes harder. Nothing. He pushes even harder. Nothing. He pounds. He kicks. He smashes. Nothing. It won't open. He tries and tries. Day after day, he batters, smashes, and claws. No matter how hard he tries, the door just won't budge. He's getting desperate.

Finally, he says to himself, "This is it. If I don't get out now, I'm going to die in here. Maybe I haven't pushed hard enough. Maybe I haven't really mustered my all." He braces himself, takes a deep breath and in a mad lunge rushes for the door. CRASH! He falls. He gets up and pushes again with all his might. He falls again. He gets up and pushes again. He's now red in the face, sweating profusely, pushing and pushing, until out of sheer exhaustion he crumples to the floor. It's over. He's trapped forever. Crying his last tears, he looks up. On the bottom of the doorknob is the word "pull."

Suddenly, it's all clear to him. The door doesn't open outward. It opens inward. He was pushing so hard; all he needed to do was pull.

Husbands and wives push and push to change their spouse and it never works because they're pushing when they should be pulling. Pull back and work on yourself to embrace your spouse for who they are. Ironically, that's when things can change. He'll feel respected and accepted. She'll feel loved and cherished. They are both far more eager to please their spouse. Does it mean their spouse will change? Not necessarily. Many things can't change. But in an environment of respect and love, at least it's possible.

Gentlemen, work on accepting your wife exactly as she is. When a woman feels cherished, she's more motivated to please you, and that increases the likelihood that she's going to change. Ladies, let your husband know that you respect him and accept him exactly as he is. Let him know that you don't want to change him.

If you get one thing out of this book, let it be that it's not your job to change your spouse. Your job is to embrace your spouse. If change is necessary, your job is to change *yourself*. If you change yourself, your spouse may change too. But setting out to change your spouse will get you nowhere.

Although this applies to both men and women, it is typically far more damaging to a man when his wife tries to change him. But there are other ways that men are sensitive, and a wise woman will try to understand them so that she won't accidentally hurt her husband.

Boys and Girls and Independence

While girls crave attachments and relationships, boys crave independence. Even at a young age, boys value self-reliance and the sense of not being dependent on anyone—certainly not Mommy! This is part of the male nature.

These differences manifest themselves in the relationship.

The Unconsulted Donation

After my wife and I married, we opened a *maaser* account. Before I'd draw on the account to make a donation, I'd ask my wife what she thought. She always agreed.

Once someone asked me for a donation and I wrote a check for $100, but I didn't have the opportunity to ask my wife. When she found out, she was upset.

"I don't understand," I said. "I've written larger checks. You never questioned my judgment then." Why was she suddenly bothered by this $100 check?

It took me a long time to understand that it had nothing to do with the money and everything to do with feeling connected. She wasn't questioning my judgment. She was questioning why I didn't ask her. *We do these things together,* was her attitude. *When you did it independently it was like you wanted to be apart from me.*

Once I understood this, it became much easier for me to relate to my wife, and it became much easier for her to understand me.

My Buddy's Coming for Shabbos

Shlomie gets a call from one of his old buddies. "Hey, how are ya? Listen, I'm going to be in town this weekend. Can I come for *Shabbos*?"

"Absolutely," he replies. "It'd be great to have you."

He hangs up the phone and tells his wife, "Good news, Ruchie. My old buddy is coming for *Shabbos*."

Her face falls. "Why you didn't ask me first?" she replies.

It takes Shlomie a minute or two to process this. She seems displeased. In fact, she looks hurt.

"Well, you always have extra food. You don't mind company. Don't you always tell me to invite guests? I didn't think you'd mind."

If we could see into their inner worlds, this is what we would find: When Shlomie was on the phone, he did think about asking his wife if it was okay to invite his buddy, but he felt awkward. What's it going to sound like? *Like I need my wife to approve it? Like I can't do anything without permission?*

The reason he feels this way is because he's a guy. For a guy, dependence on anyone, even a spouse, is bad. It's embarrassing to need his wife's consent. It implies that he's not a man. Men are independent. In charge.

The reason she finds it so hurtful is because in her world, dependence on a spouse is a good thing. If she says that she has to ask her husband, it's almost bragging. It conveys: *My husband and I are attached.* In a female world, being attached is a source of pride. In a male world, it's embarrassing.

If you think this sounds petty and juvenile, you're probably a woman. Most guys relate to this very strongly. The important thing is for both husband and wife to be aware of what's typical for a woman and a man, so that they can put things into context and understand why their spouse does what they do.

Playing Ball After Shabbos

Another example: A husband tells his wife he wants to play ball with the guys on *motzei Shabbos*. She's fine with it. "Go, it's great."

The game goes on longer than he expected. When he gets home, she's upset. "How come you didn't call?"

The truth is that he thought to call, but he was with his friends. It would be embarrassing to call his wife in the middle of a game and "ask permission," as if he's a little kid staying out past his bedtime.

This couple is upset with each other because they aren't accounting for the different needs of men and women. Men strive for independence. Women strive for interdependence.

If you don't understand this, you will completely misread your spouse.

It's Not a Matter of Being Controlling

I have heard many husbands describe their wives as "controlling."

What does she want? For me to tell her everywhere I go? Everything little thing I do? To ask her permission? She's such a controlling person.

Some women are controlling, but very often the problem has nothing to do with control: He wants to act independently, and she thinks he wants to act like he's not married. She doesn't understand that he's just acting like a guy. That's all.

She has to recognize that if he doesn't call, it's not because he doesn't want to be married to her or that he doesn't love her. For his part, he has to recognize that she is proud of their attachment and wants her to let him know where he's going.

To be a supportive spouse you have to recognize what is important to your partner. It might not be important to you, and it might not even make sense to you, but it's still true.

One of the hardest parts of marriage is learning that your spouse is different than you.

Different by nature, upbringing, attitudes, and outlooks. Even if something doesn't bother you, it still might deeply hurt your spouse.

And, ladies, I guarantee that if you don't accept your husband's "maleness," there is something that *he* will never be able to accept…

Chapter 6

A Woman's Need To Talk

WHAT'S THE MOST IMPORTANT skill in a good marriage?

If you were to present this question to a room full of people, I think most would say: communication.

That is, if you were asking a room full of women. If you were asking that question to a room full of men, I doubt that would be their answer.

I have tried this time after time and found it to be true. An article in the Journal of Personality and Social Psychology quotes a study of 264 couples who were asked this question: What is the most necessary factor to achieve satisfaction in your relationship?

Almost all the women said communication. Almost none of the men gave that answer.

Ted Huston, a psychologist at the University of Texas who has studied couple relationships in depth, observes, "For the wives, intimacy means talking things over, especially talking about the relationship itself. The men, by and large, don't understand what their wives want from them. They say, 'I want to do things with her, and all she wants to do is talk.'"

One marriage therapist describes watching this play out in real time. She was treating a couple, and the husband told her that the best part of their relationship was that they could just sit together on the couch holding hands and listening to music – they didn't have to always be talking about something. Yet when the therapist spoke to his wife, her description was a bit different. "Yeah. He'll just sit there like a lump of clay. Not saying a word. There are times I get so angry with him I want to hit him over the head with a bat."

Probably the most common complaint marriage therapists hear from women is, "We never talk."

The most common complaint from men is, "All we do is talk. We talk and talk and talk."

Now somebody's got it wrong.

The Talker

> **ספר בראשית פרק ג**
>
> כ) וַיִּקְרָא הָאָדָם שֵׁם אִשְׁתּוֹ חַוָּה כִּי הִוא הָיְתָה אֵם כָּל חָי:
>
> *And the man called his wife Chava because she was the mother of all humans.*
>
> **בעל הטורים על בראשית פרק ג פסוק כ**
>
> כ) ויקרא האדם שם אשתו חוה - על שם שמחוה. וזהו שאמרו (קידושין מט, ב) יו"ד קבין שיחה ירדו לעולם, תשעה נטלו נשים:
>
> *He named his wife Chava because she was a talker. This is what is said: ten measures of speech came down into the world, and women took nine of them.*

"And the man called his wife Chava because she was the mother of all humans." (*Bereishis* 3:20).

The *Baal HaTurim* explains that the name Chava means "talker." Adam called his wife Chava because she was talkative. The *Baal HaTurim* continues, "And this is what the Gemara in *Kiddushin* says, 'Ten measures of speech came into the world, and women took nine.'"

This *Baal HaTurim* is very difficult to understand. Firstly, "Talker" doesn't sound like a very nice way to refer to your wife. But this problem becomes magnified when we put it in context.

The Medrash explains that Hashem wanted to show the *malachim* the vast wisdom of man, so He asked them to name the animals. They couldn't. Then Hashem asked Adam to name the animals. Without hesitation, he began. "This is a shor, this is a gamal. This is a chamor…" When the *malachim* saw Adam's stunning brilliance, they were awed.

The *mefarshim* explain that Hashem wasn't asking the *malachim* to simply invent names for the animals. When we name something, we just pick a term as a convenient reference. The word in no way defines the object; it's just a label. When we need an easy way to reference something with four legs and a flat part on top, we call it a table. Something tall with roots and leaves we call a tree. The word *table* is a convenient way of referring to this object, but in no way does it *define* the object.

But Hashem was asking Adam to use a term that defines the essence of each animal, its nature and inclinations. Hashem created the world with words and the words formed the object. If one were privy to the inner nature of the object, one could infer its name. The name is practically the DNA of the object.

Hashem infused Adam with a vast amount of wisdom and knowledge. It's as if he opened his eyes and his mind contained a fully loaded Wikipedia. With stunning brilliance, Adam was able to sum up each of the creatures with a single expression that became their name.

Now the Baal HaTurim is extremely problematic. When it was time for Adam to name his wife, he called her "Talker." How does "Talker" define her essence? Even if you argue that women speak more than men, that doesn't define her. It's surely not what made her the mother of future generations. What does this mean?

Monkeying Around

In the early 1950's, Harry Harlow, a psychologist, conducted a study on how primates learn. He had difficulty obtaining enough monkeys to experiment on, so he began breeding them. He found it more efficient to bring up the monkeys without the mothers around, so right after birth he separated the baby and kept it isolated in a cell. The monkeys were well fed, but for the first twenty-four months of life they had almost no contact with other living beings.

Dr. Harlow discovered something that was surprising to scientists at the time. Although his monkeys were well-cared for physically, they couldn't socialize, they couldn't learn, and they couldn't function as regular monkeys. They weren't lacking food or any other physical need. They were lacking a mother's love and attention. Harlow presented to the world scientific evidence that the role of the mother as caregiver and nurturer is essential for the psychological and emotional health of the monkey.

This discovery was revolutionary in the early 1950s. At time, there was a debate amongst psychologists and social scientists over whether mothers were even needed. Many posited that the role of the mother was strictly to provide food, clothing and warmth, but that a nurturing bond was unnecessary. For the most part, this was accepted as scientific fact.

Mothers were warned not to have too much physical contact with their newborns in order to avoid spoiling the child and stifling her development. "Never hug and kiss them or let them sit on your lap," wrote John Watson, the American psychologist who established the school of behaviorism. "Shake hands with them in the morning. Give them a pat on the head if they have made an extraordinarily good job of a difficult task. If you must, kiss them once on the forehead when they say goodnight."

New mothers were told to ignore their most fundamental instincts and avoid holding their infant at all unless they were feeding the baby, changing a diaper, or otherwise providing very basic care. Hospital nurseries around the country followed through on the best advice that science had to offer. Not long after birth, the baby was taken from the mother and isolated as much as possible. Orphanages propped bottles and left babies unattended. Good mothers were told – in books by leading psychologists and physicians – not to pick up the baby even when she cried. Doing so would pamper and ruin the child.

When Harry Harlow discovered the deprivation factor, he offered a whole new understanding of the mother-child dynamic. "By this ingenious research," Harlow said, "we learned what had been totally obvious to everyone else, except psychologists, for centuries." Infants need warm, physical contact and comfort.

Though widely accepted now, that idea was revolutionary at the time. A baby needs its mother's touch. It needs to be loved. It needs a caregiver, a nurturer.

Who's smarter, men or women?

The next time you are at a Shabbos meal with the entire family gathered and you want to liven things up a bit, here's a trivia question to ask: Who's smarter, men or women?

While I'm sure you will get very strong opinions on both sides, in reality there seems to be no distinguishable difference. In math, science, comprehension and memory, it seems that men and women are of about equal intelligence.

Dr. Summers' Big Mistake

This is intriguing because in January 2005, Lawrence Summers, who was then the president of Harvard University – one of the most prestigious posts in all academia – made a statement that created quite a stir in the scientific community.

> "It appears that in terms of mathematical ability, and scientific ability, there is a significant difference of a standard deviation between the male and female population. And that is true with respect to attributes that are and are not plausibly, culturally determined."

Effectively he was saying that in terms of math and science, men are a lot smarter than women and therefore women are innately less suited than men to be top-level mathematicians and scientists.

Ironically, it turns out he was wrong; he missed a subtlety. Studies of boys and girls age twelve or younger show no significant difference in mathematical abilities. In terms of intellect and academic capacity they are the same. Where they differ is *interests*. As boys and girls begin maturing and their bodies begin changing, differences in what they find interesting begin to surface.

In her book *The Female Brain*, Dr. Louann Brizendine explains: "We now know that when girls and boys first hit their teen years, the difference in their mathematical and scientific capacity is nonexistent. But as estrogen floods the female brain, females start to focus intensely on their emotions and on communication—talking on the phone and connecting with their girlfriends at the mall. At the same time, as testosterone takes over the male brain, boys grow less communicative and become obsessed about scoring—in games, and in other male related interests. At the point when boys and girls begin deciding the trajectories of their careers, girls start to lose interest in pursuits that require more solitary work and fewer interactions with others, while boys can easily retreat alone to their rooms for hours of computer time."

These changes impact academic performance. When a girl reaches twelve or thirteen, she begins losing interest in subjects that require her to study alone because her desire to be with friends is far more powerful than her interest in the subject. In a boy's world, it's the opposite. As he hits twelve or thirteen, he becomes more comfortable in a solitary environment and can study alone for hours.

This can explain why there are far more male mathematicians and scientists. It apparently has little or nothing to do with *capacity* and has everything to do with *interest*. The hours required to excel in those fields are better suited for solitary study. So while there are many excellent female scientists and mathematicians, there are more males in those fields – not because of capacity but because of interest.

Hashem planted in women this inner desire to connect to others because she is the one who nurtures children. Today it's common knowledge that if the mother doesn't hold, cuddle and coo to her baby, it actually damages the child. Modern science understands that the role of the mother goes beyond providing food, clothing, and basic needs. The main role of the mother is to nurture the child so he feels secure and loved. The mother-child bond builds emotional attachment, providing security. Nurturing is built into the nature of women.

It's not just interest that predisposes women to be nurturers. The brain center for language and hearing in females has 11% more neurons than in males. The hippocampus is larger in women because that's the part of the brain that processes emotions and memory. Not only are women hormonally disposed toward nurturing, but the actual parts of the brain that processes those functions are further developed.

So while the brains of men and women are the same in terms of raw output, they're very different in terms of what they're programmed to do and how they're programmed to see things.

Brizendine writes: *The female brain has tremendous unique aptitudes—outstanding verbal agility, the ability to connect deeply in friendship, a nearly psychic capacity to read faces and tone of voice for emotions and states of mind, and the ability to defuse conflict. All of this is hardwired into the brains of women. These are the talents women are born with that many men, frankly, are not.*

There is a reason why Hashem gave women these unique gifts.

The Mainstay of the Home

A woman's role in the family is to be the *akeres habayis*, the "mainstay of the home." Her role is to cultivate, nurture, and support the family; to be a wife and mother.

Some people confuse *akeres habayis* with the term "domestic help." Women who perform that function are called housekeepers. That's not what the Torah means by the woman being the *main support* of the home. A woman is the center of the family, the one who brings them together. She is the "relationship manager" of the family. Her role is to be the one who nurtures both her children and her husband. To be suited for that role, Hashem crafted her with a unique nature, different than that of a man. While the home is certainly her domain, and housework is part of that, it is but a small part of her role.

When our kids were little, I told my wife that we needed to hire as much cleaning help and buy as much takeout food for Shabbos as possible. I specifically asked her not to bake challah. My wife said, "What do you mean? Why don't you want me to bake challah? Isn't that a woman's *mitzvah*?"

"What our family needs right now," I said, "is for you to devote your attention to our children, to be there with them, to get down on the floor with them and play. They need your time and nurturing. When they grow up, you'll have plenty of time to bake challah. Right now, your primary role is to nurture the kids."

A few years ago, I traveled to South Africa. Domestic help is very inexpensive there, and almost every *frum* home has at least two full-time, live-in maids who cook, clean, and take care of all housework. I was there on an eight-day speaking tour, but I could have brought just two shirts, because when I returned from *shul* in the morning, the shirt that I had worn the day before was cleaned and pressed and waiting for me on my bed (which was made). The Jewish women in South Africa don't have to clean, do the laundry, or cook. So, what do they do all day? They nurture, support, and bring up their children. The role of the *akeres habayis* isn't to be a maid. Her primary responsibility is to take care of her family: to nurture them, guide them, and be there for them.

This seems to be the answer to the Baal HaTurim.

How do human beings create and develop relationships? There's only one way—communication. Through speech, we create social connections. A woman *needs* to connect; she needs to express her emotions and feel other people's emotions because that is how relationships are built. Hashem designed her to seek out, build, and repair relationships because she's the mother of all future generations. She was formed with the capacity to care for her family and to nurture them.

This is why Adam called his wife Chava. It wasn't because she was chatty. Hashem gave women a talkative nature because their role is to create and build relationships. Speech is the vehicle to create attachments. When Adam called her "Talker," it's equivalent to calling her "Relationship Builder."

Man, on the other hand, was not given that nature because it's not his role. As a result, there is a marked difference between men and women in *why* they talk, *how* they talk and *what* they talk about. These differences surface in their roles as parents, and certainly in their relationship as husband and wife.

What are you talking about?

Deborah Tannen is a social linguist who has authored several bestsellers that focus on the nature of men and women as revealed in their respective styles of speech. She makes several important observations. One is that men and women talk for very different reasons.

- Men talk to share ideas.
- Women talk to connect.

For women, talk is the glue that connects the two parties in the relationship. The subject matter they talk about matters less than the fact that they are talking. Women talk to bring others into their world and bring themselves into the world of others. Women bond through talking.

Men, on the other hand, bond through activities they do together. Men talk to communicate information and ideas. *What* men talk about and *why* they talk is different than what women talk about and why.

Once I understood this distinction, I realized that I owed my mother, a"h, an apology.

When I was away at yeshivah, each time I called home my mother would ask me, "What's new?" I had a tough time answering that. What was I going to say, we learned an amazing Marharsha? We're stuck on a Tosfos?

There was little I could tell her because I was in yeshivah and that was my life. It took me decades to understand what she was asking. She wanted to connect. This was her son and he no longer lived at home. She wanted to feel attached. She was asking for the details of my life because that was her way of joining me in my life.

The Most Important Issue

Because men and women talk for different reasons, they have a hard time understanding each other. When men listen to women talk, they think that they're talking about irrelevant trivia: People and occurrences, what happened, what she said and what he said... What does it matter? In an objective sense, he's correct – it doesn't matter. It's not earth-shattering or even relevant; in fact, it makes no practical difference to him or her, or to anyone else. So why is she telling it to him? Because she's building their relationship. She's sharing her inner world, she's expressing herself, and she expects that from him in return.

The reality is that for a woman, communication is essential. It's part of her nature. She craves relationships. She needs to bond. Hashem equipped her for that via the gift of speech.

Men don't talk to build relationships. When one guy talks to another guy, he's telling him stuff. Men talk to convey information.

This is one of the reason that couples misread each other.

"How was your day?"

A *chassan* and *kallah* get married and things are going pretty well. One day, the *chassan* comes home and the first thing his young wife says to him is, "So dear, how was your day?"

"Good."

"Just good?"

"Yeah, good. It was good."

"Is that all? Nothing happened today?"

"No, no, it was good."

This is the beginning of the divide.

He's thinking, *What does she mean 'just good'? What does she think, some catastrophe happened? I said good, I mean good. Why is she asking all these questions?*

She's thinking, *Why isn't he telling me about his day? Why isn't he sharing with me?* What she hears is: *He wants to be distant. He doesn't want to be connected. He wants to be apart from me.*

So she probes a little more: "Nothing happened?"

Now he's thinking, *Does she need to know everything I do every minute of the day? Why is she so nosy?*

Neither of them get it.

He's not trying to push her away. It's just that most guys simply don't "talk about their day."

She's not nosy. She just wants to feel connected. And more than that, she wants him to share with her because she wants to feel part of his life.

The Chazon Ish writes that when a man leaves his house, he has to tell his wife where he's going. When he returns, he has to tell her what he did. These routines may be inconsequential in his eyes, but they are essential habits that make a big difference in their relationship.

Small Talk

This is one of the reasons couples have different perceptions about their relationship, and specifically the need for communication. Many young *chassanim* are shocked to find that all she wants to do is talk. Do they love their wives? Absolutely. Is conversation helpful? Without doubt, he will say. But most men will tell you that spending time talking about things is a lot less important to him than it is to her. The relationship may be important to men, but they bond through different means. For women, the primary means of connecting is talking—and often she feels that she and her husband just don't talk enough.

And this is the 6th Really Dumb Mistake that Very Smart Couples Make—they forget that talk means something different to women than it does to men.

Ma'am, You Married a Man

Once you understand this you'll appreciate why men regularly claim "we talk all the time" while women complain "we never talk." I often ask kallahs: Before you met your *chassan,* how much time did you spend talking to your friends on the phone every night? The typical answer is two or three hours.

When I ask the chassan, he says, "Maybe ten minutes."

During the early stages of their relationship – the infatuation phase, when everything feels magical – he wanted to talk for hours on end. Then the magic wore off, and the real work began. He has to learn to share and communicate. She has to learn that he's not a woman; he probably won't be able to handle as much talk as you do.

Both spouses have a responsibility to the relationship. He has to learn how to connect through conversation and sharing. She has to recognize that it's not natural for him. As a couple, they have to strike a balance. Together, they find the middle ground.

Gentlemen, if you want to have a strong marriage, spend time conversing with your wife. It may not come naturally to you, but if you want to make our wife happy, you have to communicate. It doesn't necessarily have to be deep, meaningful conversations. It doesn't have to be heavy. But the conversation should be real. And it's a good idea to make it a ritual – you talk every day over dinner or when you get back from Maariv, or whatever time works for you as a couple.

Ladies, a piece of advice: keep your girlfriends. You're probably not going to be able to share, analyze, debate, discover, vent and process everything with your husband like you can with them. Save the main things to share with him, but don't expect your husband to singlehandedly, fully meet your need to talk. It's not because he doesn't care, and not because he doesn't love you—he's simply not built for that.

But there's more to communication than just talking.

A husband and wife are on a date, having a conversation. About 20 minutes in, the woman says to her husband, "You're not listening to a word I say!"

"What do you mean?" he replies. He then repeats everything she said, word for word.

"You see," she says, "that proves you're not listening."

He's dumbfounded. He's been listening intently, and she's accusing him of not listening to a word!

If you would like to know the explanation to this great mystery, go to a *shul* during a *kiddush* and listen to the men talking. Then listen to the women talking. Pay attention not to *what* they're saying but to the *sounds* in the communication.

On the woman's side you'll hear something like this:

"Talk. Talk. Talk."
"Aaaaaaah."
"Talk. Talk. Talk."
"Oooooooh."
"Talk. Talk. Talk."
"Mmmmmmm."
Followed by, "So nice talking to you, Shira!"

On the men's side, you'll hear:

"Talk. Talk. Talk."
Silence.
"Talk. Talk. Talk."
Silence."
Talk. Talk. Talk."
Silence.
Followed by, "Great talking to you. Bye."

One of the differences in communication is that men listen in silence, and women make "listening sounds." Women do that because they are not just communicating ideas. The point of the conversation is to share, bond and connect. The woman who is listening offers feedback to show that she relates—that's how you bond.

When a wife is speaking to her husband, she wants to know that he's with her, that he understands her situation and relates to it. She doesn't care that he can repeat word for word what she said. The question is whether he *felt* what she described.

Guys need to learn to listen in a way that may not come naturally to them. Male conversation tends toward things, objects, and maybe accomplishments. We talk about politics, business, sports and hopefully learning, but not much about people or experiences.

Since we're not accustomed to communicating our emotions, we certainly aren't focused on listening for the underlying feelings being expressed.

When your wife is talking, try to identify the emotional undercurrent. What is she feeling? She describes an experience – what was it like for her? Try to climb into her emotional world.

Face to Face

There is another factor that causes men and women to misread each other.

My daughter has twin girls. At eight months, they were already the apple of my eye – not just because they were my grandchildren, and not just because they were so cute, but because any time I walked into the room they looked right at me.

Infant boys rarely look you in the face, but girls won't take their eyes off you. The face is the window to the emotions and girls are hardwired to focus on emotions.

It's not only infants and children. Watch men and women in conversation. When women talk, they usually look right at each other, maintaining eye contact. When men talk, they're not even looking in each other's direction.

When my daughter was in eighth grade, she had a friend over one Shabbos afternoon. They were sitting on opposite ends of the couch with their feet tucked underneath them, facing each other and talking. I remember thinking to myself that they look like a young married couple having an intimate conversation.

That's not the way men talk. When men talk, one guy is looking this way and the other guy is looking that way. They might be out fishing, they might be on the opposite sides of the table learning *Gemara*, but they're not usually making eye contact. They're not wired to be attuned to emotions, so they're not usually focused on the face.

Researchers took men and women of different ages and directed them to enter a room and sit down. In the room were two chairs facing forward. "If you wish to talk," they were told, "talk. If you don't wish to talk, don't talk." That's all the researcher said to each group. They found that almost invariably, when two women, young or old, went into the room, they sat down, moved the chairs to face each other, and began talking. When two men went into the room, they didn't move the chairs and would talk only sometimes.

Often, a woman feels that her husband is not listening, but he is. He might even be listening very carefully. But she doesn't think so, because he's not making listening sounds ("Oh, I hear… mmm…"), or not making eye contact. To her, that means he's not paying attention.

It's not a matter of right or wrong. It's simply a fact to be aware of. Men and women are wired to communicate in different ways. He has to work on looking at her when they're talking. She has to work on recognizing that if he's not looking at her, that doesn't automatically mean he's not listening, doesn't care, and doesn't cherish her.

There is, however, another function of speaking that might be even more foreign to guys, but just as critical to wives.

Validation

I was speaking at a shabbaton, and one of the sessions was right before *shalosh seudos*. I had opened the floor to questions, and it was getting late. One woman raised her hand and said, "Rabbi, this has nothing to do with what you're talking about, but I'd like to say a *kaddish* for my father now."

There was a halachic reason why I didn't think it was appropriate, and a number of people still had questions. So I said, "I'll tell you what, we're going to *daven Maariv* soon. Why don't we say *kaddish* for him at *Maariv*?"

She went ballistic. "WHAT'S WRONG WITH YOU? My father was a Holocaust survivor! You won't say Kaddish for him? WHAT KIND OF PERSON ARE YOU?!"

I responded, "I'm sorry you feel that way." I took the next person's question and the session was over—at least I thought it was.

At *shalosh seudas*, she approached me and let loose another barrage of complaints about me, my behavior, my yeshiva, my family—whatever. The only thing I could do was remain silent; she clearly wasn't in the frame of mind to hear anything rational. I said, "I'm sorry you feel that way," but she wasn't done. As I got my food from the buffet, she followed me around, continuing her tirade. Finally, I said one last time, "I'm sorry you feel that way," and left the room.

At the time, I thought I handled it pretty well. After all, I didn't react. Here she was attacking me mercilessly and I just held my tongue. And while that part was fine, afterward I realized that I had missed an opportunity. What if had asked myself, *why is she so upset? Why would she react so outlandishly?* It's not every day that a woman loses it like that in public. *Maybe there's something going on that I'm not seeing.*

Had I taken the critical step of considering her perspective, I might have understood that from her point of view her reaction was appropriate. After all, she wanted to do a good thing, in honor of her father. And this man, supposedly a rabbi no less, won't do it. He refuses, and for no reason!

I missed that opportunity because I heard her words, but I didn't listen for *why* she said those words. Her words were harsh, critical, and uncalled for—from my perspective. And yet, I was rude, disrespectful, and uncaring—from her perspective. She was in her world. I was in mine. Things spun out of control because we couldn't understand the situation from the other's point of view.

The ability to see another person's perspective and recognize it as valid is important for all relationships, but in marriage it is vital.

The three pillars of marriage are: commitment to work on your marriage, working on the relationship, and learning to live together. In terms of living together, being able see things from your spouse's perspective is probably the single most important skill. Every disagreement begins with two different perspectives, and it will never be resolved until you are able to at least recognize your spouse's way of thinking.

But it's more than just conflict resolution. The essence of your relationship is the sense of being one. When you climb into your spouse's inner world you are connecting to them on a deep level. You are saying, *I understand you. I get why you feel the way you feel, and it makes sense. I may not feel the same way, but we are in this together. I relate to you. I live in your world.* That process connects you.

The problem is that we often miss our cues.

Fixing the Problem

As a rebbi in yeshivah, the guys would often come to me with their problems and life issues. I would listen and offer guidance. It seems that most guys thought I gave pretty good advice. Twenty years later, they still come over to me and say, "Rabbi Shafier, thank you. I don't know if you remember, but that advice you gave me back in high school—I still use it today…"

Over the years, however, I noticed something strange. Whenever I would speak with a talmid, they walked away happy. A guy would bring some problem to me, I would listen for a while, maybe we'd discuss it, then I would offer him my approach to the situation. And generally, it seemed to work.

But whenever my wife asked me for advice, she was never happy with my answer. It was as if the moment I walked in the door my IQ dropped 80 points. It didn't make sense.

It took about ten years for me to get it. My wife was never happy with my advice because she wasn't asking for advice!

She was asking me to listen. She wanted to share her issues, her problems, what was going on in her world. I thought she was presenting a problem for me to solve. It took me a solid decade to figure out that she didn't want me to solve her problem. She wanted me to feel with her. She wanted me to relate. She wanted me to say, "Oh wow, I understand how you feel. I'm so sorry you feel that way. That must be hard."

The reason it took me so long to understand this is because I'm a guy. Guys don't work that way. If a guy is upset, he doesn't go around the dorm talking to everyone about his problems.

A guy needs to learn how to listen to his wife. It doesn't come naturally to men. They're used to problem-solving. They're not used to staying quiet and hearing out another person's feelings and emotions. This is new for men.

So here are some rules for becoming a good listener.

Two Ears, One Mouth

The first rule is not to interrupt. Just keep quiet and let your wife talk. It's a good rule for any conversation with any human being, but it's nonnegotiable when talking with your wife.

Studies show that the average person listens for just 7 to 17 seconds before starting to talk. That's all the average person gives somebody before he interjects his own opinion. The ability to listen without interrupting is a great skill in life. It's a vital skill when talking to your wife.

But it's very important that your marriage not be the training ground to learn this skill. Train yourself on others. Learn not to interrupt when speaking to anyone. In your marriage, you should be a professional listener. If you're not, act as if you are. Don't interrupt. Let your wife speak. Keep your mouth shut. Don't give advice. Don't argue.

This is especially hard for guys brought up in yeshivah, where we're trained to argue and debate. Guys even rate themselves on how quickly they can *shlug* up the other guy. That's great in the *beis medrash*. It's a disaster at home. Therefore, the first rule of listening is to train yourself not to interrupt. Just seal your lips.

For the record, it's not only men who don't know how to listen; women can be as guilty as men of interrupting and not listening to their husbands.

There is, however, another aspect of listening that might be even more crucial.

Validating, Revisited

Let's go back to the woman who wanted to say kaddish. After it was over, we went our separate ways, probably never to cross paths again, so the ramifications of our encounter aren't earth-shattering. But what did we think about each other after the event? When she began speaking in very heated terms, I looked at her like she was an alien from outer space. I believed her reaction was out of bounds, and my response and body language conveyed the message that she was overreacting and maybe even unstable.

But what do you think she thought about me? I would imagine that she believed I was cruel for not granting her innocent request. But what compounded the situation dramatically was my reaction. Not only did I stand there as if I had done nothing wrong, I looked at her like she was some kind of alien, as if she was mentally unstable, as if she were crazy! That's a pretty infuriating reaction for a woman to get when she knows that she's right.

Acknowledging her perspective is not enough, though.

Imagine if I had said, "I see you're upset, and the reason is obvious. Your father was dear to you and you want to do something in his memory. Here's a rabbi saying it's not appropriate, and that makes no sense to you. I certainly understand why you're upset. But I want you to know that it's not that I don't want to do something for your father. I just feel it's more appropriate to say *kaddish* by Maariv."

Had I said something like that, the incident would have ended. She would have heard that response to mean: *I hear you. What you're saying makes sense, but there are other considerations.*

Those words would have validated her feelings.

Validation on its simplest level means letting you know that I recognize your feelings as valid. I am able to climb into your world and I can relate to it. I may not feel the same way, but your feelings make sense. I get it. I understand it. I am with you, and I let you know that. When I validate your feelings, I validate your experience. I validate you.

We humans crave acceptance. We need to know that we fit in, that we belong, and more than anything, that we are okay. That we are normal, regular people going through life. When you act like I'm an alien, doing things or saying things that are abnormal, you certainly aren't accepting me. If anything, it feels like you're looking down at me. Maybe even mocking me.

The problem was that I didn't try to understand her perspective and I didn't validate it. I stayed in my world, and she stayed in hers.

Ensconced in our own worlds, we judge. We project. And we are always right. *There is no excuse for that behavior. That line was completely uncalled for.* The next step naturally follows: We demonize. *Anyone who says that must be… cruel, uncaring, out of their mind, mentally unstable, out of control.* Or whatever adjective neatly defines you as not being a person. Certainly not one whose opinion matters.

At that point, there's no way to bridge the gap.

Validation is conveying the understanding that although my reality may be different than yours, I see how you view things, and I accept your reality as reasonable. Seeing another person's perspective and validating their feelings opens a line of communication and allows us to reach a mutual understanding. Neither of us is crazy, illogical or irrational. We may not view things the same way, but we are two sensible people, each with an acceptable way of looking at things, so finding a solution won't be that difficult.

Just as validation drives connection, invalidation drives disconnection.

When my wife would tell me the events of her day, she was trying to share her inner world with me. She wanted me to recognize what she was experiencing and relate to it—maybe even offer solace or consolation. But more than anything, she was opening up and sharing her life, and she wanted me to be there with her. Because I'm a guy, I didn't get it. Time after time, I would try to solve her problem with my wise advice. When I would "fix her problem" what I was saying to her was, *I'm not like you. I don't feel what you feel. I don't relate to what you are experiencing.* I was driving a wedge between us. (Luckily, my wife was very forgiving; we are still happily married some 30 years later.)

Communication requires listening not just to the words, but to the underlying emotion. Then, acknowledging those emotions as normal and valid. It takes a lot practice—but the payoff is huge. It replaces distance with connection and it brings a couple closer.

"Just Validate" T-shirts

When you start implementing this new style of listening, it may feel unnatural at first.

One summer, my daughter came home from camp with a sweatshirt printed with the Nike swoosh and the words "Just validate." That had been the theme of the summer.

That would never happen in a boys' camp. I don't think the average high school boy knows what the word *validate* means. *What do you mean, "validate"? Why would he be invalid? Is he an illegal alien or something?*

But a woman is accustomed to validation. When she has a problem, she shares it with a friend. Her friend intuitively knows what she needs: She needs to talk it out, unburden herself, discuss it. She needs someone to say, "Oh, that must be terrible, oy, I feel so bad, that's horrible." She doesn't need someone to say, "You shouldn't feel that way. You should feel differently." She needs someone to recognize her feelings as real and understandable based on how *she* perceives the situation.

While I have been focusing here on the guy's need to do this, it applies to women as well. There are women who are sensitive to everyone's inner world—expect their husband's. "Oh, Moishe, cut it out. Stop carrying on. It really doesn't matter." Because she's so used to her reality as a woman, recognizing that a man has different feelings, attitudes, or points of view isn't on her radar. (More on this in the next chapter.)

There's another reason that both husbands and wives have trouble validating each other: they truly care. You don't want to see your wife suffering. You don't want her to feel hurt, or embarrassed, or taken advantage of. In your effort to shield her from pain, you try to correct the situation, or sugarcoat it. You say things like, "It's not that bad," or, "I'm sure they didn't mean it that way." Or the worst: "There's nothing to be nervous about."

In an effort to protect your spouse, you're hurting her. What she thinks is, "Here I am, clearly nervous, and he's telling me there's nothing to be nervous about. What does he think, I'm some incompetent, mentally unhinged, lost soul?" By jumping to solve the problem instead of validating her feelings, you're saying, *your feelings are wrong.* You instinctively want to solve her problem so all her pain will go away and she'll be happy again, but instead you are forcing her to either defend herself, accept that she is overreacting, or recognize that you simply don't care. None of which are at all helpful, and all of which it will damage your relationship.

So what should you say? As little as possible.

Years ago, my mother's friend lost her son suddenly. He was a young man in his forties, in perfect health. He was playing basketball, took a jump shot, and had a heart attack on the way down. He collapsed on the court and died. It was a horrible tragedy.

This woman had known me since I was a child. My mother had recently passed away, and since she couldn't be there for her friend, I felt I should go be *menachem avel.*

I knew it would be an emotional shiva, but I wasn't prepared for what happened when I walked in. The mother of the niftar looked up and said, "Barry is here. He can answer the question." Everyone in the room was silent as she said, "Why did Hashem do this? Why did this happen?"

I walked over to where she was sitting, sat down, and said nothing. When she mentioned something about her son, I said a few words about how fondly I remember him. I said little else. I stayed for about half an hour, saying nothing more. Then I left.

A month later my father told me that this woman called him to tell him that my visit brought her real *nechamah*.

Why didn't I answer her question? I'm not afraid of dealing with questions about death, or even about children dying. There is an entire Shmuz (#165) entitled, *Only the Good Die Young*. So why didn't I offer any of the valid hashkafic answers to her question?

Because there is a time and a place for everything, and this was not it. In the Bais Medrash it is proper to answer difficult questions. In a shiva house, it's not. In a shiva house the focus is on bringing nechama to the mourners. It's not the place to deal with philosophical issues. The way you bring consolation is by being there with them, feeling their pain, and sharing their experience.

The same principle applies when your wife has a problem. Say as little as possible. It's not about solving the problem or finding the bright side. It's about being there with her—sharing her troubles, worries and pain. It's about being in her life with her.

Be Curious

The first step is to say little. The second step is to be curious. Ask her to help you understand. Find out what it was like for her, and how it made her feel.

The goal is to understand why she feels the way she does. It's irrelevant how you would have felt in that situation. Your job is to discover what she's feeling and why. Don't solve the problem. Don't minimize it. Don't look for the bright side. Feel the emotion and let your spouse know you are there with them.

While we're on the topic, here's an advance warning for young chassanim: It won't be long before your wife tells you, "I'm overwhelmed!" It might be when your parents are coming for a meal, or erev Shabbos, or when she talks about work. And you're going to be tempted to say what males always say: "Calm down, it's not that bad. I'm sure it will work out."

I've met many women in my life, and I've met many men. I can't recall even one woman who doesn't get overwhelmed (at least from time to time), but I don't recall one man ever getting overwhelmed. Stressed—maybe. Nervous—okay. But overwhelmed?

It doesn't matter why it's like this. What matters is what your wife is looking for and what she needs at this moment. She needs you to climb into the pit with her and feel her pain, or fear, or worry. You don't have to agree with the cause of the worry, but you need to feel it with her. When you say "There's nothing to worry about," you're saying, "Your feelings are wrong. You don't have a right to feel that way." Instead of coming closer to support her, you are invalidating her and distancing yourself.

(Again, gender differences aren't always true. There are men who desperately crave validation. The key is to recognize the emotional realm of your spouse.)

Let's take a look at another phenomena in communication: the fight.

The Fight

Studies show that when asked to name their best friend, 80% of married men name their wife. Yet the greatest complaint women have about men is that they never want to talk—and certainly not about issues in their marriage. How can we reconcile this?

One reason we discussed is that men don't feel a need to bond through talking; they can feel connected to their spouse by spending time together and doing things together. But there is another reason: In many cases, men don't want to talk because they are deathly afraid of fighting. Men hate talking about their problems because, in their minds, it only leads to one thing: conflict.

Many men have said to me, "All she wants to do is pick a fight. I don't understand her. Every time we talk about this issue, we get into a fight. Why can't she just leave it alone?"

You're right. She *can't* leave it alone. It's really troubling her. She keeps talking about it because that's the way women deal with problems.

Do you ever find yourself telling the same story to five different friends? If you are guy, I highly doubt it ever happened. If you are a woman, I'm relatively sure that it happens (often).

Women speak not just to connect, but also to clarify and process their emotions. Because they feel emotions more acutely than men do, they spend far more time exploring what they are feeling. When a woman speaks about an event or incident, it helps her process her feelings, and then she can calm down and move on.

That's not how men work. Men don't work through their feelings by talking to their friends. When a woman tries to discuss a sensitive topic with her spouse, he's like a fish out of water. He doesn't know what to say or why she wants to talk about this, so he tries to avoid the topic. But she *needs* to talk about it, so she brings it up again. That just makes him more uncomfortable.

As an example: A young couple, married a few years, just had their second child. They are financially stable and she wants to be a stay-at-home mom, so they agree that she'll quit her job. At first, everything's fine. But soon their expenses grow and money gets tight. Since he takes care of the bills, he recognizes this first, but he shields her from any bad news. He doesn't mention they're a month late on the rent. He takes out another credit card to juggle the expenses. Then one day she discovers that they don't have money to pay the early registration for camp and now their older child can't get into camp. She doesn't tell him that she knows, but she's beginning to notice his stress.

Finally, she decides to share her feelings with him.

"You know," she says, looking directly at him, "I wish I could relax about money, but when I see you worrying so much I wonder if I did the right thing by staying home and not working this year."

He's reading a newspaper or hopefully a *sefer*. He knows that as soon as he looks up at her they'll get into an argument, and that's the last thing he wants. "Listen, dear," he says, "Don't worry. It will all work out. Really, it will be fine." Then he goes back to what he was doing.

She thinks, *Why doesn't he want to talk to me? I don't understand it!* So she says, "Maybe I'm not doing the right thing. Maybe I should go back to work. I'm just not sure."

As she utters the words, he starts tensing up. *I don't get her. We're always getting into fights about money. Whenever we bring up the subject, all we do is fight. Why is she bringing it up again? I thought we settled this already!*

He looks at her and says, "Listen, I think you're doing the right thing. It's harder to make the budget work right now but we'll get back on track. I don't think we need to hash this out again."

She's frustrated. *Why can't he open up? I just want to talk it out!*

After a slight pause, she turns to him and says, "I see you really don't want to talk about this, but it bugs me. Whenever I want to talk about this you either change the subject or get all quiet."

I can't believe she's starting a fight, he thinks. He doesn't say a word.

She looks at him and says, "You see, that's exactly what I mean. You're shutting me out again. I'm tired of it. Why don't you let me in? WHY DO YOU ALWAYS DO THIS?"

Now he's turned squarely toward her. "Why are you always starting a fight? Why can't you just leave well enough alone? WHY DO YOU ALWAYS DO THIS?"

They each stalk off — not only to different rooms but to different worlds.

Processing Emotion

This scenario is very common and if a couple doesn't learn what is really going on, the pattern will repeat itself and they will find their relationship constantly cycling between good and bad and not even knowing why.

It's not that great a mystery: each is reacting from their perspective, judging the conversation from their world. Once they learn the inner world of their spouse, it becomes much easier to avoid these conflicts.

Men need to accept that women actually feel emotions more strongly than men do. Emotions are also more central to their lives. Women talk in order to process their emotions. If a woman is upset or down but doesn't quite know what she's feeling, so she'll open a conversation to clarify her emotions.

This is easy for a husband to learn.

But what comes next is harder: To learn to be patient and listen to what his wife is feeling.

Men don't feel emotions as strongly as women, and they don't want to talk about whatever they do feel. If they're feeling scared or anxious or embarrassed, they go into their cave and figure things out on their own.

Both husband and wife have to make room for each other's needs. A husband needs to let his wife speak her mind; most likely she's just trying to unburden herself and process her feelings. If you want to be there for her, put away the phone or the *sefer,* look her squarely in the face, and listen. Try to recognize what she's feeling and why she's feeling it. You don't have to agree with her about the issue, you don't even have to agree about the feeling, but you can try to experience what she is experiencing. If you're able to do this and not try to cure her, solve her problem, or find the bright side, but just be there with her, after a few minutes she'll feel much better. Her emotional unrest will settle down, and instead of being in separate worlds, you'll be closer—maybe a lot closer. You supported her. You were there for her.

Remember, she's not trying to criticize you. She's not trying to blame you. She's not trying to start a fight. She's unburdening herself. She feels anxious or nervous and she's expressing that. What she needs is your validation; she needs to know that you understand what she's feeling and that you are there for her. If you show her that, you'll be able to actually see her relax. The angst will disappear. The edge in her voice will soften and she'll become a different person. (Try it—you might be shocked.)

Women, for their part, have to accept that men don't avoid discussion in order to shut them out. It's simply that in his world, that's not the way things are done. It requires patience and gentle explanation to let him know what you need. Maybe later, when things are calmer, you can gently explain what you would want him to do or say.

One last point:

Stonewalling

If you're married for more than a few months, you've probably discovered the inevitable truth that in marriage, there are times when things get heated. Well… maybe very heated. In fact, maybe very, very, very heated. Even in the best marriages, that's just part of the landscape. Sometimes people think, *this means we don't have a good marriage.* It's not true. Maybe if you were Avraham Avinu and Sarah Imeinu you would never quibble, but you're not. You're human. You make mistakes. Disagreements are unavoidable. That doesn't mean you don't have or can't have a great marriage. The quality of your marriage isn't based on how much you fight. It's based on how well you are able to repair the damage, move on, and learn for next time.

How do you react when things get heated?

Some people raise their voice. Some people cry. Some get nasty and biting. Some become sarcastic. Some are cruel. It seems that there's no shortage of creative ways to lose your cool. But men seem to have cornered the market on one method of dealing with emotionally charged situations—they check out. *I am not doing this again. We've been here, done that. I am not going back down that road.* No matter who started it and no matter who's at fault, the minute it gets very hot, they stonewall: they go into their zone, freeze out their spouse and refuse to discuss it further. (Women sometimes stonewall, but generally it's a guy's reaction.)

Usually it goes like this: a couple will be talking about a particular issue. They've probably spoken about this issue a couple of times recently. They hit an impasse and he says, "Look we're not getting anywhere. We're just getting angrier and angrier. I don't want to discuss this anymore." But she does want to discuss it, so she keeps talking. He repeats, "This isn't getting us anywhere. Let's just stop." Again, she persists. Finally, he's had it. He says, "That's it. I'm done. I'm not talking about this." He shuts down and walks away physically and emotionally.

From his perspective this is wise; it stops things from deteriorating further. The problem is that she won't view it as wise; she'll view it as cruel. To her, this is the best time to hash things out. We can finally deal with this and clear the air. In her world, you never just walk out of a conversation. None of her friends would just abruptly stop talking like that. When you walk out on her, what she hears is that you are so angry, disappointed, or resentful of her that you can't stand to speak to her. Or worse: you are so distant, unfeeling, and uncaring that you don't want to engage with her.

When you stonewall her, you are rejecting her. That rejection is infinitely more hurtful than whatever you were arguing about.

So, Gentlemen, hang in there. The reason your wife wants to continue talking is because women process their emotions by talking. After hashing things out, a woman will feel better. If you can let her say her piece, she'll sort out her feelings, express what she needs to, and you'll both be in a better place. You just need to wait it out. Don't lose your cool. Listen to what she says and try to understand what she's feeling—without commenting, correcting, or judging her. If you are able to just stick it out, you'll both end the conversation in a better place.

But if it's not getting better, and you feel that you are getting more and more worked up and you need to step away, here's a tip that is going to make your life much easier (read: your wife much happier).

Say to your wife, "Sweetheart, I want you to know that we're good. You're the best thing that ever happened to me. I love you and always want you—it's just that right now this conversation isn't getting us anywhere."

It's likely that the first time you say that, your wife will still continue trying to talk about the issue. Just repeat the same words again. *Sweetheart, I want you to know that we're good. You're the best thing that ever happened to me. I love you and always want you—it's just that right now this conversation isn't getting us anywhere.* Ending the conversation on that note will be much, much easier for her than just walking out on her, and life will be much better for both of you.

When a woman is arguing with her husband, she thinks her marriage is in trouble. If you walk out on her at that point, you're confirming her fear. But your marriage is not in jeopardy; all that's happening is that you guys are having a heated discussion, and right now neither of you are calm enough to have a productive conversation. That's the message you want to convey. As long as you reassure her that you guys are good, you're good. Even though you're still stonewalling, it will be a lot less painful for her, and much easier later to reconcile and make up.

It's a Two-Way Street

There are two sides to communication: he has to understand her and she has to understand him.

Women, if you want your husband to listen to you properly and validate you, remind yourself over and over again that men are different. Women like to talk about their problems, specifically the problems in the relationship. But when a man hears her bringing up issues in the relationship, he thinks, *Oh no, I'm in trouble again. I'm going to be blamed. I'm the problem. I'm the issue. I'm no good.* He's not going to be very receptive.

So be sparing about bringing things up. If something really bothers you, and you need to talk about it, make sure your husband understands that this isn't an attack on him or something he did wrong. It's just something that is troubling you and you'll feel better if you bring it out in the open.

You may have to coach him about what you need. He would love to know what to say and how to say it to bring you closer. As much as it distresses you when you pull apart, it bothers him as much. He just doesn't know what to do. All your friends know, and you've been doing it since 6th grade, but that's your world—not his. You have to help him understand what will help you and what you want him to do and say when you're upset. You have to bring him into your world.

In Summary

Hashem created Chava as a "talker" because conversation is the key to relationships. It's the key to raising healthy children, who need a close relationship with their mother. It's the core of creating the bond between husband and wife. Women were given the gift of speech—the gift of being the connector. It's built into their nature. It's part of their essence.

Hashem created women to fill the role of *akeres habayis,* the center of the home. A woman gives her husband and children necessary emotional support. Women are more talkative because their essence is to be a nurturer, caregiver, and relationship manager. That's what children need and that's what a marriage needs.

Men are also caring, giving, and nurturing, but to a different degree. A wife has to recognize that her husband may not need to talk in order to feel close. A husband has to understand that the essential nature of a woman is to seek attachment. If she lacks that in her marriage, she feels empty.

When each spouse climbs inside the very different world of the other, learning from each other and understanding that they have different natures, they relate on a much deeper level.

Instead of experiencing the pain and strife that plague many marriages, they become supportive, loving friends, helping each other get through the rough spots in life.

There is, however, another difference between men and women that makes it even harder for them to understand each other.

Chapter 7

Women are More Sensitive

WHAT'S WORTH FIGHTING ABOUT in marriage?

Obviously, spouses will have different wants and needs. They'll have different opinions. Decisions will have to be made. Compromises, too. But the question is: What issues are worth fighting about?

The answer is… none. There is nothing worth fighting about.

A court case is an adversarial relationship. If one side wins and the other side loses and they never speak to each other again, life goes on. But in marriage, fighting is a lose-lose proposition. If you lose, you lose, and if you win, you lose. You may have won the battle, but it's your best friend and lover that you just beat.

The rule in marriage is that *nothing* is worth fighting over. Negotiate, debate, discuss—but don't fight.

Yes, there are some things you shouldn't compromise on. If an issue comes up that really does seem to matter, use the five-year rule: ask yourself, will it matter in five years? The answer is almost always no. (Usually it doesn't even matter the next day.) If something does pass the five-year rule, I still strongly recommend that you be *sho'el eitzah*, ask someone for advice, because what we think is so *important* in the moment usually doesn't matter in the bigger picture.

But one thing is for sure—don't fight. It just damages the relationship.

Advice for Men

That's the advice I give to couples. But to men I give advice that is more specific: don't fight with your wife because you'll lose. Guaranteed. You are outclassed, outmanned and outgunned. It's like fighting an eighth-degree black belt. You're going to get destroyed.

Women have incredible memories. They remember everything you ever did wrong, in vivid detail, and they will bring it up over and over again. I once spoke with a woman who began listing for me all the things her husband had ever done wrong. "Ma'am," I said, "that was 20 years ago!" You can't remember what she said yesterday, but she remembers your entire history.

But here's the curious part: In academics, women don't seem to have better memories than men. They don't score better on standardized achievement tests. They're not better at remembering dates. They're not better at memorizing number sequences. So why is it that you can't remember a single detail of a given incident, and she seems to have a file cabinet filled with memories of everything you ever did, or didn't do, since you met?

To answer this, we need to take another look at the Rambam.

The Rambam told us that a husband has to:

- Respect his wife more than he respects himself and
- Love her as he does himself

A wife must:

- Treat her husband with exceeding respect as if he were nobility

Respect is vital within marriage, for both men and women, but a woman has to treat her husband with exceeding respect. In a man's world, respect is more important than love.

But why does the Rambam state that he has to treat her with more respect than himself? It's sufficient for him to love her as much he loves himself. Why does he have to respect her *more* than himself? Women don't have delicate egos and the same need for respect as men do. Why would he have to respect her more than he respects himself?

Roundhouse Kick to the Solar Plexus

My wife and I have been married for about 30 years. Not long ago, we were walking together and she tripped.

"Are you okay?" I asked with great concern as I helped her up.

"I'm fine."

As she brushed herself off, I asked her again: "Are you sure you're okay?"

"Yes, I'm fine."

"You sure?"

"Yes."

When we headed to the car, I asked her again if she was okay. And as we drove home, I asked her the same question a number of times. My wife isn't frail and she's not old. Yet I kept asking to make sure that she was okay.

When I was first married, that wouldn't have been my reaction. That's because when I was a kid, I was into martial arts. At 15, I wheedled my way into a master class for brown and black belts. I didn't belong there. Firstly, I was much younger than everyone else. Second, I was only a purple belt. The class ended with an "elimination circle." Each participant would lock arms with the person next to him, creating a large circle. The highest rank would begin with a roundhouse kick to the solar plexus of the person locked in arm next to him. Then that guy would kick the guy next to him, and so on around the entire circle. The idea was to learn how to take a kick. A person who couldn't take the pain would sit down. The kicks would go around the circle—the last man standing was the winner

The first guy kicked, thud. The next person kicked, thud. As the kicks circled around, I knew one thing—I wasn't going down. Smash! One guy sat down. Smash! Another guy sat down. And another. I made it through the first round. The second round. The third. On the fourth round, the guy next to me got knocked down. I now found myself arm-linked to Sensei LaPuppet. Sensei LaPuppet, at the time, was a fifth-degree black belt. At 6 foot 2 inches tall and weighing 205 lbs., he was a very intimidating. He was also quite respectful and used to call me "Little Brother." When I linked arms with him, he gave me a look as if to say, "Little Brother, are you okay with this?" I returned a look of my own that said, "Bring it on!"

The next thing I saw was the flash of his foot lifting off the ground. Then, as if detached from my body, I heard a *thud* as the ball of his foot plowed into my solar plexus. I didn't know which part of me was going to split first, but I knew I wouldn't be in this circle any longer. I sat down, my ego bruised a bit, but knowing that I'd be tougher next time.

In the early years of our marriage, if my wife fell, I would ask her if she was okay. If she looked shaken, I would add, "Anything broken? Internal bleeding? Hemorrhage?"

"No," she'd reply, "I just fell."

So what's the problem? I'd think to myself. *Why do you look like you got hit by a truck?* As someone who had survived a few rounds in an elimination circle at 15, getting knocked to the ground wasn't a big deal. My attitude was, if you don't have a concussion or at least internal bleeding, you carry on.

But that isn't what most girls experience growing up. Dr. Boruch Eisenberg was my children's pediatrician. He spent a few summers as a camp doctor in sleepaway camp. Each summer he'd spend two weeks in Magen Av, a boys camp, and then two weeks in Camp Sternberg, a girls camp. He told me that at the boys camp, he was on vacation. He barely saw a single camper. Unless a guy had a fracture or a fever of a least 102 degrees, he wouldn't even come to the infirmary. But in the girls camp, every morning when he opened the infirmary there was a long line of girls waiting for Band-Aids and cough drops. Girls don't get sick more often than boys. It's just a bigger deal to them.

Because my wife grew up as a typical girl, she had a very different perspective on injuries than I did. I remember the first time she hurt herself while she was cutting vegetables. "Oy, I got a cut," she said to me. I looked at her finger and said, "It's not deep. It's fine. Just put a Band-Aid on it."

She was visibly shaken, but it took me a long time to realize that a cut was a big deal to her. More to the point: It took me a long time to realize that my experience wasn't hers. To her, a cut was a much bigger deal than it would have been to me. As a young husband, it was a challenge to learn that my experience doesn't define reality. After 30 years, I think I've finally got it. A fall is a big deal to my wife – even if she doesn't have a concussion, broken ribs, or a mortal wound.

And while it's important to recognize that bruises and bangs hurt your wife more than they hurt you, it's far more significant to be sensitive to the different ways you each experience emotional pain.

> **תלמוד בבלי מסכת בבא מציעא דף נט/א**
>
> אמר רב לעולם יהא אדם זהיר באונאת אשתו שמתוך שדמעתה מצויה אונאתה קרובה
>
> *A man should always be careful not oppress his wife with words; as her tears are more readily found, so too is her oppression.*

Chazal say that a man must be extremely careful with what he says to his wife because "her tears are more readily found" (*Bava Mezia* 59a). *Chazal* are telling us that a man has to be very careful, not because she's a crybaby, but because his wife is more sensitive and will be pained more easily. She'll also feel the pain to a greater extent. He has to be guarded with what he says, because while the words he says might not bother his friend, they will hurt his wife.

This is a mistake that young husbands often make. They think that women cry over every little thing. *If she would just be a little more sensible*, he believes, *she would realize that it's not a big deal.* But she's not crying because she "cries easily." She's crying because it hurts her. She feels pain more intensely than you do. Things that would hurt you only a little, hurt her a lot. When you're in a lot of pain, you cry.

There are countless studies which confirm that the area of the brain that handles stress is more sensitive in women. Clinically, the number of women suffering from anxiety and depression is double the number of men. At a funeral, women tend to cry more than men. The reason for all these is because women are more sensitive than men. Women feel pain – as well as joy, happiness, and all other feelings – to a greater degree than men do. They feel the full emotional spectrum more acutely.

Of course, rules about genders apply to *most* men and *most* women, *but not all, always.* A husband may be more sensitive than his wife. But as a general rule, women are far more sensitive than men. Chazal state this as a general principle; husbands have to accept that their wives really feel those feelings, and any attempt to dismiss them damages the relationship. Expressions like, "Come on, you're exaggerating," aren't fair, and definitely aren't helpful. She's not exaggerating. She really is feeling that bad. Telling her it's wrong to feel that way invalidates her and sets off a chain reaction of even stronger feelings.

If you were drunk, you'd be drunk

The Chofetz Chaim offers a parable related to this. Two men are standing outside a bar. A drunkard comes out of the bar, falls to the floor, and rolls in the dirt. One man says to the other, "Look at that. If I got drunk, I would never act that way."

"Fool," the friend replies, "if you were drunk, you'd be drunk. The reason you're saying that now is because you're not drunk."

The Chofetz Chaim says something similar about our attitude toward wealthy people. Many people say, "If I had a lot of money, I wouldn't be like *him*. I wouldn't put my name on buildings all over town. I would be very humble." The Chofetz Chaim explains that great wealth affects a person. It gives him an inflated sense of importance and a belief that he's worthy of honor. If you aren't wealthy, it's easy to say, "If I were rich, I wouldn't be that way." But if you were rich you would feel very differently than you do now. You don't know how you would act if you felt that way. You're like the sober guy saying how he would act if he were drunk.

He Must Respect Her More Than Himself

This seems to be why the Rambam says a husband must treat his wife with more respect than he does himself—because she's more sensitive. She feels things more acutely. Pain hurts her more. She doesn't need the respect in the same way he does, but her feelings are very delicate. She feels things more intensely than he does. That's why he has to more careful with her honor than his own.

This principle carries a powerful message.

> **ספר בראשית פרק יב**
>
> ח) וַיַּעְתֵּק מִשָּׁם הָהָרָה מִקֶּדֶם לְבֵית אֵל וַיֵּט אָהֳלֹה בֵּית אֵל מִיָּם וְהָעַי מִקֶּדֶם וַיִּבֶן שָׁם מִזְבֵּחַ לַידֹוָד וַיִּקְרָא בְּשֵׁם יְדֹוָד
>
> *From there he moved on to the hill country east of Bethel and pitched his tent, with Bethel on the west and Ai on the east; and he built there an altar to the Hashem and invoked Hashem's name.*
>
> **רש"י על בראשית פרק יב פסוק ח**
>
> אהלו - אהלה כתיב בתחלה נטה את אהל אשתו ואח"כ את שלו. ב"ר
>
> *HIS TENT — This word is written with a ה suffixed instead of the usual ו so that it is read "her tent," to intimate that first he pitched a tent for his wife and afterwards one for himself.*

Parshas Lech Lecha opens with Hashem telling Avraham Avinu to leave his land, his birthplace, and his father's house, and journey to Canaan. Many events happened along the way, and the Torah tell us the details of Avraham's life that are relevant for generations. We are told that at one stop "he pitched his tent." But the Torah uses the feminine suffix, so it reads, "he pitched *her* tent." Rashi explains that this teaches us that first Avraham set up his wife's tent, and only after that set up his own.

A man is obligated to honor his wife more than himself. By erecting his wife's tent before his own, he was showing her honor (*Siftei Chachamim*).

Why do we need to be told this small, inconsequential detail? Because it's not a small and inconsequential detail. The Torah is teaching us a foundational concept: Shalom Bayis is made up of many small acts. These small acts may seem like trivial, simple things that don't matter—yet they do. They create an undercurrent of respect that tells a woman that her husband holds her in high regard.

This is what the Torah is teaching us about Avraham and Sarah. It's true that they had the most perfect marriage ever known to mankind, but it wasn't by chance. Their relationship was carefully nurtured and developed. A big part of a successful marriage is in the myriad small details—showing respect in the daily, mundane activities, showing deference and regard; setting up your wife's tent first.

Ladies First

Unfortunately, the world has lost much of its sense of propriety. Basic expressions of decency and manners have been abandoned. The world has become coarse, vulgar and unrefined, and humanity pays a heavy price for it.

But that isn't the Torah's way, and it doesn't belong in a Jewish home. When I was growing up, the concept of "ladies first" was a given. My mother drilled into us that you act differently toward a woman. You speak differently—certain terms and expressions that are fine amongst the guys are not appropriate when talking to a woman. And while this may sound radical now, the idea of opening the door for your wife used to be the basic expectation of a *mentsch*. That was just the way things were done. That was how respectable people acted. These aren't small, irrelevant niceties, relics of the past; these acts demonstrate in word, deed and action that you are important to me, you are cherished.

This concept carries much further than outward signs of respect. It means respecting her as an individual; respecting that her feelings are real and that she is entitled to them; respecting that she will feel things that you don't and things that don't bother you might cause her great pain. There are very real differences in the way men and women feel things.

She's Not One of the Guys

One of the first things a husband must learn is that his wife is not one of the boys. The jokes that work with his buddies won't work with his wife. This reality can take a long time to learn because even though men and women function similarly in many ways, and might be intellectually equal, they have very real differences in emotional sensitivities. Understanding your spouse's emotional world is one of the keys to being successfully married.

This is why women have uncanny recall for every detail of every incident between them and their spouse. They don't have better memories—they feel things more acutely. A guy can't remember what happened this morning because to him it was just words—a passing moment, then he went on to the next thing. But she really felt those words; to her, they were deeply troubling. They cut into her essence. Those words play over and over in her mind, like an endless looping video. She sees it pop up, she relives it; she reviews that conversation dozens, maybe hundreds, of times. And that's why she will remember every detail of a fight that he forgot long ago. She doesn't have a better memory, she just felt it more strongly, and the details came back to her time after time. How can she not remember it?

Her emotions also function differently than his. If something is bothering her, she has to deal with it. She's not bringing it up again to be vindictive or vengeful. She feels it and she needs to process it; that's just the way she's built.

When Rashi says that "a woman's pain is closer," he's telling us that a woman is more sensitive to emotion—she feels things intensely. When the Rambam says "you have to be more careful with your wife's honor than your own," it's because she is more sensitive to dishonor. She's going to feel the barb, the disapproval, and the pain, more acutely than you.

That's why it's so difficult for a woman to let things go. "Why can't she just move on," cries her poor husband. "I said I'm sorry—why can't she just forget it?"

Usually, the best way for her to let it go is to talk about it. Talking helps her process her emotions and she'll feel better. As a husband, one of the greatest favors you can do for your wife is to listen to her. Hear her out without interjecting any observations about how she could have done better, without fixing her, without showing her why she shouldn't be worried or hurt. Just be there with her. Understand that she's not attacking you; she's not bringing this up to make trouble or cause a fight. She's bringing this up because it's her emotional reality, and the best thing you can do is just be there and feel it with her.

This is a fundamental principle for human relations in general, but especially in marriage. Spouses live in discrete emotional worlds that are very different from each other. The problems start when spouses do not learn to understand the landscape of each other's emotional world.

Mind Reading

One last point, for women: Ladies, *nevuah* (prophecy) ended with the destruction of the second *Bais Hamikdash*. Your husband cannot read your mind.

An example: A couple is sitting on the couch, talking. They're even looking at each other. He suddenly notices that she has a long face. "Dear, you look upset. What's the matter?"

"Nothing."

"No, dear, really. I see you're upset. Please tell me what's wrong."

"No, no, no. It's nothing."

"You sure?"

"Yeah. It's nothing"

He stops asking.

At that moment she starts thinking, *What's wrong with him? Doesn't he see that I'm upset? Doesn't he realize I'm hurt? Why doesn't he ask me? He's such a cold, callous person!*

The reason he stopped asking is because he's male. If a guy is bothered by something and wants to share it, he's going to say so clearly. If a woman says she doesn't want to share it, he believes her. She can't assume that her husband knows what she *really* means—that she wants him to help her open up.

Or maybe she's upset that he doesn't *know* what's bothering her. Maybe she's thinking, *if my husband really knew me, if he really cared about me, he would know what's bothering me.* But that's the point. He doesn't know. Not because he doesn't care, but because he's male, and if you want him to know how you feel, you need to tell him.

But even when you get really good at understanding the opposite gender, there is a quirk in human nature that makes really understanding any person on the planet difficult—very, very difficult—maybe near impossible.

Chapter 8

Learning to Live Together

Up on the Chair

Moshe has been married for about six months. As he makes his way home after a long day, he says to himself, "Boruch Hashem, I married such a put-together woman. Not one of those flighty emotional wrecks. She's grounded and intelligent and fun to be with. I'm so fortunate!"

He opens the front door of his apartment, walks in, and sees his put-together wife standing on a chair, screaming.

"Sara, what's wrong?"

"There! Over there!"

"What? What is it?"

"There," she shrieks, pointing to the ground. "Over there!"

He looks. "What?"

"There!"

"There WHAT?"

"A... a... a... COCKROACH!"

"A cockroach?"

"*Do something!*"

He looks up at her on the chair, then calmly walks over to the cockroach, stomps on it, and says, "You can come down now."

He's thinking, *Grounded? Put-together?* But he doesn't give it too much thought.

Two weeks later he's in the *Beis Medrash* learning and his phone rings. It's his wife.

"Moshe! Moshe!"

"What happened? Is everything okay?"

"No! Please come home!"

"But... I mean, I'm in the middle of learning. What happened?"

"THERE ARE TWO OF THEM! PLEASE COME HOME."

He hangs up the phone and says to himself, *I don't believe it. She wants me to leave the* Beis Medrash *to come home to kill two cockroaches? Is she kidding?*

He gets in the car, fuming. *I can't believe it. What's the matter with her?*

He enters the apartment and there she is again, up on the chair, pointing to a spot on the floor. "There! Over there!"

He walks over to the two cockroaches, stomps on one, stomps on the second. Then he turns to his wife and says, "I hope you're satisfied." He turns around, storms out the door and heads right back to the Beis Medrash.

Who is Right?

Here's the question: Who is right? Was she right in calling her husband home because she felt she needed help? Was he right in being upset at her for interrupting him for something so trivial?

Some people will say, of course right she's right—how could he be so callous?

Some people will say he's obviously right. How can she have so little regard for her husband's learning?

So, who's right?

The Question is Wrong

The right answer is that the *question* is wrong. In fact, probably the single most *damaging* question you can ask in a marriage is *Who is right?* That's a fine question for a labor dispute or for a court of law (maybe a divorce court), but it's not a helpful question to ask in a marriage.

A marriage is a union of friendship and love between two unique individuals, each with their own strengths, weaknesses, and idiosyncrasies, and each with their own needs, desires and wishes. The problem is that often his needs and her needs compete with each other, and there are limited resources. There's only so much money we have to spend, there's only so much time in the day, there are only so many things we can do, and we certainly can't be in two places at once.

The reality is that there will be many occasions when you won't get what you want. For a marriage to succeed, a couple has to find a working balance between their needs. Any situation where one spouse feels that their needs don't count, or that what they want doesn't matter, damages the relationship. This certainly doesn't mean everything will always go your way, and it doesn't mean all of your needs will be met every time; there will be many situations where your needs will not be met and where you'll have to do things you don't want to do. But if your feelings are valued, then within a framework of friendship you'll be willing to sacrifice your preferences, knowing that your spouse sacrifices many things for you as well.

This kind of sacrifice can only exist within the context of love and friendship, where both sides know that their needs count—that *they* count.

So rather than asking who's right, a far more productive question to ask is, *What is each person asking for?*

What was Sara feeling when she called her husband home? What was Moshe feeling when his wife called him home?

To figure that out, you need to climb into their inner worlds. When she was up on that chair, she was thinking, *Baruch Hashem, now I'm married, I don't have to deal with these dreadful things anymore. My best friend, my husband, will come and save me.* But then when he kills the bug and gives her that disgusted look, she says to herself, *I'm really scared and he doesn't even care. I didn't want to call him home. I value learning as much as he does. He's making me feel stupid, like I'm a little kid. Then he has the audacity to say "I hope you're satisfied!" What a callous, uncaring creep!*

On the other hand, he's thinking, *I can't believe that she called me home to kill a bug! Why couldn't she just step on the stupid bug herself? I can't believe how little concern she has for my learning.*

This is a classic example of a couple hurting each other and each one not understanding why the other one is hurt. They're each stuck in their own mindset, so what their spouse is doing makes no sense.

The secret to detangling so many of the complications in marriage is to figure out what your spouse is feeling.

It's Never the Issue

When a couple argues, they think they're arguing about an issue, like how much money should be spent on a specific purchase. But they're not arguing about the issue itself. They're arguing about the underlying mindset, and what the issue *means* to each of them. The reason the discussion becomes contentious is because each spouse is living in their own world and judging the other based on their own emotional reality.

You and your spouse experience things differently. You have different natures, temperaments, and feelings, and will respond to things with different emotions. That's typical and normal. The problem is that we all tend to feel that our experience defines reality. *I've always felt this way. Doesn't everyone feel this way? Is there any other way to feel?* And it is often difficult to realize that this is *your* experience, but that doesn't mean others experience it the same way.

I don't know why, but many women are afraid of bugs, and many guys aren't. When my youngest son was two years old, he used to play with bugs. When one of his big sisters found an ant in her room, she would call in her baby brother to save her (she just had to make sure he didn't eat the bug). To the young wife up on the chair, based on her nature, temperament, and inclinations, bugs are terrifying—especially large bugs with lots of legs and big antennas. This experience was frightening for her. But to her husband, based on his nature, temperament, and inclinations, bugs aren't scary at all. For him, there was nothing to be afraid of.

He judged her based on how he feels ("bugs are not a big deal"), and determined that by calling him home she was clearly overreacting. He thinks she should just get a grip and be normal ("normal" being defined as "like him"). But it's unreasonable to expect her to feel the same way he feels.

She judged him based on how she feels ("bugs are terrifying") and determined that he was insensitive and callous. She thinks everyone knows that bugs are scary ("everyone" being defined as herself). But it's unreasonable to expect him to feel the same way she feels.

To make this dynamic clearer, let's change the scene slightly. Imagine that Moshe was alone in the apartment and two large German shepherds charged through the front door. How would he react? He wouldn't be standing on a chair. He'd be out the fire escape and down the block. Large dogs are frightening.

In his experience, dogs are scary and bugs aren't. The problem is that he used his experience to *define* reality. When *my* experience defines reality, I can't understand why *you* do what you do. It just makes no sense.

As long as he allows the way he feels to dictate reality, he'll never understand her. Because it's true that in his world bugs aren't scary. But in her world they sure are.

If you judge your spouse based on the way *you* feel, it's going to be very hard for the two of you to live together in peace. You can be a reasonable, kind person, but there's a limit; what she's doing makes *no sense*, what he's doing is *ridiculous*. Each person reacts to things differently, feels differently, has different experiences, and therefore their realities are distinct. If you're not aware of what your spouse is experiencing, you can't be sensitive to their needs and you will inevitably hurt them.

This is the 7th Really Dumb Mistake That Very Smart Couples Make: judging your spouse based on your own experience and allowing your experience to define reality.

While this mistake is a great challenge in marriage, it actually plagues all relationships. It stems from a universal handicap.

Chapter 9

Mind Blind

IMAGINE YOU DRIVE WITH your friend to the mall to go shopping. You park your car on the third level of the underground parking lot and you say, "Listen, I have to stop in at the wine store first. So let's meet back at the car at 5:30 and then we'll shop together. And don't forget, we're parked on the third level, row G, space 46." With that, you both head into the mall.

About 20 minutes later you remember that you promised your brother that you would pick up his clothes from dry cleaners, and they close in 10 minutes. *Oh well,* you think, *it's not far.* You rush back to the car, drive out to the cleaners and pick up the clothing. When you arrive back at the mall you to find thar the parking lot is jammed and there isn't a single space on the 3rd level. No big deal, you drive up a level. Still no parking. Another level. Still no space. Finally, on the roof of the garage, you find an open spot. As you get out of your car you realize that it's now 5:30, exactly the time you arranged to meet your friend back at the car. You agreed to meet on the 3rd level, and your friend doesn't have a cell phone. "No problem," you say to yourself, "I originally parked on the third level, but now I'm on the roof. She'll just meet me up here, because this is where I am."

Obviously, that internal dialogue would never happen. Just because *you* know that you moved the car to the roof, doesn't mean that your friend knows. At 5:30 she'll go looking for you on the third level where the car was supposed to be.

In this case, it's obvious that just because *you* know something doesn't mean *someone else* knows it. But it's not always so clear.

One of the features of autism spectrum disorder is *mind blindness*, meaning difficulty perceiving what is going on in someone else's mind. Mind blindness is a failure to grasp that if I feel one way, it doesn't automatically mean that you feel the same way. And if I know something, that doesn't mean you know it.

Mind blindness isn't restricted to people on the autism spectrum. Realizing that each person has a different mind, and therefore different thoughts, feelings, and worldviews, doesn't come naturally to everyone. In fact, we all suffer from mind blindness on occasion.

To demonstrate, let's try a thought experiment:

Imagine that I were to tap out the beat of song that we both knew, and I asked you to guess what the song is. What are the odds that you would guess correctly? Very likely? Somewhat likely? Very unlikely?

Tappers and Listeners

Elizabeth Newton earned a PhD in psychology from Stanford University by asking just this question. For her doctoral thesis, she conducted what seems like a simple experiment. She organized participants into two groups. She called one group the "tappers" and the other group the "listeners." Each tapper was paired with a listener. The tappers were given a list of well-known songs, like Happy Birthday and The Star-Spangled Banner, and were directed to tap out a song. The listeners' job was to guess which song they were tapping.

Almost none of the listeners were able to guess the song correctly.

The surprising part of the experiment was that Newton asked the tappers to predict the odds that the listener would identify the song correctly. She tried this with hundreds of participants, and over and over, the tappers predicted at least a 50/50 chance that the listeners would figure out the song, but almost none of them did. Only about 2.5% of the listeners identified the correct song. Time after time, the tapper assumed the listener would get it. And time after time, they didn't. It's almost comical to watch videos of the experiment. While the listeners sit there clueless, the tappers faces are full of disbelief. *How can you not get it? It's so obvious!*

The fascinating part is *why* the tappers assumed that the listeners would easily guess the song. When you tap out a song, you're playing the song in your head. Because you hear it in your head, the song is so obvious to you that you can't imagine that anyone would fail to identify it!

The recognition that what's playing in your mind isn't playing in the other person's mind is essential for dealing with other people.

Creamer in the Coffee

Most Shabbos mornings, I get up pretty early. The house is quiet and I can learn undisturbed. When my wife wakes up, I bring her a coffee in bed. This has been our routine for many years.

Almost every time I prepare the coffee, I open the refrigerator and reach for the creamer—and freeze, because my wife prefers her coffee with skim milk. Now, everyone knows that coffee tastes so much better with creamer—or at least full-fat milk. It's just so much smoother—skim milk doesn't even change the color!

And that's true—in my experience. I like my coffee that way. I want my wife to enjoy a good cup of coffee, so I automatically reach for the creamer, to give her the best... even though my wife doesn't like her coffee with creamer.

The odd part is that we're married for over 30 years, and I still have to consciously stop myself from giving her the creamer because it's so *obvious* to me that coffee tastes better with thick cream. It's not simply that I *like* my coffee this way—it's that I think this is *the way* to enjoy coffee.

This seems to be a quirk in human nature—the belief that your own experience defines reality. A critical ingredient in marriage is the recognition that what I perceive as normal is just that: *my* perception of what is normal, and your perception may be completely different.

This is critical to learning to live together.

Love is vital to the success of a marriage, but many couples who love each other can't live with each other. No matter how hard they try, no matter how fine their middos are, they keep ending up in squabbles and disagreements, and they can't understand why. They don't have a clue why their spouse is upset. They don't have a clue because they're mind blind.

Living together necessitates recognizing that the way you experience things is only the way *you* experience them. It doesn't define reality. Your wife may experience the same thing in a markedly different way.

This dynamic surfaces over and over again every day.

It's freezing in here

I was learning with a chosson, preparing him for his upcoming marriage, and he commented, "You know, it's so interesting. I'm always hot and she's always cold. It can be 80 degrees and sunny, but she's cold and needs a sweater, and I'm sweating away. When we drive, I open my window because it's so hot, and she asks me to close it because she's freezing. Isn't that strange?"

"Welcome to the first test of your marriage," I said. "I'm not a *navi*, but I'd like to make a prediction. When you first get married, everything will be fine. When she says she's cold, you'll say to yourself, *it isn't cold. Come on—it's 72 degrees! But, hey, she's uncomfortable.* And since you're a *mensch*, you'll have no problem raising the thermostat. Everything will be fine.

"But then one night, maybe six months after you're married, you'll wake up in a sweat. You're going to look at your wife and say to yourself, *what's her problem? It's not cold. I'm paying hundreds of dollars a month to heat this place like a sauna! Why is she like this?* And it's at that moment that your marriage begins in earnest, because then you'll be faced with that great challenge—can you accept that your spouse's reality is different than yours? That just because *you're* not cold doesn't mean that *she* isn't?"

While this may seem like a simple point, it's a major source of friction in many marriages (and it impacts almost every other relationship). We tend to view the way we do things as the right way, the normal way, *the* way. We may be tolerant of people who do things differently, but in our hearts of hearts, we know they have it wrong. If they could just learn to do things the right way, life would be much simpler.

Happy Birthday and WWIII

A couple called me. They're in the middle of their own personal World War Three. What's the issue? He forgot her birthday.

They're both fine people who love each other and normally get along well. "It doesn't make sense," the husband told me. "Why is she getting so bent out of shape? What's the big deal?"

The big deal is that they had very different upbringings. In his family, a birthday wasn't a big deal. In hers, it was; the entire family got together and threw a party. Each spouse came to the marriage with very different experiences and expectations. To him, if you remember to give a birthday card, you deserve a medal for going above and beyond the call of duty. To her, if there's no party with lots of friends and family invited over, it's an egregious violation.

"I know," he told me, "that in her family birthdays are a big deal, and I know how important it is to her, but I forgot."

Why did he forget? Not because he doesn't care. Not because he doesn't love her. Because his experience wasn't the same as hers, and he hasn't yet learned how to make her experience his. Learning that can take time. But if he works on understanding how important it is to her, he won't forget. (Life hack for husbands: What's the best way to make sure you never forget your wife's birthday? Forget it the first year you're married.)

But it's not just he who has to work on understanding his wife's world. She has to appreciate that her experience isn't his. If she can understand that he grew up thinking birthdays were no big deal, she'd be able to better understand *why* he forgot, and not feel so hurt. Yes, he should be more sensitive. But she has to try to crawl into his world too, and not overreact.

Marriage requires that you break out of your own world and learn that your spouse experiences things differently. In these examples so far, the problem is limited and can usually be sorted out. But the issue becomes far more complex when it involves core differences.

His and Her Interpretation

I got a call from Yosef and Chani. They were married a little over a year and had a baby. I first spoke to them individually.

She described him as "the cruelest person I've ever met. He's so controlling. Everything has to be exactly his way. If not, he's furious."

His description of her wasn't much better. "You should hear the way she talks to me. She screams at me about every little thing. She's vicious."

I asked each of them to describe what their relationship was like when they were dating.

"It was wonderful," she said.

"Gan Eden," he said.

The strange thing was that they were a mature couple, and they had dated for a long time. During that period there was real chemistry between them. But the infatuation wore off almost as soon as they got married. Things got progressively worse until, within a year, they were on the brink of disaster.

As I started digging, their story became clear.

Yosef owned a business. When he was dating Chani, he was distracted from work. Once they got engaged and began planning their wedding, his focus on his business dropped some more. By the time they got married, he had neglected his business for months and things had started to slide. It was a major concern, and it needed attention. He explained to her that even though he would love to spend as much time with her as when they had been dating, his business had been slipping, and in order to get things back on track he needed to spend more time on it. She understood, and everything was fine.

But then the trouble started. He would come home fairly late each night. They would spend some time together, but not much. After a while she began seriously suspecting that he didn't really like her. "It's obvious," she told me. "I spend two hours a night talking to my friends, and my own husband doesn't want to be with me more than twenty minutes. It's clear to me that he no longer likes me. I don't know what happened."

She didn't give up, though. She said to him, "Maybe we should talk more. Maybe we should try to spend more time together."

"I would love to," he'd said, "but you know my business needs my attention. Once I get things back on track it will be different."

She tried to believe him, but after a while she couldn't help but feel that he just wasn't interested in her. It started eating at her. *This isn't the man I dated!*

One night he came home while she was on the phone and said, "Hi, Chani."

"Hi, Yosef," she replied—and went back to her phone call.

He said to himself, *That's strange. I come home, and she has no time for me?* He went about his business and then to *Maariv*. When he came back, she was still on the phone. The same thing happened the next night.

Pretty soon the situation had worsened.

"Hi, Chani. How are you doing? Is supper ready?"

"No, I was busy."

She wasn't trying to be malicious. She was very hurt. She felt rejected. So she stopped behaving lovingly toward him. She was curt. Sometimes she was rude. Occasionally she was downright nasty.

I don't treat her that way! he said to himself. *Why can't she speak respectfully? This isn't the woman I dated!*

He began distancing himself from her.

When that happened, her hurt grew deeper. She lashed out. The cycle continued. By the time they called me, they were on the verge of divorce.

This tragic cycle plays out whenever people allow their own experience to define reality.

When she sees that her husband isn't spending time with her, she *knows* exactly what's going on: He's not interested in their marriage. Naturally, she'll feel hurt and offended. She won't be so nice and sweet anymore.

When he sees that she's acting curt and or even nasty, he *knows* exactly what is going on: She's trying to get him mad, she just likes to fight. Naturally, he distances himself further.

They each translate the situation according to their own realities. They are mind blind to their spouse's reality.

An outsider might wonder, why were they both so clueless? She should have sat down with him and said, "Yosef, dear, it hurts me when you stay away. It hurts me when we don't talk. We're not bonding. We're not connecting." Why didn't she just explain it?

And why was he so thick? Why didn't he just say, "You're acting so different. Did I do something wrong? What's bothering you?"

They didn't do that because it never even occurred to them that their spouse didn't understand their feelings. They were each so stuck in their perception of events that they never even considered that there might be an alternate interpretation.

And even though he explained himself, it didn't matter—we become so locked into our way of thinking that words don't penetrate.

In marriage more than any other relationship

Sadly, this happens often. He doesn't get her and she doesn't get him. Usually, there's nothing fundamentally wrong with them or their marriage. They're just not understanding each other's needs and styles.

Most men don't understand women. Most women don't understand men. And that's okay — until you get married. Once you get married, you're responsible for the emotional wellbeing of your spouse and the relationship. You're not supposed to make your husband better or change your wife, but you're responsible for the emotional climate — the love, bonding and affection, the togetherness of you as a couple. To do that, you have to learn to understand your spouse's inner world.

This is particularly vexing because most of the time your spouse isn't much help when it comes to you learning to understand them. We are so accustomed to our viewpoint that we don't even recognize that our version of reality may not be the way others view things. If you don't recognize that your reality is just your isolated experience, you can't explain it to your spouse. It would like asking a fish to explain what water is. As a result, we are mind blind. We don't understand the emotional needs of our spouse, which means we can't possibly address them. And we aren't able to view life from their perspective, so it's inevitable that we are going to hurt them and not even have a clue to what we did wrong.

After many years of counseling couples with this problem, I've found a technique that solves this quandary. In fact, it is almost a foolproof way to improve any relationship.

Let me start with a trivia question.

That's Strange

What are the two most important words in a marriage?

If you were to ask that question to a group of people, I'm sure you would get a long list of answers:

- Thank you
- You're welcome
- I love you. (Okay, that's three words.)
- You're right.
- Yes, dear.

While all of those are good, and in fact very important, words to use often in your marriage, I've found that these are not the two most important words. There is another two-word phrase which will have a much greater impact on the health of your relationship.

"Eureka—I've got it!"

The story goes that around the year 250 B.C.E., Hireon the king of Syracuse gave his goldsmith a fortune of pure gold to fashion a crown. When the crown was delivered, the king suspected that the goldsmith had substituted some silver in place of the gold and had kept the change for himself. The problem was that the weight of the crown exactly matched the weight of the gold the king had given him. How could the king prove that it was filled with silver instead of gold?

To solve this enigma, the king hired Archimedes, the famous mathematician. Archimedes pondered the question for weeks and couldn't find an answer. One day, while entering his bath, he noticed that water was displaced by his body and spilled over the side. The more he sank into the bath, the more water was displaced—and he realized that he now had a simple method to measure volume. Since silver is lighter than gold, it would take more silver to achieve the same weight as gold. In that case, the crown would have to take up more space, and would then displace more water. All he had to do was measure how much water that weight of gold displaced and compare it to the amount of water displaced by the crown. He was so excited about his solution that he ran straight from the bath to the king shouting, "Eureka!" *I've found it!*

Whether the story is true or not, the word "eureka" has long been associated with scientific findings. However, the words that preempted almost every scientific discovery are not, *Eureka, I've found it!* but *Hmm, that's strange.*

Almost every discovery began with a scientist noticing something that didn't make sense. *Wait a minute. That doesn't fit. Why is that? I mixed A and B and got D. That's strange.*

The openminded search to understand, beginning with the words "That's strange," prompted some of the greatest scientific breakthroughs in history.

In 1928, Alexander Fleming was looking for a cure for infections and experimenting with staph bacteria. He went on vacation, leaving some unwashed culture dishes near an open window. When he returned, he found that mold had grown on the culture dishes, and the mold killed any staph bacteria it had come in contact with. *That's strange,* he thought. He began to experiment and eventually discovered penicillin.

In 1946, Percy Spenser was working on magnetron tubes (used in radar) when he realized that the peanut bar in his pocket had melted. *That's strange,* he thought. He had discovered the power of microwave technology, and eventually invented the microwave oven.

In 1884, a man spent years trying to improve rubber but had little success. One day, a piece of rubber accidentally landed on the sizzling surface of a potbellied stove. When he scraped off the rubber, he found that around the charred area was a dry, springy brown rim. *That's strange,* he thought. *It should have melted.* Charles Goodyear had discovered a new substance, weatherproof rubber. He invented the rubber used in tires.

Similarly, in marriage, the two words that are critical to success are "that's strange." It is going to happen that your spouse is going to act in a way that's utterly inexplicable. There will be no rational explanation. Your natural reaction will be to judge them – and judge them by *your* standards, by your gender, by your experience. But instead of judging them, try the words *that's strange.*

That's strange. She's normally a sane, sober person. Why is she reacting that way?

Or, *that's strange. We were talking about whatever, it sure sounded innocent enough, and then he got all mad. What might be bothering him?*

When you train yourself to say *that's strange,* you open your mind to discover the inner world of your spouse. (But please, make sure that you say those words to yourself, not aloud!)

To be a good spouse, you have to know and understand your partner. Love is never enough—you have to know what matters to them and what counts in their world. You have to know how they look at things and what they value. You have to know what hurts them and why it hurts them. You have know what they need and why they need it. If you don't know their inner world, you can't meet those needs and you are (inadvertently) going to cause a lot of pain to the one you love—and you won't even know that you did.

What makes this particularly difficult is that both of you are handicapped because your experiences are those of your own gender. Guys spend their lives in a male world. Women spend their lives in a female world. Even if you had brothers and sisters, it's just not the same. One of the most common refrains you'll hear from women is, "*Men.* Who can understand them?" And one of the most common refrains you'll hear from men is, "Women! Who can understand them?"

The ability to climb out of your world and enter the world of your spouse begins with a "that's strange" moment.

I don't get it. Why is he taking offense? Why is she all upset? That's strange.

That's when you begin to discover their world.

But being open to your spouse's emotional world isn't enough. For a marriage to work, you also need flexibility.

Uni-mind to Incompatible

There is a progressive transition in people's attitudes from the getting-married stage to the being-married stage. Sometimes a *chosson*, and more often a *kallah*, begin with a "uni-mind."[1] Uni-mind means *we are one*. We think alike. We look at things the same way. Our marriage is going to be perfect. He likes vanilla ice cream; I like vanilla ice cream. I like slow music; he likes slow music. Our marriage is going to be wonderful because we are one.

Then they get married and they discover that they're not one. He'd rather go to his parents for Shabbos, she'd rather not. He thinks the neighbors are bums, she thinks they're great. He has his way, she has her way.

"You want to serve fish on Shabbos morning? No one does that!"

"You want to paint the walls blue? That's absurd; you can't possibly think that!"

"Why do you always leave the lights on?"

"Why are you always turning off the lights?"

"You're driving so slow—we'll never get there."

"You're driving so fast—you're going to get us killed."

"I hate coming late."

"Only nerds come on time."

Sometimes these differences seem so pronounced that one of them (or both of them) wake up one day and say, "We don't agree on a single thing. Everything we like, everything we want to do, is so different. We're just not compatible."

---

[1] I want to thank Rabbi Donni Frank for the use of this term

And it's true— you and your spouse are radically different. But so are you and every other human being on the planet. Because people are different. And learning to join two lives together requires changing the way you do many things—and change isn't easy.

"But I have tons of friends, Rabbi. I went to camp and got along with all sorts of people. I never had all these problems."

That's correct—because you never shared your life with another person. You shared a room. You did some things together. But you were never in a situation where every move you made had to be balanced and weighed with another person in mind. Put any two people so closely together and you'll find many, many differences that need to be navigated.

In marriage you share a life –which means everything you do, you do together. If one spouse isn't punctual, you're both late. If one is sloppy, you both live with the mess. If one is rigid, you both have to deal with the fallout. It's the first time in your life that you are actually joined together with and dependent upon another—you go from "me" to "we." It sounds romantic, but it's not easy.

Loving your spouse is easy but *living together* isn't. Living together takes a lot of work. Hashem gave us many tools to build the bond of love, and if you use them properly it is relatively straightforward to maintain the love. The hard part is living together. It doesn't matter how flexible you are or how easygoing you are. You and your spouse will have vastly different ways of doing things because every human is vastly different from every other.

No Two Alike

People come in all types of flavors, shades, stripes, and textures. Each of us is a unique blend of temperament, nature and inclinations. And just as no two faces are the same, so too no two people are the same. Some people are extroverts, some people are introverts. Some are loud, some are quiet. Some are high energy, some are mellow. Some are spontaneous, some are methodical. Some are morning people; some are night owls. Some need to fit in, some have no need to fit in. Some easily accept things as they are, some always need to challenge the status quo. Some are organized; some are chaotic. Some make lists, some rely on memory. Some get things done right away, some procrastinate. Some are easily hurt, some are thick-skinned. Some are risk-averse, some are risk-takers. Some work best in groups, some work best alone. The list goes on and on and on.

One of the hardest things to accept is that despite what you or I may recognize, understand, or feel, there is no right way and wrong way. The Myers-Briggs Inventory lists 16 personality traits, and you will find highly successful people in every category. No one type is automatically successful. No one type is automatically a failure. People are people and all people are different. There's no "way" that is categorically better or worse.

But the difference that overshadows every other difference between you and your spouse is that you are different genders—more accurately, opposite genders. We all know that men and women are vastly dissimilar—until we get married, and then we expect our spouse to be just like us. And when they aren't, we become dismissive. *Why can't they just stop it and act normal?*

If that's your attitude, it's going to come out in your relationship and your marriage will suffer. And while most of us won't voice our opinion quite that strongly, the natural bias remains: My way is the normal way, the right way, the way things are done. Any other way of doing things isn't really to be taken seriously.

Many nice, sweet, and polite men and women are difficult to be married to because they are highly dismissive of doing things in a manner different from what they are accustomed to.

Getting used to another way of doing things requires keeping an open mind. It means resisting the urge to be dismissive by just saying things like, "That's ridiculous," or "No one does it like that."

"The right way to cut meat is…"

"Everyone knows that…"

It might be true that that has been your way, but your way isn't the *only* way, and learning to accept another way of doing things and taking into account another person's priorities is vital for a happy marriage.

Why does everything have to be her way?

This brings us to a very important point.

When you begin the process of melding together two lives, you need to compromise on many things that you've been used to doing your way: how you celebrate birthdays, what indoor temperature is comfortable, what time you go to sleep, what time you get up, what you do to have fun or relax. Attitudes towards money, in-laws, risk taking, priorities, neatness, punctuality, what's important and what's not. Religious issues, values and beliefs. Leaving dishes in the sink overnight—or not. What to talk about and when to talk and how much to talk. How to socialize, when to socialize, and how much to socialize. What to eat, when to eat, how to eat…

Realistically, there will be thousands upon thousands of situations where your spouse does things differently than you, and there is no one right way to do it, just different styles and different approaches. Getting used to so many changes in so many areas of life isn't easy. It will feel strange. You might find yourself thinking, *Why does everything have to be done in a strange way? Why can't we do things normally?* But, hey, it's not a big deal. You're a flexible kind of guy. So you come up with a fair compromise – 50/50. Half my way, half her way.

Watch what happens: If on any given day there were only ten situations where you have a difference of opinion, that means there are going to be five things in your day that you're going to do in a new way. Things like:

- what time you leave
- how you handle paperwork
- how you drive

Those five things might surface numerous times during the day, and pretty soon you get frustrated. *This is the fifth thing today that we are doing in a non-conventional (read: wrong) way. Why do we always have to leave early? Why do we always have to do paperwork like a CPA? What's so bad about driving over the speed limit?* It starts to feel not like five things, but like everything. *Why does everything have to be* her *way?!* To your mind, the fact that there are five things that you're doing *your* way doesn't count, because that's just regular—the way things are "supposed" to be.

One of the things that makes living together so difficult is that we are very kind to ourselves. We give ourselves a lot of space. But we're not so forgiving to others. When you give in and do something her way, you deserve full credit. *Look what I'm doing for our marriage!* When she gives in and does it your way, you think, *I mean, that's the normal thing to do. Do you want a medal for being normal?*

If you don't learn to accept that your spouse is an equal partner and her different ways of doing things are valid, things will devolve quickly.

"She's so bossy. She has to have everything her way!"

"He's so demanding Everything has to be his way!"

It's not enough to love each other. You have to also have an open mind and be willing to accept new ways of doing things. If you remain mind blind and trapped in your own world, marriage becomes a huge challenge. You will feel like you are constantly being asked to do things that seem to you to be different, wrong, incorrect, improper, abnormal and uncomfortable. As long as your internal dialogue says "my way is *the* way," living together is going to be difficult for you.

The only way to make this transition smooth is by being open to a different way of doing things.

The next stage in growth

One of the motivations to do this work is that you are going to need this skill to be a good parent.

When your children are little, your responsibilities are straightforward. Feed them, clothe them, put them to bed—take care of their physical needs. As they mature and their personality begins to emerge, your role becomes far more complex. Now it becomes your responsibility to pilot your children along the path of their emotional, social, intellectual, and religious development. You are there to escort them and show the way.

This presents many challenges. When you parent a child who is similar to you, you will quickly recognize what your child is doing and why they are doing it, and you will be able to offer direction. There will be times when your advice will be heeded and there will be times when it won't be. There will be times when you find yourself at your wits end, wanting to scream, "You don't have to make the same mistakes I did." But you'll probably need to let them scrape their knees and take their falls, because your wisdom only came through decades of living, and there are many things that have to be learned the hard way. But when they do fall, you'll be there for them, and you'll understand them well enough to help them pick themselves up.

It's harder to parent a child who is unlike you. You find yourself in uncharted waters. You just can't relate to your child. Why would she do that? Why would he react that way?

Here is where your years of learning to climb into another's world come into play. To be able to discern what your child is thinking and what's motivating them when they don't have the same personality type as you, will require you to step out of your own experiences and relate to what your child is feeling in the given situation. But by then you will have had years of practice doing this within your primary relationship—your marriage.

Which brings us to another point:

How to parent

The following question is one of the most common questions I get.

"My husband is too strict with the kids. I feel like he's damaging them, but if I try to talk to him about it, it will hurt our shalom bayis. How can I protect my children without sacrificing our marriage?"

Or:

"My wife is too indulgent with the kids. I feel like she's damaging them, but if I try to talk to her about it, it will hurt our shalom bayis. How can I protect my children without sacrificing our marriage?"

What do you tell someone who asks that type of question?

The first thing I say is that I assume that we aren't dealing with actual abuse and you guys have discussed this openly and calmly for a good while, but it's still not getting you anywhere. It that's so, then let's focus on the issue at hand. You are at an impasse—you feel strongly one way, your spouse feels another way and the issue at hand is very serious. What do you do?

The first thing you do is speak to whoever you ask your life issues to, hopefully a rav, or at least someone older and wiser. An outside party with an objective, clear perspective should be able to give you guidance and direction.

But let's say you can't ask. Now what? Do you sacrifice your children or sacrifice your marriage? Which one comes first?

The first step is to recognize that anything that damages your marriage will damage your children (probably far more than anything your spouse might be doing). To your children, especially when they are young, Totty and Mommy are 10 feet tall. When you bicker, you act petty, vindictive, and mean-spirited. You are modeling for your children exactly what you don't want them to be. But even worse, if your child doesn't feel that your relationship is secure, their entire sense of security is jeopardized. You are the center of their world. If the union of Mommy and Daddy is unreliable, then everything is unreliable. If Mommy and Daddy cannot be taken for granted, nothing can be taken for granted; nowhere is safe. In most cases, the damage caused by your spouse's style of discipline is far less than the damage caused by parents who fight.

But the deeper question to ask is, are you correct? Is it really damaging to your children if you are too strict? Is it really hurtful to your children if you are too lenient? What makes you feel that way? What makes you so sure that you are right?

When my children were young, their principal suggested that we get outside help for an issue relating to one of our kids. We asked around and a number of people recommended a psychologist named Dr. Rita Underberg. She had been the head of the psychology department of Rochester University, had studied under Dr. Chaim Ginott, and spent decades in research and teaching. She had recently retired from the university and maintained a private practice working with couples to help them with parenting issues.

We went to Dr. Underberg for a few sessions and she taught us an approach that resolved the issue with our child. But even when the issue was resolved, my wife and I kept going. Week after week after week after week. The woman was brilliant. She gave us incredible insight to the world of a child. I would sit there each session writing page after page of notes. I gained a wealth of knowledge and understanding from her, so much so that I begged her to write a book (sadly, she passed away before completing it).

One of the things I learned from her was that there is a lot more to learn about parenting than most of us know—and it could be that your approach is wrong. But the bigger lesson was that most parents parent their children based on their own worldview and life experiences. The simple truth is that most of our parenting style stems from our personality—not from a careful consideration of what is best for the child. If by nature a man is laid back, that's the approach he'll use to raise his children. If by nature a woman is rigid and structured, that will affect the way she raises her children. Both will believe they are using the right approach.

The reason it's so clear to you that your way is the right way is because it's *your* way. You become mind blind to the possibility that your spouse could have a valid point.

To sum up: You need to work on maintaining love in marriage, but living together often requires even more work. Many couples are very good at infatuation, and they learn to maintain love, but they find it very difficult to live together because it's hard to do so many things your spouse's way. Even if you consider yourself an easygoing person, if you remain stuck in your own perception of reality, every one of the little things your spouse does differently will bother you every time, and it will be hard for you to live together. Learning to accept the fact that your spouse is different and trying to do things their way requires hard work, but it's essential for a happy marriage.

To be a supportive partner you need to recognize that your spouse's way of doing things is legitimate. Not because it's better, smarter, or more efficient, but because it's my spouse's way and that's okay.

The Rav Auerbach story that's not famous

The following story has two parts. One part is famous, the other isn't.

When Rav Shlomo Zalman Auerbach, *zt"l,* was maspid his wife, he said, "Normally, the *minhag* is to ask *mechilah* from your spouse. But I'm not going to ask my wife for *mechilah* because there is nothing to ask mechila for."

That's the famous part of the beautiful story. Two *tzaddikim,* the Rosh Yeshivah and his rebbetzin, joining together in peace and harmony. It was a beautiful marriage.

But there's a sequel.

After a young man became engaged, he visited Rav Shlomo Zalman to get advice. He knew the famous story, and who better to learn about *shalom bayis* from than the great Rosh Yeshivah. Rav Shlomo Zalman was very generous with his time and explained to him various ideas about *shalom bayis.*

The young man got married. About six months after his wedding, he saw Rav Shlomo Zalman at a *chasunah* and went over to him. Rav Shlomo Zalman recognized him and asked him how married life was going.

"*Mei menuchos,*" answered the young man. "Waters of tranquility." Total peace. We get along perfectly.

Reb Shlomo Zalman asked, "Are you married?"

"Yes."

"So how's your marriage?"

"*Mei menuchos.*"

Rav Shlomo Zalman asked again. "You got married, right?"

It became clear to the young man that something was amiss. "I don't understand," he said, "why the Rosh Yeshivah is so surprised. Wasn't the Rosh Yeshivah the one who said he doesn't have to ask mechila from his rebbetzin?"

"We had many differences of opinion," Reb Shlomo Zalman responded. "How could two human beings not? How could two people possibly look at the everything the same way? There were many things we disagreed on. The reason I didn't have to ask *mechilah* is because we spoke to each other with respect. In that regard there was nothing we said that was improper. But, of course, we had to compromise on many things, because it's impossible for two human beings to agree on everything."

A marriage is comprised of different people – not people who are slightly different, but a man and a woman of vastly different natures. It's only when you open yourself up to the truth that *my reality is not her reality, the way I experience things is not the way he experiences things*, that each of you can begin to bridge those differences. You have to climb into each other's world. Only then can you do what you're each supposed to do.

That's when your marriage becomes the special, fulfilling relationship that it's supposed to be.

Recognizing that your experience doesn't dictate reality is a paradigm shift that validates your spouse's inner world and allows you to build a beautiful, nurturing relationship. Mind blindness is a challenge, but it can be overcome.

But there is another aspect to living together that might be even more difficult. It's not there we're blind, it's that we see too much.

Chapter 10

You Become an Expert at What Your Spouse Does Wrong

WHENEVER I GIVE A marriage seminar, I hand out a worksheet before I start. It lists the following question:

> Every marriage could use improvement. Assuming your marriage is good, great, or somewhere in the middle, please list two things in your marriage that, if changed, would make it better.

I don't hand it out to find out the answer. I know the answer. Time after time, it's two things *your spouse* does or doesn't do. It's never two things y*ou* do. The answer is always: *My marriage would be much better if my spouse would.…* No one ever writes: *My marriage would be much better if I would.…*

Most people spend their married life blaming their spouse. Even if your marriage is very good, there's a belief that if your spouse would be different, your relationship would be better.

At the beginning of this book we met Shayna and Bentzi, the all-American couple—the case of Mr. ADHD married to Miss Anxiety. They spend the first 20 years of their marriage trying to change each other, only to find out that it doesn't work; it can't work, because that is the way their spouse is built. They might be an extreme example, but every couple has it—the "one thing" about their spouse that if only it would change, life would be so much better.

Notice that it's always the one thing that your *spouse* should change.

My Strength and Your Weakness

The "one thing" is usually something that is your strength and your spouse's weakness. If you're punctual, it's your spouse's lateness that's causing problems. If you're a flexible thinker, it's your husband's rigidity that's the issue. If you're organized, it's her disorganization. If you're creative, it's his need to conform.

If you're brutally honest, you will likely find that it's your winning trait and your spouse's lack of it that causes trouble in your marriage.

A fellow once asked me for help. He said, "I can't respect my wife. First off, she loses it with kids. Second of all, no matter how much we talk about health and eating right, she just doesn't make it a priority. I've lost all respect for her."

Because I knew him pretty well, I understood where the problem lay. I said, "You're not being fair. What's easy for you isn't easy for her." He is one of the most goal-oriented, self-disciplined people I have ever met. He wakes up 5:00 am every day, jumps into a freezing cold shower (just to master himself), works out for 45 minutes, and then plans his schedule. By 6:15 am he's ready to take on his day.

"The reason you can't understand your wife," I said, "is because these things come easily to you. It's not difficult for you to be disciplined—it's part of your nature. But you can't to expect that of someone who doesn't have that gift. You are using *you* as the scale and demanding that your spouse measures up."

Your spouse's "flaw" will crop up over and over again until it seems that you can't help but see it everywhere you look. She may have many positive traits that far outweigh this deficit; other people may not even be aware of this shortcoming; but to you it will be right there, front and center, visible all the time.

There is a reason for this.

Filtering Mechanism

Did you ever notice that when something unusual catches your eye, you suddenly start seeing it everywhere? It could be a striking color, or a beautiful bird, or anything that creates an emotional response. Maybe you like cars and you spot a red Tesla. *Wow! Great car!* Suddenly you start noticing that car everywhere you go.

The human mind is astonishingly complex. Whether awake or asleep, we are constantly assailed by a massive array of visual, audio, and kinesthetic stimuli. To allow us to make sense out of the world and function effectively, Hashem equipped the brain with an automatic filtering system. Without our being aware of it, our brain processes all the incoming data and tunes out the vast amount that isn't relevant so that we can focus on what matters. All the things that aren't relevant stay in our peripheral focus so we can respond in case of emergency, but these things don't register in our conscious attention. That's why a new mother can sleep through the noise of passing freight train, but one whimper from her baby and she's awake in an instant. Even when she's asleep, her brain is scanning, looking for warning signals, only bringing to her attention those sounds that have been deemed important.

When you're driving on the highway, you'll see hundreds and hundreds of cars. None of them make an impression on you. Your filter keeps them beneath the surface of your attention. There could be blue Fords, green Hyundais, silver Camrys—none of it registers with your conscious mind. But then there's this unusual red car. It catches your attention. You take notice of it. Your subconscious mind gets the message that this car is significant and flags it as something to look out for. From then on, you won't notice any of the black, silver, or white cars, but whenever a red Tesla comes into your field of vision, your brain will bring it to your attention.

When you notice something that your spouse does wrong, it creates an emotional response in you. Your brain perks up, flags this occurrence as important, and points it out to you every time it happens again. Out of the millions of things that your spouse does every day, the vast majority just pass under the radar, but when she comes late – ding-ding-ding, you notice it. Pretty soon you just can't help but notice it all the time. Before long, you start to expect it, and you may even see it when it's not even there!

In short order, you become an expert at what your spouse does wrong. You don't mean to be critical. You don't mean to be judgmental. But you spend so much time together, and every aspect of your lives is so intertwined, that you can't help but see over and over how much better life would be if they would only be punctual, or organized, or articulate, or whatever the flaw is.

This is a formula for misery. You're upset because your spouse isn't good enough, and your spouse is upset because you think they aren't good enough. The relationship suffers.

But what can you do? You can't help but see the flaw. You're only human.

One Change Guaranteed to Make Your Marriage Better

I have a mussar exercise that I believe can solve this great challenge, if you are willing to do the work. I call it *work* because it isn't going to be easy.

If you would like to have a better marriage, and if you are serious about self-improvement in general, I want you to walk up to a mirror, look at the face staring back at you, and say these words aloud three times: "I am a difficult person to live with."

I am a difficult person to live with.

I am a difficult person to live with.

I am a difficult person to live with.

I, not my spouse, am a difficult person to live with.

As you say those words, a voice might well up inside you. *No. That's not true. It's my spouse that's the problem.*

Your spouse might be flawed, but you also have stuff. Every human being has quirks, idiosyncrasies, shortcomings, and flaws. We're either too late or too punctual, too sloppy or too neat, too uptight or too chilled. I guarantee that you're a difficult person to live with. How can I guarantee it? Because Hashem created you imperfect and put you on the planet to perfect yourself. (If you were perfect, you wouldn't be here. Your job would be done, and it would be time to leave. So let's hope that I'm right and you're not perfect.) You, like every other person on the planet, have habits, tendencies, and weaknesses that need improvement—which means you are difficult to live with.

That doesn't mean you're an obnoxious person. It means you're human. Every human being, no matter how put-together, no matter how good their middos, has things that make it difficult for another human being to live with them.

The reason that you don't see yourself that way is because people have a basic instinct of self-protection—we can't help but be kind to ourselves. The problem is that we don't apply that standard to everyone else.

When you actually do this exercise and look in the mirror, for a rare moment you can see yourself honestly. While you have many strengths and talents, you also have things you need to work on. When you recognize that, it becomes a lot easier to accept your spouse.

The Only Solution

The only way to really live in peace is to accept your spouse as they are. That becomes much easier to do when you recognize that you didn't create yourself, nor did you create your spouse. Each of you were created by Hashem, each given different strengths and talents with fantastic potential, and each of you are imperfect in your own ways. Each of you were given the perfect mix of gifts and limitations. You didn't get to choose. That decision was made by the wisest of all—your Creator.

Our task in this world is to use our strengths to grow and accomplish, and a large part of that is self-perfection. But self-perfection means exactly that—you are charged with perfecting *yourself*. It's not your responsibility to perfect your spouse. When you're done your job on this planet, you won't be asked, *How much did you transform your spouse?* You'll be asked, *How much did you perfect yourself? How much of your potential did you reach?*

Within each of us is a need to grow, to change our essence and become more like our Creator. The problem is that change is very difficult. One of the traps that we fall into is that we divert that need to grow and focus it on other people. It's far easier than focusing on your own growth, but not only doesn't it work, it's not your job, it's not fair, and it takes your attention off your own responsibility to change yourself.

To embrace my spouse as they are, I have to accept that her nature, disposition, and temperament wasn't something she chose. She was put into a body, given a mission, and granted all the tools that she needs to fulfill it. And you were, as well. But your mission isn't her mission, and her mission isn't yours. You are two individuals joined in life, but each with your own personal directive—each with your own charge. Your duty is to accomplish your mission. Her duty is to accomplish hers.

The difficult part is that nothing short of truly embracing your spouse *as they are* will do. No matter how committed you are not to criticize her. No matter how much you refrain from helping him change. If you don't actually *accept* your spouse for who they are, your feelings will come out. You won't realize it, but your spouse sure will. That sense of disapproval is toxic. It erodes the relationship.

People wonder, *Why doesn't he like me? Why is she so defensive? I'm not being critical!* And that might be true. You didn't say anything negative. You wanted to, but you held yourself back. But as long as you think it, your spouse knows it, and the damage is done.

In Dale Carnegie's classic, *How to Win Friends and Influence People* (a must-read for marriage and for life), he writes that the surest way to get people to like you is to compliment them, and the surest way to get people to dislike you is to criticize them.

We humans crave acceptance. When I know that another person accepts and respects me, I feel good about myself. When I know that someone disapproves of me, I feel badly about myself.

It's natural to want to feel good about yourself, so it's human nature to like people who approve of us and dislike people who don't. This applies even more strongly to the person I am supposed to be closest to and spend the most time with. When that person makes me feel inadequate, it hurts, and I can't help but dislike that person.

Nothing short of actually accepting your spouse as they are, blemishes and all, will allow you to live in peace (or, more precisely, will allow your spouse to live in peace with you).

He Knows What He's Doing

Anyone who says that marriage isn't hard work was never married (or at least, not happily married). Marriage is the closest of all relationships, and it is the most demanding. There is no relationship that is as supportive, joined, and connected. Marriage also demands more self-growth than any other relationship. But self-growth means you working on *you*. In a proper marriage, the two of you become one. But you aren't two *halves* who join together and become whole. You are two *whole* people, each with your own identity, personality, and will, charged with joining together to become part of a greater whole.

There may be times when you are tempted to say, "Hashem, I don't mean to be insolent, but when You put us together, what were You thinking?! We're so different. I mean, we're *opposites!*" And that's correct. You are two distinct individuals, coming from different homes, brought up in different ways, with different perspectives and outlooks. You each have different personalities, interests, and desires. Yes, you are opposites. Yet you are ideally suited to live together, because you aren't opposites that conflict. You are opposites that match perfectly. Opposites that *when aligned*, fit together seamlessly to form a complete whole—far greater than the sum of its parts. That *alignment* might take time, and certainly much effort.

In marriage, as in all things in life, you have to trust Hashem. He Created you, and He knows your strengths, your weaknesses, and what you need. Hashem chose for you the perfect counterpart. You and your spouse balance each other perfectly. But that doesn't mean it will be easy for you to adjust, and it doesn't mean there won't be a few bumps along the way. It means He chose the perfect match to accompany you on this journey of growth and change that we call life.

It's helpful to remember that Hashem knows what He's doing. It's not by accident that He made men and women so different. He didn't have to create so many different types of personalities and then mix them up, swapping and switching so that each person is a unique blend of traits, tendencies, and inclinations. He did it because this world is the great workshop of personal growth. Hashem put us into this world to develop. Much of that development is internal. The ultimate goal is to be as much like our Creator as any human can be. Hashem is the source of all good, and He created this world to share His good with others. By mastering your nature, and becoming other-centered, you do just that—you become more like Hashem.

Marriage requires you to put someone else's interests ahead of your own, and often in a way that's not easy, not comfortable, and foreign to your nature. As such, it is a catalyst for growth. That growth is some of the most important that you will ever engage in.

Let me not put a damper on things. Marriage is the most rewarding relationship in the human experience. It's just the fairy-tale version of marriage that needs editing. *Boy meets girl, they fall madly in love and live happily ever after* – that version is just a fantasy. Never happened. Never will. Marriage takes work. A good marriage requires a good amount of work. A great marriage requires a great amount of work.

This pillar of marriage, learning to live together, is where the self-growth happens. This is arguably the most difficult area. It requires reaching beyond what seems obvious; It requires asking questions before you react. More than anything, it requires learning and adapting to the needs of another person. It demands that you become a bigger, better person.

But there is another pillar, love, which really means working on the relationship. This is the fun part. In terms of the health of your marriage, it might have the greatest impact. Because while love alone is never enough, if your relationship is strong then you are married to your best friend. You are both kind, tolerant, and forgiving, so it's a lot easier to put up with each other's stuff.

But even more significantly, if there is a strong bond of love, you both have the energy and motivation to do the difficult work it takes to change. So let's get started on that—the second pillar, working on the love in your marriage.

Chapter 11

Tools that Bond

> **ספר בראשית פרק כט**
> יח) וַיֶּאֱהַב יַעֲקֹב אֶת רָחֵל וַיֹּאמֶר אֶעֱבָדְךָ שֶׁבַע שָׁנִים בְּרָחֵל בִּתְּךָ הַקְּטַנָּה
> כ) וַיַּעֲבֹד יַעֲקֹב בְּרָחֵל שֶׁבַע שָׁנִים וַיִּהְיוּ בְעֵינָיו כְּיָמִים אֲחָדִים בְּאַהֲבָתוֹ אֹתָהּ
>
> **ספורנו עה"ת ספר בראשית פרק כט פסוק כ**
> כ) ויהיו בעיניו כימים אחדים. שחשב שהיה ראוי לתת מהר רב מזה: באהבתה אותה. שהאהבה מקלקלת השורה

IN PARSHAS YAYEITZEI, YAAKOV sets out to find a wife. He meets Rochel at the well. He recognizes her as his *bashert* and they agree to marry. Yaakov then approaches Rochel's father, Lavan, to ask his permission. They negotiate a bride price and settle on seven years of labor. In the words of the Torah, "In his eyes they were but a few days." The Sforno explains that Yaakov grossly miscalculated—seven years' labor was well beyond the typical bride price. Since love blinds, he mistakenly thought he was getting a great bargain. But because of the great love that he felt for Rochel, those years seemed like just a few days. (Sforno, Bereishis 29:20).

This is very difficult to understand. How can the holy Yaakov Avinu, one of the Avos, see Rochel and instantly fall in love? Real love takes years and years to develop. The Torah doesn't say he was infatuated – a temporary, illusionary state. The Torah says he loved her. He loved her so much that it blinded his judgement. How could he love her instantly?

To answer this, we need to revisit the concept of *bashert* (predestined).

Two parts of one whole

When we think about *bashert*, we take it to mean that before you were born Hashem searched through millions of possible matches and said, "Yes! This is the one. This is the perfect match for you." But that's not exactly how it works.

The Raishis Chachma explains that before you were born, you and your spouse were one neshama. Hashem split that neshama into two. Each of you were placed into a body. For your formative years, you were assigned to different families. You were given the mission to find your other half, join together, and create a union. When you are each finished your jobs here on this earth, you will leave and join together again as one unit to share in the World to Come forever.

Your job now is to learn to live in peace and harmony and overcome any obstacles that stand between you. Marriage is such a great challenge because even though you began as two halves of one whole, in your current state you are very different from each other. Hashem gave each of you a life with its own reality. You were each brought up in different homes with distinct values and priorities. You were put into a body that has a specific level of intelligence with a preset temperament, nature, and inclinations. One of you were placed into a male body and the other female

– opposite in nature, interests, and desires. Joining together to live in peace and harmony is far from simple.

Answer for Yaakov Avinu

But that is for us mere mortals. The Avos lived in a different reality and saw the world with different eyes. Yaakov spent decades perfecting himself, and normal physical limitations didn't blind him. When he looked at Rochel, he saw her. Not her outer shell—not the physical form that she wore. As a cloak isn't the man, so too the body isn't the person; it is merely the housing that temporarily holds them. Yaakov perceived the essence of Rochel and saw her inner greatness. He loved her for what she had become, loved her for who she was. Even more, he had a prophetic understanding that this woman was the right one. They belonged together. She was his lost half. That sense was so profound that he felt complete with her, and he loved her. They lived in that state of love and dedication throughout their time together in this world.

Lavan asked for a price for Rochel, but to Yaakov there was no price—she was precious beyond any value, and seven years' labor was a bargain. Yet, as the Siforno points out, it was only because love blinds that he miscalculated.

The Avos aren't mile markers

This is a beautiful illustration of the level of perfection a person can reach. But it's also important to remember that we aren't the Avos and Imahos. They were spiritual giants and were almost above physical limitations. We study their ways and wish for the time "when our actions will reach theirs" ((insert source)). At the same time, we need to remain realistic about what is expected from us. As we journey through life, the Avos serve as our North Star, a guiding light directing us toward greatness and expanding our understanding of what is possible. But they aren't mile markers—we don't measure our progress against their accomplishments. We have our challenges, just as they had theirs, but the two are vastly different. They may have existed in this world, but they lived miles above. We aren't them. We live very much in this world. We have needs that are very real. For us, loving another doesn't come easily.

There's another reason why it's difficult for us to connect to another person, and that has to do with the very nature of the human personality. To understand this, we need to take a quick tour of the soul.

> Man was created from elements that are very different, whose essence are opposites, and whose very natures are in competition. They are his body and his soul. Within man, God implanted drives and desires that are necessary for the continuation of the human species; these are all of the desires for physical pleasures. They are [present] in man as in all animals. If man makes use of them, he will strengthen his physical standing, and the human race will flourish. In addition to these, God implanted within the human soul strengths, which, if man uses them, will cause him to look down on his position in this world and make him desire to separate from it. This is his spiritual part. *–Duties of the Heart 3:2*

Within this short paragraph we have been given the formula of man's nature. When Hashem created man, He joined two diverse elements to form man's essence: the spiritual soul (what we call the neshama) and the animal soul. The conscious sense of "I" that thinks and feels is made up of both parts.

The neshama comes from beneath the throne of Hashem's glory. It is pure and lofty, holy and sublime. All that it wishes for is that which is good, proper, and noble. Because it comes from the upper worlds, it derives no benefit from this world and can't relate to any of its pleasures. This is the part of you that only wants to serve Hashem, help others, and do what's right.

There is, though, another part of man – his animal soul. It is exactly like that of an animal, with all of the desires and instincts necessary to keep him alive. If we wish to understand man, to make sense of what drives him, and relate to what matters to him, then as much as we need to understand the neshama, we need to understand this other part of his soul as well.

An animal has a living essence. Just like man, it has an inner essence that directs it. A dog is attracted toward certain types of objects and repelled by others. It likes to do certain things and detests other things. It will form attachments to its master and will even risk its own life to defend him. Every animal has a part of it that is vibrant and living, and just like a human soul, that part isn't physical. That part of the animal is its inner essence, its animal soul.

Hashem implanted into the animal soul all of the drives that an animal needs for its survival. A cat hunts mice by instinct. A bird eats worms because of an inner urge. It would be difficult to imagine a robin thinking, *Based on my nutritional needs, as well as my capacity to hunt for, capture, and digest such foods, coupled with the general availability of such items, I have surmised that it would be best for me to utilize the worm as my food staple.* The bird simply hungers for a worm. It has a natural pull, an inborn inclination, toward its optimum food.

Studies show that even animals raised in captivity, when released, instinctively hunt for the ideal food for their species. Siberian tigers that were orphaned at birth and brought up on bottled milk began hunting deer when allowed into the wild. Deer is the natural food source for Siberian tigers, and that's what they pursued, even though these tigers had never before seen a deer, let alone watched one being hunted down and eaten. The tools, the aptitude, and the inclination to capture and consume the types of food that best assures its survival, is inborn in every animal.

So too with mating. Two bullfrogs don't sit down to discuss their future, with one saying, "Kermit, I think it's time for us to settle down and raise a family." Hashem implanted in each animal all of the necessary drives for its survival as an individual, as well as the survival of the species as a whole. Those instincts are part of its animal soul.

Man, as well, has an animal soul. There is a part of him that yearns for physical things. He desires to eat, sleep, and procreate. Hashem put into man's animal soul all of the inclinations he needs to stay alive. If he follows these instincts, he will survive, and the species of mankind will continue.

The animal soul is part of you. You don't say "my body hungers for food." You say, "I'm hungry."

That "I" is made up of two parts: pure spirituality and base animal instincts. One part of me is more sublime than the angels, and one part of me is as impulsive as any member of the animal kingdom. When a dog feels the mating instinct, there is nothing that stops it; instinct rules the animal. Such drives live in man as well. Within me are instincts for physical activities and pursuits. The greatness of the human is that the other part of me, the part that is guided by intelligence, can control the animal instincts.

These two elements of man are opposites, and they fight for primacy and control. As a result, man is in a constant state of flux. The more he uses either side, the stronger and more influential it becomes. Much like a muscle that becomes stronger with use and atrophies with disuse, if a person uses his spiritual soul to control his animal soul, it becomes stronger, and he becomes elevated. If he gives in to his desires, the animal soul gains command, and his desires become more intense and frequent. They demand to be fulfilled more often and with more force — and man becomes progressively more controlled by these drives.

In this regard, man's animal soul is different from what is found in the animal kingdom. An animal's desires are set to a certain intensity at birth. They will fluctuate based on seasons and circumstances, but all within a given range. Man, on the other hand, has less restriction on the intensity of his desires. If he controls his animal instincts, they lessen, so it becomes easier for his spiritual side to dominate. He becomes their master. But if he allows his animal instincts to rule, they become stronger and more extreme until they are in command. Then, man is but a slave to his drives.

Life is a battle between these two forces. Ideally, a person uses his pure spiritual soul to harness his animal soul to keep himself alive. Like a captain steering his ship by the wind, he uses the animal soul and its energy to accomplish his objectives and goals. He eats to maintain his health so that he can perform his mission on this planet. He engages in intimacy to create a harmonious, loving marriage and to bring children into the world. The pleasures that he takes from this world are also for a purpose — so that he should have the peace of mind to pursue the elevated path that will lead to eternal joy.

By using the animal soul to further his spiritual goals, not only does he increase the control that his neshamah has, he elevates everything that he does. Mundane, physical activities necessary for human survival are elevated into holy acts, mitzvos, and the he functions on the utmost level of spirituality — an angel wearing the form of a man.

However, if a person allows his animal desires to prevail, they become stronger, eventually ruling over him. At that point, he is no longer able to make decisions based on intelligence. Rather, like an animal, he is dominated by whims and governed by passions until he loses control of himself, and ultimately even loses the ability to choose. He becomes more animal-like and less God-like, eventually becoming nothing more than an animal in the shape of a man.

The challenge of life is to perfect ourselves by finding the path that brings about our growth and allows our instinctive desire to do what is right and noble to win out. The difficult part is that it's *I* who is in contradiction. It's *I* who wants to grow — and it's the very same *I* who wants to roll in the mud. It's *I* who wants to shoot for the stars, to reach the heights of humanity — and it's *I* who is satisfied to go on living without a plan, without direction, just taking life as it comes.

To help man succeed, Hashem gave us a method that allows the part of you that is great to come to the fore. He gave us a program for spiritual development, a system for accomplishing our life's mission. That system is the Torah and mitzvos.

The Torah provides us with guidelines and a system of living that allows all that is great in humankind to flourish. It's the program that allows the spiritual part of man to grow and dominate the animal within him. The Torah is replete with commandments and precepts, many of whose meanings are readily understood, and others that take great work to understand. All of these focus on one goal: to strengthen man's spiritual side, to allow it to emerge victorious and to ultimately gain primacy.

The challenge of being human

When you understand the composition of your personality, you can begin to understand life.

We are a living contradiction, made up of two parts completely opposite in nature. There are many things that we know are true, but we don't feel them. You could be davening, speaking directly to the Creator of the heavens and the earth, and then your mind drifts and you are 3,000 miles away. If a person were standing in front of you, you wouldn't space out. So why can't you concentrate when you're speaking to Hashem? Because the person is *there*, you *know* it. Your spiritual soul knows that Hashem is present, but your animal soul, which is a full half of you, denies it, so it's difficult to feel it.

It's difficult to care about another person. When I hear about a young mother with cancer, half of me cries out, "Oy! That's terrible. What can I do to help?" But there is another half of me that couldn't care less. The animal soul is made of hungers and needs; it can't feel someone else's pain. It isn't equipped to relate to others. That's why it's very difficult for us to really love another person. You may want to. You may know that it's the right thing to do, but a full half of you cannot relate to anything other than your own needs.

Marriage is one of the greatest exercises in self-mastery and growth. We enter marriage with this lofty concept of looking out for the good of your spouse, being dedicated to their welfare, and putting their interests before your own, but it doesn't happen easily. You may be a nice guy and always be willing to lend a hand to a friend, but marriage is far more demanding.

For the first time in your life, you are called upon to give up your wants and desires for someone else's, not once in a while, but day in and day out, and often in a way that often doesn't make sense (*this wouldn't bother me, why is it such a big deal to her?*). Learning to value someone else's reality goes against your nature.

If life is the laboratory of growth, marriage is both an aid and a catalyst. It is an aid in the sense that you have a partner to accompany you on the journey. It is a catalyst in that you are constantly challenged to put aside your interests for the good of another. In that aspect, marriage coaxes you to be giving, kind, and loving—to act as much like Hashem as you can. Do it often enough for long enough and you become a vastly different person—an angel wearing the suit of a man.

Marriage requires you to constantly give to another. The greatest force to make one want to give to another is love. If I love someone, I want their best. If I love someone, I want to give to them. If I love them enough, I may even be willing to give up of my needs for them. But to actually love another person, a person you didn't grow up with, a person you just met as a full grown adult, is tough. Because the journey is a long, tough climb, and there are many obstacles we encounter along the way, Hashem gave us a number of tools to make it easier. These are **tools that bond** spouses to each other. These tools, when used properly, create a profound sense of love between a husband and wife and allow them to become one. Some of these tools function on a physical level.

To understand these, let's return to Yaakov and Rochel.

> **ספר בראשית פרק כט**
>
> ל) וַיָּבֹא גַּם אֶל רָחֵל וַיֶּאֱהַב גַּם אֶת רָחֵל מִלֵּאָה וַיַּעֲבֹד עִמּוֹ עוֹד שֶׁבַע שָׁנִים אֲחֵרוֹת
>
> *Yaakov came also to Rachel and he loved Rachel more than Leah, and he worked for him another seven years.*
>
> **רמב"ן על בראשית פרק כט פסוק ל**
>
> ל) ויאהב גם את רחל הזכיר הכתוב שגם אהב רחל יותר מלאה, והטעם, בעבור כי הטבע לאהוב יותר האשה אשר ידע האדם בראשונה, כענין שהזכירו חכמים בנשים (סנהדרין כב:) ואינה כורתת ברית אלא למי שעשאה כלי והנה רחל אהב יעקב מלאה שלא כדרך הארץ, וזה טעם "גם":
>
> *The pasuk mentions that he also loved Rachel more than Leah because nature is to especially love the woman whom a man knows first... That Yaakov's love for Rachel was greater than his love for Leah was not according to the normal way of the world, and that is why it says "also."*

After working the agreed-upon seven years, Yaakov approaches Lavan and says, it is time for me to marry Rochel. Lavan, however, had other ideas. During this time, his wealth had increased dramatically. He recognized that it was because of Yaakov's presence. Everything that Yaakov touched turned to gold. Lavan desperately wanted to delay Yaakov's leaving, so he schemed to switch brides. If Yaakov married Leah, he would be forced to work another seven years to marry his beloved Rochel.

But Lavan faced one obstacle. A wedding, even in those days, was a very public affair, and he had to invite the entire town. The local people knew the greatness of Yaakov. They had interacted with him on many occasions and recognized his extreme modesty, honesty and holiness. He was very well-liked and respected and everyone knew his plan to marry Rochel. If Lavan would try to switch Rochel for Leah, the townspeople would warn Yaakov.

Lavan decided to take the direct approach. He told the townspeople, "You see how much success we have enjoyed because this tzaddik is in our midst. He wants to marry my daughter Rochel, but if he does, he will leave, and our prosperity will cease. We need to keep him here longer. My plan is to switch brides. In place of Rochel, I will give him my daughter Leah. He will then be forced to stay another seven years to work for Rochel." He swore them all to secrecy. Immediately prior to the wedding, Lavan told Leah to take Rochel's place.

As they were walking the bride to the chuppah, the townspeople wanted to warn Yaakov. But Lavan was a powerful man, not one to trifle with. While dancing, the guests began singing, "Hilei, hilei, hilei." Sung quickly, it sounded like *"hee Leah"*—she is Leah. (This is where the Sefardi custom of crying *hilei, hilei, hilei* at weddings comes from.) (Medrash)

The people were not successful in warning Yaakov. He married Leah. In the morning when he awoke, he realized he was tricked.

He complained to Lavan, "Why did you dupe me?"

Lavan replied, "In our place, it isn't the custom for the younger daughter to marry before the older. If you work another seven years, you can have Rochel as well. Finish this week of celebration, and then you can marry Rochel." Yaakov agreed and a week later he married Rochel.

After he had married both, the *pasuk* says, "And he *also* loved Rochel more than Leah." The Ramban explains that the Torah uses this word "also" to teach us a lesson. The nature of a man is to feel a special love for the woman he was with first. Since Yaakov married Leah first, he should have loved her more. However, Yaakov felt that Leah deceived him, so he harbored some ill will against her. Therefore, contrary to nature, he loved Rochel more.

This Ramban is very difficult to understand. The Ramban is saying that by nature Yaakov should have loved Leah more than Rochel because he was with her first. The only reason he didn't love her more was because he had a complaint against her. But why should he love Leah at all? He didn't want to marry her. He wanted to marry Rochel. That's who he loved. Besides, although he married Leah first, he thought she was Rochel; he believed he was with Rochel. Why should marrying Leah in error cause him to love her more than the one he really wanted?

To understand this, let's jump back to the animal kingdom.

The Loyal Emperor Penguin

Most animals are not monogamous. An ox will mate with any cow that happens to be nearby. Stud horses are taken from mare to mare. When a dog is in heat, it will search out any compatible mate and then leave it, searching for a new one as soon as the mating instinct kicks in again. Most animals form no allegiance or attachment to a partner. Mating is a physical act that leaves no connection between the male and the female.

But some animals are different.

Together Forever – The Swan

Many species of birds mate once and then remain together for a season or for life. Swans form lifelong pair-bonds. A male and female will engage in a courtship dance; if successful, they mate, and from that moment on, they are bonded. They fly together, hunt together, build a nest together, and take turns incubating their eggs. Another female swan does not tempt the male swan; another male does not tempt the female. They remain faithful for life. Season after season, they remain together. When one dies, its partner will appear to be mourning, and typically won't seek another mate.

Emperor penguins demonstrate this trait to an extreme. They live in Antarctica, and breed in the winter when the temperature dips to 40 below zero. The female lays a large egg and gingerly balances it on her feet. If it touches the icy ground it will crack, and the chick inside will die. She waddles carefully over to her mate and nudges the egg onto his feet. The male covers the egg with feathered skin known as a brood pouch. He will then stand completely still, keeping the egg warm. The female goes off to hunt. She has to eat enough so that when she returns, she will have the reserves needed to feed the newly hatched chick.

It's not a short journey. She will walk 50 miles or more on frozen ice to find an area of open water. She then jumps in and begins hunting for many weeks. She needs to build up her body fat. All this time, the male stands in place protecting the egg. Despite the 90 mph winds and the blistering cold, he will remain in place, protecting the egg and keeping it warm until the female returns. For over two months he stands there, not moving, not eating, losing up to 35% of his body fat. Finally, the egg hatches and the female returns to feed her chick.

The remarkable part of the process is that Emperor penguins huddle together in very large groups to maintain warmth. The female will waddle through a group of up to 25,000 penguins, passing by every male until she finds her mate. When she finds him, they change roles. The female takes over caring for the chick and the male leaves to hunt. About four weeks later, he returns. On his way back, he too passes by thousands of females and heads straight to his mate. From then on, the pair takes turns caring for their little one.

The pair-bonding effect, where mating creates an almost inseparable attachment, isn't relegated to the animal kingdom alone. Hashem put it into man as well.

The term *onah* ("time of") is used in halacha to refer to marital intimacy. The Torah says וְעֹנָתָהּ לֹא יִגְרָע "do not take away from *onasah*—her time." The Ramban defines *onasah*, her time, as ועת דודיה לא יגרע ממנה, "time of love." It is a time when a couple join together in love and creates love.

Sometimes people feel awkward about the concept of physical intimacy. It may seem foreign, almost animalistic. It may take time to get used to and appreciate. One of the reason that it takes getting used to is that you are completely, utterly vulnerable. There is nothing to hide behind, there are no separations. But that's a significant aspect of its power: intimacy breaks down barriers. You and your spouse can become one.

> **ספר בראשית פרק ב**
> כד) עַל כֵּן יַעֲזָב אִישׁ אֶת אָבִיו וְאֶת אִמּוֹ וְדָבַק בְּאִשְׁתּוֹ וְהָיוּ לְבָשָׂר אֶחָד
>
> *Therefore, a man should leave his father and his mother, and he should cling to his wife, and they should become one entity.*

One Entity

The Ramban explains that when a husband and wife join together physically, this brings them to view themselves as one entity. When a man leaves his parents' home and clings to his wife he creates his own family, his own home. One of the primary tools to do this is the act of intimacy. Through it they become *"basar echad,"* one flesh, one entity. They are now joined as one complete whole.

Much like the swans that mate once and pair-bond, Hashem put the capacity for fidelity within the physical nature of a human being. The *neshama* started off as one unit, and though it separates into two when it comes down into this world, the *nefesh habehami* has the power to reunite the halves. When a man and woman join together, they view themselves as one. It's an act of bonding.

The Emotional Connection

This is what the Ramban is telling us about Yaakov and Leah. Yaakov was with Leah first, and physical intimacy is so powerful that it should have caused him to love Leah more – even though he *thought* he was with Rochel! Yaakov Avinu was pure, so the potency of intimacy was powerful and undiluted, and the natural consequence of intimacy is love.

But he had complaints against Leah, so the power of intimacy didn't work properly. Therefore, despite his being with Leah first, he loved Rochel more. Still, the rule remains: regardless of whom he wanted to marry and who he thought he was with, he should have loved Leah more, because that's what intimacy accomplishes.

This Ramban is fundamental to understanding an aspect of marriage that many people don't understand.

Intimacy brings a couple together emotionally. It's a physical act that results in an emotional attachment. The physical act causes them to love one another.

It is through this joining in love that they bring children into the world. The intention while doing a mitzvah plays a powerful role in the outcome; it is only through a total joining together in peace, love, and harmony that holy children can be born. So it is appropriate that an act of love brings children into the world.

But the function of intimacy goes beyond having children. In the animal world, the mating instinct exists to perpetuate the species, but people would want to have children even without the desire for intimacy. The desire for intimacy serves a different purpose for humanity: to create a loving bond between husband and wife.

Intimacy creates a loving attachment between husband and wife. It plays an important function in a couple being happily married. It causes them to feel connected to each other. Although initially it may take some getting used to (typically more for women than men), it is special, holy, and appropriate.

A man in a tuxedo isn't a penguin

The bond created by marital intimacy is different than the pair-bonding that penguins and swans experience. A penguin has no conscious mind. There is no "I" that makes decisions. The penguin is driven by instinct. Hashem programmed into the species an automatic bonding effect. The male penguin doesn't have to like the way the female treats him. The female penguin doesn't have to be satisfied with their relationship. They are bonded with each other and joined for life.

Humans, on the other hand, are far more complex. The bond caused by intimacy is powerful, but not unbreakable. Penguins have only an animal soul, but humans have both a neshama and an animal soul, and a conscious mind that decides which one to listen to. While penguins act on instinct, humans have to make choices. Intimacy creates an attachment between a couple, but there are many things that can weaken that attachment. If the couple does not build a strong and healthy relationship, and guard that relationship, the attachment created by intimacy will be countered by negative feelings. Intimacy is a powerful tool, but it remains only one tool in a bigger picture. Even this powerful tool needs some assistance.

> **תלמוד בבלי מסכת נדה דף לא/ב**
>
> תניא היה ר"מ אומר מפני מה אמרה תורה נדה לשבעה מפני שרגיל בה וקץ בה אמרה תורה תהא טמאה שבעה ימים כדי שתהא חביבה על בעלה כשעת כניסתה לחופה
>
> Why is it that the Torah made a niddah forbidden for seven days? Because he would become accustomed to her and he would loathe her. The Torah says, Let her be impure for seven days and she'll be as precious to her husband as when he took her originally under the chuppah.
>
> **רש"י נדה דף לא/ב**
>
> מפני שאדם רגיל באשתו - כל שעה שירצה
>
> Any time that he wants.
>
> קץ בה - מאוסה עליו אמרה תורה כל שעה שתראה תהא טמאה שבעה כדי שלא יהא רגיל בה ותתחבב עליו
>
> She will be disgusting to him, says the Torah. She should be impure for seven days so that he won't be accustomed to her and she will be beloved to him.

Two Weeks On, Two Weeks Off

When you teach a *chosson* and *kallah* about *hilchos niddah* and tell them it's going to be two weeks on and two weeks off, sometimes you get a *look*. "What? That's crazy! I waited all these years, and now you're going to tell me two weeks on and then totally separate... That's inhumane!" It's not until you're married for a while that you understand the beauty and wisdom of the system.

Our Creator, Who understands our nature, gave us a powerful force and put it within a precise cycle. The act of intimacy needs to happen regularly because the couple has to constantly reconnect. At the same time, intimacy is only one part of the relationship cycle. The other part is the *niddah* period. Chazal tell us that "if it wasn't for this separation, a husband would become accustomed to his wife and loathe her." Temporary separation is an essential part of total togetherness. Just as food never tastes as good as it does right after a fast, the Torah commands husband and wife to separate for a time. When they join together again, she'll be as precious to her husband as when he originally took her under the *chuppah*.

Rabi Meir explains that when something is always available, it no longer feels special. It becomes ordinary. If she were always available to him, he would lose desire for her and intimacy wouldn't create that powerful bond. Therefore, Hashem instituted a separation period. When she is a *niddah,* husband and wife have to separate completely. No contact. A total physical separation.

During these two weeks, there is a shift in the relationship. With the physical relationship on hold, the couple is focused on their emotional connection. It's very important to remain in close emotional contact during this time. You still speak words of endearment. You still compliment each other and express your love for each other. The key distinction is that the focus is now on emotional closeness, not physical closeness.

There's another shift during this time. The desire to be together begins building. You can't help but look at each other differently. As more time passes, the desire increases. As you remain romantically connected during this time, a sexual tension builds and draws you toward each other. This drive increases as time passes, and when you do join together again, it is new and special, a synthesis of desire, love, and commitment that bonds you again as one.

This cycle of two weeks on, two weeks off is part of the success of a Jewish marriage. When people get accustomed to anything, even intimacy, it loses its power. In fact, secular marriage therapists often advise struggling couples to try a two-week physical separation. It revitalizes the marriage because it eliminates the monotony that naturally follows availability. New is always exciting.

Approaching from opposite directions

One of the profound secrets to a happy marriage is understanding that Hashem knew what He was doing when He created us. He created many tools to bring a couple together. In order to use the tools, you just have to know what they are and how they work.

The tool of physical intimacy is a little tricky because it works differently in men and women.

Men have a natural drive for intimacy. It's part of their nature. Women also have this desire, although typically it's not a driving force to the same degree. But the larger distinction is what arouses desire.

Men's desire for physical intimacy is inborn, instinctive, and self-igniting. If he channels it correctly, it will bring him closer to his wife; intimacy creates connection. For men, the desire leads to love.

For women, the sequence is the opposite. First comes love, then desire. Unlike men, women's desire is not constantly simmering under the surface. A woman's desire is kindled by her love for her husband. When a woman loves her husband, she desires to be with him. When she feels that her husband cherishes her, that arouses her desire for intimacy.

For both, intimacy is a necessary tool to increase their love and attachment. The difference is that when she feels close to her husband, she'll desire intimacy; if she doesn't feel close, she likely won't be interested in intimacy. For men, it works the other way around: intimacy arouses the close feelings.

It's almost like men and women approach intimacy from opposite directions. Men were created with a need for intimacy; when this need is fulfilled it causes him to love is wife. Women were created with a need to be loved; when this need is fulfilled, it causes her to desire intimacy.

When the couple is in sync, the system works like magic. He showers her with love and attention, and she wants to be with him. Being together fuels his love for her, and he showers her with more affection, which causes her to want to be with him more. It's a cycle of love.

The problem is when the cycle breaks down and one spouse feels they aren't intimate often enough. There may be physiological or emotional factors contributing to this, in which case it's imperative to speak to a professional who can help. Often, small adjustments can make a huge difference and transform a marriage. But sometimes we are dealing with a healthy, well-adjusted couple—and yet, there is a problem.

So let me address the men first and then I'll get to the women.

Gentlemen, if you find that your wife isn't interested in intimacy, you need to ask yourself how she feels about your relationship. Does she feel like you deeply care about her? Does she feel that you cherish her? When did you last take her out? When did you last buy her a card or leave her a love note? Barring factors like health issues, pregnancy, and nursing (or other hormonal factors), a woman will naturally want to be with her husband when she believes that he loves her.

But there's a point here for women as well. Women often don't realize how much intimacy serves to create emotional closeness for a man toward his wife. It's not by accident that Hashem gave man a stronger drive for intimacy—it's something that he needs in order to connect to his wife. Men's emotions function differently than women's do. Intimacy is a tool that fosters love and connection.

Sometimes couples reach an impasse. She says, *if he was more interested in the relationship, I'd be more interested in intimacy*. He says, *if she was more interested in intimacy then our relationship would be stronger*. They get stuck.

The cycle of the relationship

The sad part is that the one who's hurt most is you. When the marriage is troubled, both spouses suffer. The ability to move forward takes courage. Both husband and wife are probably right about what the other is doing wrong—which means they're both right and they're both wrong. That's part of being human. We can all be better. We all make mistakes. One of the secrets to a great marriage is for each partner to ask themselves, what can *I* do to improve the marriage?

It's tempting to think, *it's not fair! Why do I have to do all the heavy lifting? Why do I have to do all the changing? Let him change first.* But the more you focus on what *you* can do to improve this relationship, the more likely you are to succeed.

Changing the cycle means moving forward. Whether you think it's your spouse's fault or not, whether they "deserve" it or not, whether it makes sense or not, take the first step.

The little steps make a real difference. Small changes transform the climate of the relationship. You act a little different, your spouse senses that and acts a little different, you react to that… The trajectory of the relationship changes.

The Real Goal

It is important to understand that the intimate relationship changes over time. In the early years of marriage, it is largely driven by physical desire. That's normal, appropriate, and holy; it connects a husband and wife. As you age, the physical drive diminishes. After twenty, thirty, or forty years of marriage, the desire isn't the same. But by that point, if the marriage has developed properly, the bond of love is deeper and purer. Intimacy then is driven by love and a yearning for connection. Either motivation is holy and proper; it brings a couple closer, and that's what Hashem wants.

In the highs and lows of marriage, intimacy also serves to heal the relationship. There is no other relationship as volatile as marriage. Most couples find that although their overall relationship may be great, from time to time there is a falling out. One spouse makes a thoughtless comment, the other reflexively snaps back, and in the blink of an eye both are hurt, humiliated, and angry. Very hurt, very humiliated, and very angry. Suddenly you are no longer lovers and friends, but miles and miles apart. The speed in which a couple can cycle from one state to the other can be dizzying.

We are all vulnerable. We all have needs and expectations, and we all make mistakes. It's not possible for your spouse to know everything about you (there are plenty of things you don't even know about yourself), so it's inevitable that feelings may be hurt. Sometimes so hurt that you'll find yourself more pained than you have ever been in your life. At that point, you might say things you've never said to anyone before, or act in way that you can't understand. You won't even recognize yourself. You'll find yourself wondering, *how can I ever get past this? How could I forgive the one who caused me this much pain?*

You can. Not only can you move past those strong feelings, there are tools to repair the rift and make your connection even stronger. One of the tools is intimacy. When there is a falling out, you ask forgiveness and assure each other that it won't happen again. But even after talking and explaining and sharing and apologizing, there is still a distance between you. Intimacy brings a complete healing and rejuvenation of love.

There is no other relationship that is as delicate and volatile as marriage, and there is no relationship that can be as easily repaired. If your sister hurts your feelings, it could take a long time to feel close again. If a friend wasn't there for you when you needed them, they may never regain your trust. But in marriage, you can travel much further apart and yet come back more quickly than any other relationship. You can repair the damage and be even closer than you were before. That's the power of intimacy.

Intimacy is a powerful tool, but it isn't the only tool; there are many. Another related tool that may be just as vital for the success of marriage is touch.

Touch

> **ספר בראשית פרק מח**
> י) וְעֵינֵי יִשְׂרָאֵל כָּבְדוּ מִזֹּקֶן לֹא יוּכַל לִרְאוֹת וַיַּגֵּשׁ אֹתָם אֵלָיו וַיִּשַּׁק לָהֶם וַיְחַבֵּק לָהֶם
>
> *The eyes of Yaakov were heavy with age, and he couldn't see, and he brought them close to him, and he kissed and hugged them.*
>
> **ספורנו עה"ת ספר בראשית פרק מח פסוק י**
> וישק להם ויחבק להם. כדי שתדבק נפשו בהם ותחול עליהם ברכתו
>
> *[He did that] so that he would feel attached to them, and his blessing would rest on them.*

External Actions Awaken Internal Feelings

Yaakov married Leah and then Rochel. Leah had child after child and Rochel was barren. She davened for many years and finally she had a child, Yosef. Yaakov treated Yosef differently than his other sons. This was the child of his beloved. After Rochel died, Yosef held a special place in Yaakov's heart. It was all he had left from Rochel.

Yosef was sold into slavery. After much suffering and many travails, Yaakov traveled to Mitzrayim for a dramatic reunion with his long-lost son. When Yosef presented his two sons, Yaakov said, "I didn't expect to ever see you alive, and now I get to see your children." Ephraim and Menashe were very dear to Yaakov.

At the end his life, Yaakov wanted to give a parting *bracha* to his beloved grandsons. The *pasuk* says, "Yosef brought them close, and Yaakov kissed and hugged them." Only after doing so did he give them the *bracha*. The Sforno explains that Yaakov wanted to have as much *kavana* as he possibly could. He first kissed and hugged them so that he would love them even more, and thereby increase the effect of the bracha.

The Sforno is saying that he hugged and kissed them *so that he could love them more*. This seems backwards. Isn't it because you love a person that you hug and kiss them? Besides, Yaakov loved them already. How would hugging and kissing them change anything?

The Sforno is teaching us a fundamental principle, something we come across many times in Chazal: *External actions awaken internal feelings*. Feelings are very difficult to control, but we can control our actions. Our actions, in turn, influence the way we feel. The way to change the way your feel is to change the way you act.

When you hug your child, it may be an expression of love, but the action also increases your love. Yaakov Avinu already loved Efraim and Menashe, but hugging and kissing them caused his feelings to grow. These actions brought him to a new state of love, and now he could give them the *bracha* with complete devotion.

Touch, which includes (but is not limited to) hugging, kissing, and hand-holding, is another one of the tools that bond. When used properly, touch is a powerful force to bring a husband and wife closer. This closeness can even be measured on a physiological level: While hugging, the pituitary gland secretes oxytocin, a neurotransmitter that creates a sense of attachment to another person. (Scientists now believe that oxytocin, along with vasopressin, are the two hormones that cause lifelong pair-bonding in animals.)

Like romantic love, physical touch brings a couple close and needs to be used on an ongoing and continual basis. It changes the way you feel about each other and changes the climate of the relationship.

Touch affects the way you feel about your spouse, the way you speak to your spouse, and the way you look at your spouse. You could be sitting on the couch talking, but it's a very different conversation when you're holding hands. It's hard to be angry with someone when their arm is around your shoulder. You're not going to snap at someone when you're acting affectionate. Touch brings you closer, changes the mood, and changes the way you think about each other. It reminds you that you have a unique relationship. It makes you feel loved and attached. And part of its efficacy is that it can and should be used regularly.

Touch might become challenging once a couple has children, but it should not be abandoned. The connection between husband wife requires constant infusions of energy. If left on its own, the bond of love will dwindle. That's just a reality. One of the great challenges of marriage is to keep the relationship vibrant during the busyness of life. We live in pressured times. We are frazzled, harried, overtaxed and overburdened, running from responsibility to responsibility. Maintaining a vibrant and passionate relationship requires stopping and intentionally creating it. One of the tools that helps is touch.

Touch includes almost any form of physical contact: Holding hands, a small touch to say "I'm here," hugging and kissing. The rule of thumb is that anything that is forbidden when a woman is a *niddah* is significant and should be used when she isn't. Chazal were masters of the human nature; they understood what brings a couple closer, and they forbade particular activities because of the danger of getting too close when a couple aren't permitted to be together. That's exactly why those actions should be used during the permitted times—they bring the couple close. Simple gestures like a touch on the arm, or an arm around the shoulder, convey the message that your relationship is unique. The way we act toward one another is different than the way we act toward anyone else in the world.

Us, Not Me and You

In the animal kingdom, swans become pair-bonded for life, and nothing can separate them. But that's not the way we human beings work. Hashem gave us *bechira*, and Hashem put us each into a body, and that body has desires, interests, and agendas. Putting two unique individuals in close proximity inevitably causes friction; it's built into the design. Each spouse has a voice inside screaming, "I'm in charge!" "No, I'm in charge!" "This is what I need." "No, *this* is what *I* need." Unlike the swans, we have a lot of work to do. The tools that bond are powerful forces and are necessary for a marriage to be successful.

Intimacy and touch are requirements for a close, bonded marriage. You need them. Everyone needs them. Hashem wants marriages to be long-lasting, loving unions. He created these tools and wants us to use them.

All of these tools — infatuation, romance, respect, attraction, appreciation, friendship, touch, and intimacy

— are methods of achieving pure love that is not dependent on anything. All are holy and proper as tools to create that connection.

Life Partners

My rebbi, Rav Henoch Leibowitz zt"l, constantly used the expression "life partner." Husband and wife are partners in life. Everything they do, they do together. They're one unit. They began as one *neshama,* Hashem separated them into two bodies, and now they're joining together again. The goal is to live in peace and harmony. But it takes work – a lot of work – and it takes time. Often, a couple will take two steps forward, say the wrong thing or do something careless, and end up taking three steps back. It's a cycle. They'll be close and then grow apart, join together and separate, and that's part of the process of becoming one. It's a long process, but as long as you continue along the path, things have a way of working themselves out. Sometimes it takes a while, but the relationship slowly gets better and better, until you reach the goal of being one.

In order to get there, you have to understand the system and use the tools. Intimacy and touch are powerful tools to achieve oneness.

There are other tools, maybe not as powerful, but still very much needed for a marriage to flourish.

Chapter 12

Attraction

Mirror, Mirror, on the Wall...
I went to Chofetz Chaim Yeshivah, and the Rosh Yeshivah followed the *mesorah* of the Alter of Slabodka, emphasizing *gadlus ha'adam*, the greatness of man. The Rosh Yeshivah felt that there should be mirrors in the yeshiva dorms so that the *bachurim* could make themselves presentable. Many yeshivahs don't have mirrors; the roshei yeshiva there feel it's not appropriate for a ben Torah to be preoccupied with his appearance. Some yeshivahs have mirrors and some don't – each approach has a basis in Torah. If you're looking for a yeshivah for your son, either one is fine.

However, if you're looking for a seminary for your daughter and you find out that they don't allow mirrors in the dorm, stay far away. Putting a young woman into that environment is unhealthy, unnatural, and damaging. Hashem created a desire to be attractive as part of the essence of a woman. It's not learned or taught. It's instinctive. Three-year-old girls put on nail polish and dress up in mommy's high heels—it's built into their nature. Three-year-old boys don't.

When my oldest daughter was getting married, my youngest daughter was eight years old. To her, the wedding preparations were a dream come true. The gown, the updo... She was ecstatic. Her younger brother, who was five, wouldn't even try on a suit. He had no interest whatsoever in what he was going to wear or how he would look. Even on the day of the wedding, he had to be coaxed into putting on his suit. At which point my daughter said, "Boys are so dumb. They don't even know how good it feels to look pretty."

Women's need to be attractive corresponds perfectly with a man's attraction to beauty. When husband and wife channel their natural inclinations toward their spouse, attraction is a tool that bonds a couple.

> **ספר החינוך - מצוה תקפב**
>
> מצוה שישמח חתן עם אשתו שנה ראשונה
>
> שנשב עם האשה המיוחדת לנו להקים זרע שלמה מעת שנשא אותה כדי להרגיל הטבע עמה ולהדביק הרצון אצלה ולהכניס ציורה וכל פעלה בלב, עד שיבא אצל הטבע כל מעשה אשה אחרת וכל עניניה דרך זרות, כי כל טבע ברוב יבקש ויאהב מה שרגיל בו, ומתוך כך ירחיק האדם דרכו מאשה זרה ויפנה אל האשה הראויה לו מחשבתו ויוכשרו הולידים שתלד לו ויהיה העולם מעלה חן לפני בוראו.

A man is commanded to spend the first year of his marriage together with his wife. He shouldn't leave her for any length of time, not even to go to war, nor for any other reason. Rather he should spend an entire year, from the day he gets married, together with her.

The reason for this mitzvah is because Hashem wishes for men to be faithful to their wives. Therefore, He commanded a man to sit together with his wife in order to accustom himself to her ways, so that her image and her nature should enter his heart. Her way of doing things becomes to him the way a woman does things, and she becomes to him the definition of a woman, till any other woman is foreign to him. (Sefer HaChinuch, Mitzvah: 582)

Shanah Rishonah

The Sefer HaChinuch is teaching us that a person can shape their thoughts and desires, and even what they are attracted to. A man can habituate himself to his wife until "her ways" become "the ways of a woman." *This is the way a woman walks. This is the way a woman talks.* The image of his wife becomes the definition of a woman. He will have eyes only for her because to him, only she is a woman.

Hashem gave us the ability to program our brains. Desire isn't going to change, but *what* you desire can be changed.

In fact, what people desire changes all the time. Over the course of history, the measure of beauty has transformed. Until recently, most civilizations barely had enough to eat. An abundance of food was only for the wealthy and powerful. As a result, in many cultures, being fat was a sign of wealth. When a man was heavy, it was considered a badge of honor and a sign of wealth. In those societies, a heavy woman was desirable—the larger, the more desirable. There's a story told of an African king who wouldn't marry a woman until she was so fat that she couldn't walk. Only then was she fit for the king.

As strange as it sounds to modern ears, fat was considered attractive. Today, it's the opposite. Slim is in. Since we've been brought up in this culture, it's what we find attractive. But slimness is not *intrinsically* attractive. For hundreds (maybe thousands) of years, it was considered unattractive. But now, we've been trained by society to view it as appealing.

Another example is skin color. For centuries, lily-white skin was considered a sign of beauty in a woman. In eighteenth century

Europe, women painted their skin white. In China and Japan, women walked with parasols to keep the sun off their faces. Peasants worked in the fields and had no protection from the sun, so their skin would grow tanned and dark. Pale skin color was associated with wealth; tanned skin was low class and unbecoming. Today, it's the opposite. Despite the potential health dangers, there are over 25,000 tanning salons in the US. The culture considers it beautiful.

What we consider attractive is a *learned* taste. Usually, we absorb these tastes from the environment without being aware of it and we aren't even cognizant that it's not inborn.

Imagine a fellow brought up in China. His parents are Chabad shluchim, and from his earliest memories, every woman he's seen had straight black hair, a slight build, and almond-shaped eyes. When he's 18 he goes to a yeshiva in America to learn. A few years later he is presented with a possible match. He's stunned at what she looks like. "What? I mean, what's with the yellow hair and those large eyes? And besides, she's huge."

The *Sefer Hachinuch* is teaching us a significant principle for marriage and for happiness. What a person is attracted to may seem inborn to him, but it's not. It's learned. The good news is that those changes can happen by choice: It's possible to reprogram what we desire.

Hashem wants a *chassan* and *kallah* to spend a full year together so that her beauty becomes imprinted in his mind until she becomes to him *the* image of a woman. He's interested only in his wife because she alone is a woman.

Like a fine Wine

Some women might read this and panic. *Am I beautiful enough? Do all other women pale in comparison to me? Where does this leave me?*

Besides, it's one thing when a woman is 18 and she's beautiful. But what happens as she ages? She might still look good at 28. And even at 38. What about when she's 78? No matter how attractive a woman was when she first got married, she won't look that way forever. How is a man supposed to think his wife is beautiful in later years?

> **תלמוד בבלי מסכת סוטה דף מז/א**
> אמר רבי יוחנן חן אשה על בעלה.
>
> *Rabi Yochanan said, a woman is gifted with chein in her husband's eyes.*
>
> **רש"י סוטה דף מז/א**
> חן האשה – תמיד על בעלה ואפי' היא מכוערת נושאת חן בעיניו.
>
> *The favor of a woman is always on her husband; even if she is objectively ugly, she is beautiful in his eyes.*

There's a special *chein* that a wife finds in her husband's eyes. (Sota 47a)

Rashi adds, "She'll find favor in his eyes always, even if she's ugly." Even if on an objective scale everyone agrees that she's not attractive – and not just unattractive, but actually ugly – Hashem gives her a special *chein* in her husband's eyes. He will find her appealing.

Your heart is in your hands

The *Sefer HaChinuch* explains: "It is in the hands of a person to train himself... His heart is in his hands, on everything that he desires." This isn't just *possible* – it's part of the system.

There's a mitzvah to not covet and not desire something belonging to another person. How can the Torah command me not to feel a natural emotion? If I see a beautiful car, or house, I want it.

The *Even Ezer* explains, "Most mitzvahs are to straighten a person's heart." We are commanded not to be jealous, to judge your neighbor favorably, to love your fellow Jew, not to hate in your heart, not to bear a grudge, among other mitzvos that direct us on how we should shape our thoughts.

The is what the Sefer HaChinuch means when he writes, "It's within the capacity of person to control their thoughts and desires." Desire is very difficult to restrain. But *what* we desire is within our control, and we can change what we think and what we want.

That's what happens in a marriage when a couple uses the tool of attraction properly. Attraction grows even as she ages. As their love builds, so too does her allure. It grows stronger as time goes on.

Hashem wants marriage to succeed, so He gave us many tools to connect, one of which is attraction. Hashem gave a woman a certain grace in the eyes of her husband that lasts through every age and stage.

Which brings us to a final point.

The Household Champ

Dovid and Yocheved have been married for two years. They're invited to a wedding called for 7:30. It's about an hour's drive to the hall, so, they decide to leave the house by 6:30. Dovid comes home early, freshens up, and by 6:20 he's ready to go. Yocheved is still busy getting ready. He sits down on the couch and waits patiently. 10 minutes pass. 20 minutes pass.

"Yocheved, dear, I don't want to rush you, but it's 6:40."

"I know, I just need a little more time."

No problem, he says to himself. *Shalom bayis comes first.* He takes out a sefer to learn. Another 10 minutes pass, and another. He's getting a little anxious, but hey, marriage comes first.

By now it's 7:15. He already *chazered* the entire *daf...* twice. Soon it's 7:30 and he's getting hot under the collar.

Finally, a full hour and a half late, she's ready. He's all but bursting inside, but he bites his tongue and repeats to himself, *shalom bayis comes first*. All he says is, "Okay dear, let's go." They walk to the car, and he feels like a hero. He held his tongue.

He is a hero for holding his tongue—but he also missed a huge opportunity. His wife just spent two hours making herself look beautiful—it's obviously very important to her. A wise husband would say, "Wow, you look great! I love that dress. You look fantastic!"

He forgot that women need to feel beautiful. Instead, he did what we always do: he viewed the situation from his own perspective. *What's taking her so long? How long does it take to get ready? And besides, who cares what you wear?* And it's true—for a guy.

But a woman *needs* to feel attractive. She craves it—it's a part of her essence. Just as women need reassurance of their husband's love, they need reassurance about the way they look. Don't ever believe a woman who says, "It's not important." The beauty industry is estimated at $500 *billion* per year. That's half a *trillion* dollars spent on beauty products. It's *very* important! An astute husband will notice and compliment his wife on how she looks. When he says, "What a great dress, you look wonderful," it helps her, it helps him, and it helps their marriage.

Women and Fashion

When I was married for about five years, it became stylish for women's dresses to feature huge bows. Not just any bow – gigantic ones. The bigger the better. They looked like something from a comic strip, a dress that Minnie Mouse would wear. But that was the new fad.

One day it happened. My wife came home with a dress, held it up for me and said, "Look what I bought. What do you think?" Right there on the back of the dress was a huge Minnie Mouse bow.

Baruch Hashem, I was married long enough to know the right answer. "Wow, that dress is beautiful… and the best part is that bow. It looks great!"

Gentlemen, there will be times when your wife is going to dress in a way you're not going to like. Let me share a secret. *Women dress for other women.* When she comes to a wedding, all her friends say, "I love your dress! Where did you get it? You look amazing." Not once in thirty years has a man come over to me and said, "Rabbi Shafer, I love your tie!" Or, "Great suit! Where did you get it?" It's not part of our vernacular. But women take great pride in the way they look, and they want admiration and approval from other women (who know what really looks good). They assume that when they look so great, of course their husband will find them attractive.

Sometimes it's true and sometimes it's not. The bottom line is, gentlemen, you're not going to change her. It's wise to learn to appreciate *her* taste in fashion. A wise woman tries to dress for her husband, but a wiser husband pays attention to his wife's style, whether it's his taste or not, and lets her know he appreciates the way she looks.

Having said all that, no matter how a woman looks, her personal character is far more important. A beautiful woman can destroy her marriage in many ways – with her tongue, or by trying to control her husband, or with constant criticism, or in other ways. There are many ways to ruin a good thing. Not only does it ruin his feeling for her, but she becomes ugly to him. When all he gets from her is disrespect, negativity, nagging and complaining, she loses all beauty in his eyes.

A Lifetime Tool

There are two parts to utilizing attraction. The husband has to train his eye and mind to avoid that which will draw him away from the Torah's ideals. The wife has to make herself attractive to her husband. No woman (or man) can look their best all the time, but she does need to be aware, and make the effort.

When they go out once a week, she should get dressed up. Her attitude shouldn't be, *Well, it's just my husband, he doesn't care.* She should put on nicer clothing, makeup, her *sheitel* – she should look good (and so should he).

At the same time, he has to appreciate her efforts and compliment how she looks. It's a two-way street. This should continue throughout their married life, not just at the beginning of their marriage. Attraction, as a tool of bonding, is meant to be used throughout a couple's married life. A person shouldn't think that once they hit thirty-something it's no longer important. Throughout a couple's entire married life, he needs that sense of attraction and she needs to know that she is attractive to him.

This applies to men as well. Many guys let themselves go and it becomes a challenge for their wives to feel attracted to them. She too needs to be attracted, and that includes dress and every else that goes along with being well groomed and well mannered. Both spouses have needs that must be met. If you use attraction as a tool of bonding, the marriage prospers.

There is, however, another tool that is far more subtle, yet equally important for the long-term health of a marriage.

Chapter 13

Appreciation

IMAGINE A MAN WHO, at age thirty-five, becomes blind. Being a fighter, he struggles for ten years to create a productive life and succeeds — to a degree. One day, his doctor informs him of an experimental procedure that, if successful, would enable him to see again. He is both frightened and exuberant. If it works, he regains his sight. If it fails, he might die.

He gathers his family to discuss it, and after much debate he announces, "I am going ahead with it." The operation is scheduled, and the long-awaited day arrives. Paralyzed with dread, he is wheeled into the operating room. He is sedated and sleeps through the entire ten-hour operation.

When he wakes up, his first thought is to open his eyes. He prepares himself for the moment. He will now find out how he will spend the rest of his life. He gets ready, musters up his courage, and flexes his eyelids. They don't move! In a panic he cries out, "NURSE!"

The nurse explains that his bandages won't come off for three more days. So he waits. Each moment like a decade, each hour a lifetime. Finally, it's time. With his family gathered around, with the doctors and nurses at his side, the surgeon begins removing the gauze. The first bandage is off, now the second. The surgeon says, "Open your eyes." He does. And he sees!

For the first time in ten years, he looks out and experiences the sights of this world — and he is struck by it all. Struck by the brilliance of colors and shapes. Moved by the beauty and magnificence of all that is in front of him. He looks out the window and sees a meadow covered with beautiful, green grass. He sees flowers in full bloom. He looks up and sees a clear, blue sky. He sees people — the faces of loved ones that have been only images in his mind, the sight of his own children that he hasn't seen in ten years. Tears well up in his eyes as he says, "Doctor, Doctor, what can I ever do to repay you for what you have given me? This magnificent gift of sight!"

Appreciating Our Gifts

We should be that man. Each morning we open our eyes and we see. Every day we enjoy the remarkable gift of vision. And, we can experience the same feeling of elation that he felt on a daily basis… if we train ourselves to feel it. Sight is a precious, unparalleled gift that we are supposed to stop and think about. Not once in a lifetime. Not even once a year. Every day.

Part of our spiritual growth is learning to appreciate the gifts that we have. One of the blessings we say each morning thanks Hashem for this most wonderful gift of sight. It was designed to be said with an outpouring of emotion.

We humans are a curious breed. We can have treasures for years without ever thinking of them, not once stopping to appreciate the wealth we have been given… until something happens. Then it is, *"Hashem, why me? Of all the people on the planet, why did You pick me?"* Till then there wasn't a moment of reflection.

Not one thank-you. Not even a recognition of it being a gift. But once it is gone, the complaints find their home.

Unfortunately, we don't take the time to think about the many gifts that we have. We become so accustomed to them that we almost don't know they exist. How many times do we stop and appreciate that we have legs, arms and hands? How many mornings do we wake up and just take the time to recognize that we have our health and well-being? How much richer is our life because we have eyes with which to see, fingers with which to feel, ears with which to hear, a tongue with which to taste, and a nose with which to smell?

Each of these senses was created by Hashem with great wisdom and forethought so that we should live fuller, richer, and more complete lives. There is so much about this world that was custom-designed for our enjoyment. But it takes focus and training to gain an appreciation for the riches that we possess.

To illustrate this point I would like to ask you a question.

Are you rich?

I don't mean in terms of relationships, or meaning, or family. I mean materially. Are you financially wealthy? Are you rich?

I've spoken to many audiences in many communities, and I have asked this question countless numbers of time and the answer invariably is: No.

Regardless of age or education. Irrespective of the socioeconomic level, no one is rich. Comfortable? Maybe. Able to make ends meet. Boruch HASHEM, Yes. But rich? Come on. I'm not rich.

This is intriguing, because in the course of history there has never been a generation of people who enjoy the material possessions and wealth that we do. If you were to describe our prosperity to people of a different generation, they wouldn't believe you.

Certainly, in terms of luxuries and comforts, we are unrivaled in the course of history.

My grandmother grew up in Poland before the First World War. Her family was considered well off; they lived in a two-room house. That meant two rooms. One for the parents, and one where the kids slept, ate, played, did chores, cooked, bathed, and cleaned their clothes. That was it. Two rooms, period. And believe me, the rooms weren't large, and the families weren't small.

Today, when we go on vacation and "rough it" by putting the whole family — parents and two kids — in one motel room, it's cute and cozy... for an evening. But that was the amount of space people lived in with all of their belongings, all of the time. That was home. On floors made of dirt, with furniture consisting of the barest table and a few chairs, with wood-burning fireplaces that had to be stocked by chopping trees — they lived. Their walls were filled with cracks that let in the cold air of winter and held in the sweltering heat of summer. They drove horses to the market and bathed only on special occasions — without phones, without internet, without running water or electricity, people lived. Regular people. Our people. Our grandparents and great-grandparents lived.

We aren't any different than they were. They walked, ate, slept, and breathed as we do. They weren't born on a different planet, and they didn't live a thousand years ago. Yet their lives were so different from ours that it is difficult for us to even imagine ourselves in that setting.

Luxuries of Yesteryear

My great aunt, Tante Perel, came over from Poland before my grandmother. When my grandmother arrived in America and visited Tante Perel for the first time, Tante Perel told her in an excited voice, "You must see this! You won't believe your eyes! Our building has a bathroom in the apartment itself!" It was a standard of luxury beyond what they could have imagined.

While it may sound like ancient history to us, it wasn't that long ago that people used outhouses. In the freezing cold of winter, they would don a coat and go out to the back where they found a bare hut. In that world, there were no such things as cars and planes and buses. There were no paved roads and highways. If you had somewhere to go, you got into a horse-drawn wagon and bumped along a stone path for hours until your insides wanted to come out.

Heat was a thing for the rich. My father had a friend who went to yeshivah in Poland before WWII. This man had a handy way of telling whether it was a cold morning. He would leave a vessel filled with water next to his bed each night so that he could wash as soon as he woke up in the morning. Before washing, he would look into the vessel. If it had iced over, he knew it was a cold day!

I want to remind you that water doesn't turn to ice at 58 degrees. And not at 48 either. He slept in the very room that the water froze in! These days, we set our thermostats to a comfy 72, and if it goes below 62, someone will complain, "Hey, it's freezing in here!" If your furnace goes out, you immediately call the heating company — it's an emergency! And if they say, "We'll have a technician come out to look at it in the morning," you'll go to a friend's house for the night. "It's 50 degrees in my house! How can anyone survive in that kind of cold!?" Yet people did survive — people who were no different than you or me, and at temperatures well below 50 degrees.

We Are So Wealthy

The comforts and material possessions that we take for granted today were unimaginable a few generations ago. If you walk down an aisle in Wal-Mart, everything you see is available to be had — in whatever color, shape and texture you like. And for the most part, we have the money to buy it.

Here is another example. If you own a house built before World War II, you will probably notice that no matter how large it is, there never seems to be enough closet space. The home might have sizable rooms, plenty of bedrooms and lots of living space, but tiny, undersized closets. Why is that? Why didn't they build closets to match the size of the house?

It's because the house was built for people living in those times. No one then would dream that we would own the amount of clothing that we do now. I spoke to a woman who grew up in the 1930's, and she told me she had two dresses: one for weekdays and one for Shabbos. She wasn't poor; she came from a typical home. That was considered normal. So they built homes back then with closets that were ample for the wardrobes of those times.

Our Clothing

Now we have racks and racks of clothing: suits, shirts, slacks, sweaters, winter coats, summer jackets, light fall coats, ties, belts, pocketbooks, and matching accessories, not to mention shoes. My rebbe, R' A. H. Leibowitz, zt"l, grew up in America in the 1920's. When he was a young boy, he wore a hole in the bottom of the one pair of shoes he owned. He didn't have the heart to ask his father for the twenty-five cents that it would cost to have new soles put on. So he figured out his own solution. He put a piece of cardboard inside the shoe so that his socks wouldn't rub out on the concrete when he walked. It worked well until the first rainy day. He walked outside and right into a puddle — splash! His new soles were gone.

Do we know anyone today who doesn't own a number of pairs of shoes? In black, blue, and brown — some for casual wear, others for dress. Gotta have at least one pair for running, another for basketball, and still others for bowling. Do you play golf? Of course, only an entirely separate wardrobe is fitting. And Heaven forefend to play tennis in basketball shoes!

Compared to Other Times

If we were to describe our wealth to people of a different generation, I don't think they would believe us. Kings in prior times didn't enjoy the luxuries that we do. If you look at portraits of King George, monarch of England before the Revolutionary War, you'll see him sitting on his throne in the comfort of his palace wearing layer upon layer of robes, topped off by a fur covering. Did you ever wonder why he was wearing all of those layers? The reason is that it was mighty cold in the king's palace! The King of England with all of his wealth had to stay warm by huddling up to a smoky fireplace that heated up only the part of his body that was facing it, not the rest of him that was facing the other way. His Highness had to walk through dimly lit, dank hallways at night. He had to sleep on a mattress of stuffed feathers. (Keep in mind, there were no chiropractors around to care for his aching back as he sunk down into thirty-six inches of duck feathers.) And when his brother, the Duke, was getting married, traveling to the wedding meant enduring a backbreaking carriage ride for the better part of a week. The crown jewels couldn't buy him the luxuries that we take for granted today.

The reality is that we are wealthy beyond belief. We enjoy comforts and abundance that are historically unprecedented. And it's not just the extremely affluent. The average tax-paying citizen of today lives in opulence and splendor that previous generations couldn't dream about.

Appreciation Training

Let's come back to the question we started with: are you rich?

"Come on, I can barely afford my mortgage payments — rich? Me?"

You can have all the money in the world and not be rich. In fact, you'll never be rich, until you what wealth is. Wealth is plenty, abundance. I have my needs met, and then some. Every one of us has such wealth. The food we eat, the clothing we wear, the cars we drive. With a touch of the gas, the power of two hundred horses pulls me at lightning speed, and all I have to do is pull up to the pump, fill it up with gas, and go.

And the astonishing thing is that if you don't train yourself to appreciate it, you might as well not have it, because it's almost like it's not there.

I would be the first to thank G-d, if...

It isn't unusual to hear a teenager say things like, "I would be the first one to thank HASHEM, *if* there were anything to thank Him for. But what is there to be grateful for? My life stinks." In his mind, he has nothing. His health, his well being, his youth! The home that he sleeps in, the clothing that he wears, the education that he is receiving are all... whatever. He is the recipient of tremendous good. The problem is that he doesn't see it that way.

This phenomenon isn't limited to teenagers; it seems to be endemic to the human. There is not a person amongst us who isn't grateful – when we have something to be grateful for. But no one does anything for me. We have no problem with being grateful. We have great difficulty recognizing what we have to be grateful for.

The very expression *ha'karas ha'tov* doesn't mean be "grateful for the good". "It means to *recognize*, to discern the good". Chazal were teaching us that this issue pivots on perception. We are all grateful. The problem is there is nothing for me to grateful for. That's why the work is learning to appreciate the wealth we have and then naturally I'll be grateful for all the blessings in my life.

What does this have to do with a happy marriage?

Appreciation is one of the TOOLS THAT BOND. And just as we need to train ourselves to appreciate the riches that we have, and if we don't, it's like we don't have them, so too we have to learn to appreciate what we receive from our spouse.

We receive—we just don't recognize it.

I once gave a six-week intense Marriage Bootcamp. Most of the couples were married for over ten years and many were experiencing trouble in their marriages. Some of the issues were deeply entrenched. The sessions were highly interactive and after a few weeks of hearing the complaints each spouse had about the other, I felt they needed some perspective.

I reached out to a support group for older singles, I explained what I was looking to accomplish, and I asked them if they would be willing to share their stories of what it was like to be an older single in the *frum* community.

A number of them volunteered, and it was heart wrenching. Story after story of never knowing where to place themselves. Never fitting in. Every Yom Tov a nightmare having to rejoin family and watching everyone else's life go by, while they are frozen in place. The constant questions: Nu? Anything doing? And worst of all, what it's like attending the wedding of a much younger sibling or niece.

I was trying to share with these couples the bracha that they have—but seemed to have forgotten. It seems to be a natural tendency that we might seek something for years, and once we have it, we forget that it's a gift.

What would life be like

The Steipler goan writes that one of the ways a person recognizes the benefit he has from their spouse is to imagine what my life would be like now if I were still single. Imagine that I'm thirty, thirty-five, forty — and still not married. How would I feel? What would my days and nights look like? When you climb into the world of someone who still isn't married, and you see the void, the emptiness they experience, you recognize that could have been you and you begin to appreciate what you have.

Unfortunately, it's rare for either a husband or wife to appreciate how vastly improved their life is because they are married, and what their spouse does for them. It seems to be human nature that the more frequent the favor, the less we appreciate it. The more she cooks, cleans, takes care of the family the more likely he'll take it for granted. The more he works, learns and supports the kids the more likely she's won't notice it.

A guy once said to me, "My wife, she's just a freeloader. I work so hard and she's taking it easy, how can I appreciate her?"

It was interesting because he'd recently had a baby and he looked well rested. I said, "Who gets up with the baby?"

"She does."

"I see. Who feeds the baby?"

"She does, of course."

"Who changes the baby?

"She does."

"Who buys the clothing?"

"She."

Who buys the food?

"She."

Who cooks the food?

"She does."

Who takes care of the house?

"She does."

If you look at the long, long list of what a woman does for the home, you begin to realize how much of your life is organized, structured and vastly improved because of your wife.

If you're not convinced yet, let's try a small experiment. Open your dresser draw and look at the neatly arranged socks. Did you ever wonder how they got there? A few days ago, they sure didn't look (or smell) like they do now. A heads up: There are no elves that come at night and tidy up. Your wife laundered them, folded them and put them there.

Look at the clothing, the bedding, the towels, the pots, the dishes and everything else around the house. A man will quickly see that he owes his wife a tremendous debt of gratitude. Of course, it goes much further than laundry, cooking and cleaning. It's humorous when a wife goes away for a few days and leaves her husband in charge. She spent three weeks preparing everything for him, and yet he's frazzled. He's got to go here, remember this, do this and that…and Rochi has a dentist appointment…Gentlemen, if your children are clothed and showing up to school healthy, happy and well fed, you owe your wife a deep debt of gratitude.

At the same time, women owe their husbands a tremendous amount. If you're feeling it, think back to that time when you were going out and weren't really sure if you would ever find your bashert. Most women have had that moment of doubt and fear. If you could go back to that moment and sit in it for a while you will find yourself incredibly grateful that you have a husband, and everything that he does for you. But like so many of the blessing that we enjoy, within a short amount of time, everything they do just becomes part of the background of life, not something that you even notice.

If you want a great marriage, here is a two-part exercise. Let's start with part one.

Take a sheet of paper and write down the benefits you receive from your spouse. If you're the husband, you'd better bring two pads of paper. If you don't come up with a very long list of what you owe your wife something is wrong. But, if that's the case, do the next step: What if she wasn't in your world? If she wasn't here, what would fall apart? Just go through the house. Think of your children and your daily routine. (If need be, put yourself back in the dorm, back in that state of being unsettled, no place of your own, no home, no family.) Now write it down. Ladies as well.

Once you've written your list, every day for the next thirty days, read that list out loud to yourself. For ten minutes focus on exactly what you receive from your spouse. How vastly improved your life is because of them. If you do this, you'll feel closer and more appreciative and, it will be a whole lot harder for you to get upset.

I remember times in the early years of my marriage when I felt upset with something my wife did, and might have wanted to say something, but I said to myself how can I? She's doing her job and mine as well. She's taking care of the kids and the house and the laundry and the cleaning and the cooking and since I was learning in *kollel*; she was working. That's my job. I signed a *kesuba* that says: Ana eflach v'okir v'izun v'afarnes yisi,

- I'm will work
- I will treat you with respect
- I will feed you
- I will clothe you.

It is my obligation to be the provider. Not only was she doing her job, she was doing mine as well. How could I say anything when she does so much for me?

So, part one of this exercise is to take stock of what you receive from your spouse, write it down, and review it over and over until you actually feel it.

The irony is that as much as this will help you feel appreciative, it might have a greater impact on your spouse.

A woman once said to me, "My husband does nothing for me. He's a good provider and he's responsible and he tries to spend time with the kids, but he does nothing around the house-I take care of everything. It's like he checks in at night and checks back out in the morning. I get nothing from him".

"Okay," I said. "You live in a house, a very nice one, in fact, right?"

"Yes."

"You drive a nice car, right?"

"Yes."

"You have a bunch of kids, and a number of them are learning in *kollel,* right?"

"Yes."

"Let's do the math. What do you think you pay in tuition and in support for *kollel*?"

"I don't know."

So, I helped her with the math, and between supporting two sons-in-laws and six kids in yeshivah, it was about $100,000 a year. That is $100,000 after taxes—so he probably had to earn $130,000 before taxes—that's a lot of money!

"Tell me", I said, "What time does your husband leave the house?"

"About six in the morning."

"What time does he come home at night?"

"About eight or nine."

"He probably takes a two hour-long lunch, right?"

"No, he quickly gobbles a sandwich."

"I'm sure he takes off a couple of afternoons a week to play golf, right?"

"No. He never takes time off."

"I stopped for a long pause and said, "do you appreciate what your husband is doing for you? He's slaving away, working day and night, so that you and your children should have a house, food, clothing, and a Torah education. Look around your house and see what you have. Then say the words, "What my husband gives me is astonishing."

"But it's not the kind of husband I wanted."

"Listen to what you just said! He loves you. He takes care of you. He takes care of the kids. He's a good provider. You see so many positive traits, how can you not appreciate him? How can you not feel an overwhelming sense of, wow, look at what a great husband he is? You can't see it is because you only see one thing. Over and over in your mind plays that tape. He's not the husband I want. This isn't the kind of relationship I envisioned. Till everything else pales in comparison. You don't realize it but you're brainwashing yourself. You're literally creating a reality that has no connection to what's really going on."

Let me be clear, I don't think that husband is doing his job. She didn't articulate it, but, she was lonely. She felt as if she didn't have a husband. She had a a big house, and cars and money but she felt that she didn't have a marriage. It's a husband's responsibility to give her the attention that she needs. He has romance his wife. That's his part. But she as well has to appreciate what he does do for her. What she didn't understand was how much harder she was making it for him to want to spend time with her.

I was twenty-one, living in the Yeshiva dorm and one morning I woke up, and with eyes half opened headed down for a coffee. I'm not sure how much I noticed it, but the dining room floor was wet, having recently been moped. There wasn't much time till davening, and the prospect of shacharis without coffee wasn't—so I walked across the floor made myself a cup of coffee, was about to leave when I heard:

"WHAT'S THE MATTER WITH YOU!? CAN'T YOU SEE THE FLOOR IS WET!"

I looked up to see the Janitor, an otherwise reasonable fellow, beet red. He went on, "Look what you done, I just moped that floor. Now I got to mop it again."

I said, "I apologize. I guess I wasn't thinking"

And then he said: "That's my work you walked on. When you walk on a man's work, you're walking on that man."

Those words struck me, and to this day, they play over in my mind when I see a recently mopped floor.

It is demoralizing to seeing your work going unnoticed. One of the main reasons employees leave jobs is because they feel undervalued. A staffing firm in NY reported that 66% of employees say they would "likely leave their job if they didn't feel appreciated."

People switch careers because don't feel appreciated. People stop donating money to causes because they don't feel acknowledged. People leave shuls they davened in for years, because they don't feel valued. And while we like to think that it's only other people who are so fickle, we are more vulnerable and sensitive that we like to imagine. And no matter how dedicated and giving you are if you feel your work is ignored, it hurts, and it makes it difficult to continue doing it—even if you weren't doing the work for the praise, and you really want to continue doing that work.

Sadly, a common reframe that both husbands and wives say is: "I don't feel appreciated." I work, I slave, I cook, I clean, and I don't even get a thank you. Why do I even bother?"

If you work in Buckingham Palace you are taught that when around royalty, make yourself invisible. Do whatever you can not to be seen, not to be noticed. If directly addressed, you respond, if not you are part of the scenery. This might work well if you are the Queen of England and these are your servants—but it bodes poorly for a marriage.

Let's go back to that woman who complained that her husband did nothing for her and ask what was it like for *him*? I would imagine his inner dialogue went something like this:

"I don't get it. I work myself to the bone. I do everything I can for her and the kids and she says "I do nothing for her". I put in 12-hour days, 6 days a week. For what? I don't take breaks. I don't take time off. I don't even exercise, I put in everything I have just to make her happy. And what do I get back? Do I even get one word of one work of thanks? Nothing I do is ever enough for her. She's never happy.

I am not making excuses for him. Even if he isn't getting recognition, he still needs to do his part and spend time with his wife. But it sure makes it on lot harder on him to like her when he gets so little back from her. And it sure makes it harder for him to want to spend time with her when he feels so unvalued and unappreciated. She's right he's not giving her the attention she needs, but she's not giving him the recognition he deserves. To him earning a living is his first priority. You and I might both agree that he's taking it too far, but he's not a flighty guy and he's not doing for his pleasure, and right now, this is him. His work is his identity.

A man takes great pride in taking care of his family's needs—and rightfully so. In this case he also happens to be doing a great job of it. And what does he get back? Nothing. Radio silence. Not a peep. Not a single word of appreciation. She is denying his work—which means she is denying him. And it is mighty hard to want to spend time with someone who all but denies you even exist.

Only too many times we become so accustomed to what our spouse does for us that we no longer notice it, and while we don't mean to be hurtful, but we are. You can't acknowledge what you don't see, and since you don't see it you send a message: What you do doesn't matter. What you feel doesn't matter. You don't matter. The utter silence screams out— You don't exist. That is a bitter pill to swallow and makes it very difficult for your spouse to feel all warm and fuzzy towards you.

If this isn't motivation enough to work on gratitude, there is another even reason.

I was once working on a Shmuz about appreciation, and I realized that I had been an 11th grade Rebbe for about 12 years, and in that time, I think I had received two compliments—one from my father for grilling the chicken well. I'm not a sensitive person, and I'm not that beholden to what other people think about me, but I am human, and I found it curious.

Shortly after we moved to Monsey. Chofetz Chaim had a branch there, and I began giving a shiur in the High School. One day Rabbi Maza, the Rosh HaYeshiva, told me that Rabbi Chaim Fuerman, z'l will be coming in to critique the Rebbeim and give them pointers to improve their teaching and classroom management.

It's universal to hate criticism —and I wasn't looking forward. What made this worse was that I was quite fond of Rabbi Feuerman. He had been my principal in elementary school, he was now an educator's educator and I would call him to discuss various issues. Now he's coming to tell me "How I could improve" (spelled: What I'm doing wrong.) This did not promise to be fun.

The next day, I'm giving shiur and Rabbi Maza and Rabbi Feuerman walk in and sit down in the back. I continue teaching, and out of the corner of my eye I see Rabbi Feuerman writing away on his notepad. Each time I looked, he's writing and writing and writing. After the shiur was over, Rabbi Feuerman asked if he could speak with me in the office. I walked in knowing what was coming.

I sat down and after a few pleasantries, he got down to business:

He said: "That shiur was excellent. Your presentation, the engagement of the students, it was superb."

"Thank you" I said. And I waited for the next part.

He didn't say anything.

I said, "but…"

No. That's it. You did a fantastic job. The clarity of the way you presented, the way the students were involved, it was excellent.

Now, I'm bright enough to know that they don't bring in a world class Mechanech, an expert in education to tell me I did a good job.

I said, "I appreciate your kind words, but…"

"No but. There is nothing else. You did a great job."

I was dumbfounded. That's it. Nothing more. I thanked him and walked out a bit dazed. I'm mean nothing? Nothing wrong. No criticism. I did a good job and that's it?

And I realized that at that moment, if he were to ask me to fly to the moon without a spacesuit, I would ask, "where's the launch pad?"

The power of praise

Even more than we hate being taken for granted, we love acknowledgement. It's a human trait to love praise. A sincere compliment is uplifting and invigorating, it puts wind in your sails and gas in your engine. You feel a sort of warm glow inside, a smile comes to your lips, your walk gets lighter, your whole self-lights up. You might have been in a bad mood suddenly the sun is shining; the band is playing, and everything is right in this world.

There is nothing like a compliment to get someone else to like you. I used to teach "People Skills" to my shiur. The first lesson was simple:

- Rule 1- If you want people to hate you, find what they do wrong and let them know it.
- Rule 2- If you want people to like you, find what they do right and let them know it.

One of the greatest favors you can do for another person is to find something that they do well and let them know it. We all crave approval and acceptance. Praise tells us we did good, we are good. Everyone wants to count. Everyone wants to matter. Everyone wants to feel they make a difference. The problem is that this need so often is unmet.

While we enjoy unprecedented material wealth, it seems the one thing we don't get is acknowledgment and recognition. We hunger for it. We seek it. When we get it, we are happy, when we don't, we are lacking. Unsure and unsteady, doubting ourselves and maybe even our worth. If look around a room you'll see all types of people with all types of needs, the one need that everyone has is the need for approval and acceptance.

live 2 months on one compliment

Mark Twain wrote "I could live for 2 months on one good compliment." Many husbands and wives live for years without receiving one from their spouse.

If you count the number of sincere words of thanks that spouses say to each other—it's pitifully few. If anyone else were to do a fraction of what a spouse does, we'd sing their praises. But it's only my wife. That's my husband's job. Isn't that what he's expected to do? (What if that man who worked so hard for his family had donated that $100,000 a year to a Yeshiva? How many dinners would he be honored at?). What if anyone else in the world prepared a meal for you? What if they cooked, cleaned, took care of all your needs? How much would you feel you owe them?

The problem is that it happened yesterday, and the day before and the day before that—and now it's just a given. That's what happens. And in no time at all—it becomes part of the background. Not noticed. Not seen. And certainly not acknowledged. And if you don't stop and think, you won't even see it anymore. Much like material wealth that we all possess—yet no one is rich. No matter how much your spouse does for you if you don't train yourself to see it, it becomes a given, part of the background.

If you don't work on appreciation, you lose out on both ends. You don't see what you spouse does for you—so you don't feel close to them. And you are giving up one of the most powerful tools to get your spouse to feel close to you.

People Skills

I used to teach "People Skills" to my shiur. The first lesson was simple:

- Rule 1- If you want people to hate you, find what they do wrong and let them know it.
- Rule 2- If you want people to like you, find what they do right and let them know it.

The heart is reciprocal. We almost can't help disliking people who dislike us and liking people who like us. And there is nothing that works like a genuine compliment to get someone else to like you.

One of the reasons that the stage of infatuation works so well is that the Chosson and Kallah can't help but notice each other. When he speaks she is all ears. When she walks in the room, he stops what he's doing. They shower each other with the type of attention that speaks volumes. You are important, you are significant. And that message just feels good. What you think matters. What you say matters. You matter. It is natural to admire and love people that appreciate us. And this pulls them towards each other. How can he not like her when she meets such a deep craving? How can she not like him when she gets such sincere recognition?

The trick is not to abandon this powerful tool, once you get married. If you don't work on this it's almost like you become a stingy miser, unable to speak words of praise.

Here is the oddest part. In the entire world there is no person as important to you as your spouse. You would do anything for them. And they have a deep emotional need that isn't met—and you can so easily meet it. It costs you nothing. You lose nothing by giving it. So why would you hold it back? Of course, you wouldn't hold back something so significant, you just didn't notice. And that is the great enemy, we become so accustomed to what is, that it becomes a given, then it's like it's not even there.

Here's a simple observation: your wife prepared Shabbos. Which means, she planned the meals, she shopped, she prepared, she cooked. Besides cleaning and polishing and setting. How many hours went into the Friday night meal? The Shabbos Day meal? Shaalos Seuodos? When was the last time you said to your wife: "Dear, that was a beautiful Shabbos, I really want to thank you for all your hard work?" Or when was the last time you got up from a

Shabbos meal and said, "Wow, Chanie, you outdid even yourself this time." (For the fun of it ask an organized housewife to see her check list of things to do before Shabbos. And when you notice that there are 30-50 check boxes you might begin to get a sense of the sheer amount of work that goes into it.)

But here's the problem: you can't fake it. You can't just thumb through your list of nice things to say, pick one out and deliver it on cue. Your spouse will see right through it. You actually have to feel it. And that's where the first exercise comes in. You have to take stock and review what your spouse does for you and not take it for granted. You have to return to your list over and over again. Adding new things refreshing old ones.

And now you are ready for the second part of the exercise.

You go over to your spouse and let them know how much you appreciate what they do for you.

"I can't tell you how much I appreciate how my laundry is always cleaned, folded and arranged in my draws."

"I know I haven't said this in a while, but you are doing such an amazing job with the kids. I know it's not easy. It takes an awful lot of patience, and the amount of love and care you give them is amazing."

Or how about: "I'm so proud of your learning. I always wanted to marry a Ben Torah and the fact that you're so dedicated makes me so proud."

Or: "It makes me feel so secure that I can always rely on you." You are always there for me.

It's not enough to think the words, you have to say them! If you're a little shy, write it in a card or a note and hand it to your spouse, but not just a generic thank you card, a detailed account of exactly what it is that you so appreciate that your spouse does for you.

When you first do this, you'll may feel uncomfortable. You're uncomfortable because you're not used to doing it. But as you get more accustomed, it becomes natural and just part of the way you treat your spouse. After a while, you make it a habit, just something you do on an ongoing and continuous basis. And watch the results. It works like magic. You'll suddenly find that your spouse feels differently and acts differently around you. Almost against their will they are forced to like you.

The challenge of appreciation is that unless you work on it, unless you really focus on it, it doesn't come naturally. But once you get in the habit of doing it changes your relationship. A. You being to actually recognize how much your spouse does for you and naturally you feel closer to them. B. When you express that recognition to your spouse you lift their spirits, give them that which we so crave, acknowledgment and they feel closer to you.

Do it for Yourself

As an aside one of the motivations to work on this should be purely selfish. One of the rules in the workplace is if you don't show appreciation to the ones that deserve it, they stop doing the things you appreciate. When you receive recognition for something you want to do it more. If you want your spouse to continue doing what it is that they are doing—thank them. It's not the reason you are doing it but it's very nice perk.

And if you want your children to be happy, wholesome appreciative people, make sure that they see you complimenting your spouse. It's very easy for parents to wonder why their children aren't appreciative of what Mommy does for them, what Abba does for them. Until you realize they never see you complimenting Mommy. The never see you praising Abba. You create the culture in your home. The way you treat each other sets the standard for the way people are expected to act. If you want your children to be grateful, model this behavior for them.

Bringing two people together to be one requires a powerful bond, maintaining that connection through all of life storms requires much effort. HASHEM gave us many tools to bond and you have to use all of them. Appreciation is a little understood and even less frequently used tool. If you use it along with the other tools, the way you look at each other changes and your relationship changes. Having a great marriage is a choice. It's the choice of many small actions that all add up. Throughout life there will be many forces that will pull you apart, and many life situations that test your commitment and try to wear down your try to unravel the connection and wear at your relationship. By continuously using the various tools that bond you keep your relationship vibrant and strong. You both will change over time, and the circumstances of life will change. When you make a commitment for life it is exactly that for all of life. While the words are easy to say, keeping that commitment for the long haul requires new innovations and renewals.

Let's move on to one last tool that bonds, maybe the most important one.

Chapter 14

Best Friends Who Love Each Other

IT'S SIX THIRTY AT night. A young man comes home from work, enters his apartment, plops himself down on the coach, pulls out the newspaper, and buries himself in the news. Meanwhile, his wife over in the kitchen can't believe her eyes.

"Here I am slaving away making dinner. The kids destroying the apartment, and he's going to just sit there?"

She doesn't say a thing. But the steam starts to rise, and it's not from the pot on the stove.

One kid pulls down some books. Another one knocks over the chair. And finally, she's had it. She stalks over to him, points a finger and lets out: "ALL RIGHT, MISTER. UP OFF THAT COUCH! You are either cooking dinner or taking care of the kids. But you are sitting there any longer."

He dutifully gets up and goes over to help with the kids.

Was she right in what she did?

Most women would answer: "Absolutely!" Many would say, "She's a hero". Most men as well, would agree she's right. If your wife is cooking dinner and the kids are wrecking the apartment, get up and help! Yet, while it's clear that he was wrong, she might have damaged her marriage.

Let's play out the scene.

After being read the riot act, he gets up and takes care of kids while she finishes dinner. Then together they feed the children, bathe them, and finally put them to bed. It's now nine o'clock, everything is quiet, and she settles down to spend time with her husband. She sits down next to him on the couch. And for some reason (that she can't fathom) he sort of moves away. She moves closer. And he sort of moves further away. She moves closer. He moves even further away. For the life of her, she can't figure it out.

What she isn't aware of is that for the past two hours in his brain her words have been replaying like a recording, "ALL RIGHT, MISTER. UP OFF THAT COUCH! You are either cooking dinner or taking care of the kids. But you are not sitting there any longer."

And it's been playing again and again and again. "ALL RIGHT, MISTER. UP OFF THAT COUCH! You aren't sitting there any longer. "ALL RIGHT, MISTER. UP OFF THAT COUCH!" "ALL RIGHT, MISTER. UP OFF THAT COUCH!" "All RIGHT, MISTER..."

Until finally he reached the chilling observation, "I don't believe it. I married a DRILL SERGEANT!"

And as correct as she might be, she made the Ninth Really Dumb Mistake that Very Smart Couples Make:

> **תלמוד בבלי מסכת כתובות דף ח/א**
>
> שמח תשמח ריעים האהובים כשמחך יצירך בגן עדן מקדם ברוך אתה ה' משמח חתן וכלה
>
> *Be joyful beloved friends like your Creator caused you to rejoice in the Garden of Eden of old. Blessed are You, Hashem, Who gladdens the groom and bride.*
>
> **רש"י כתובות דף ח/א**
>
> ריעים האהובים - החתן והכלה שהן ריעים האוהבים זה את זה
>
> *Beloved friends - The groom and bride who are friends who love each other.*

Under the *chuppah*, the couple is blessed, "Be joyful, be happy, *reyim ahuvim*." Rashi explains that *reyim ahuvim*, refers to the *chassan* and *kallah,* who are "friends who love each other." That expression defines the relationship. Note that it's "friends" first and "who love each other" second. There's an order. It's *reyim ahuvim.* Friends first, lovers second.

Best Friends Who Love Each Other

Successful marriages don't just happen. Couples don't just meet and live happily ever after. Marriage is the most beautiful relationship, but it requires work -- a lot of it. Hashem gave us many tools to succeed, infatuation, romantic love, respect, and attraction. One tool that's widely misunderstood is friendship.

The *pasuk* calls a man's wife, "*Chevrascha* – your friend" (Malachi 2:14). Targum Yonasan explains that it means "*shutfascha* -- your partner. Many times, I heard my Rebbi, the Rosh Yeshivah, use the expression, "life-partner." Marriage means sharing life together -- the good, the bad and the in-between. A husband and wife are partners in this thing called life.

This is where that woman went wrong, she stopped acting like a friend. Friends are forgiving, even when a friend acts dumb. Friends don't boss each other around. Friends don't demand, even when they are correct. Friends communicate when their needs aren't met. And you can be a hundred percent correct, and your spouse completely wrong, but if you act like a boss or a tyrant or anything but a friend, your marriage will suffer.

Are you still friends?

I'll ask a couple who have been married ten years, "Are you guys friends?"

"Well, we love each other."

"Yes, but are you friends?"

"What do you mean? We're married for more than a decade."

"Yes. But are you freinds."

"Well, we used to be friends," they finally admit, "but now we don't know."

Friendship is another one of the tools that bond. And like all the tools it needs to used, but first we have to understand it. I would like to share with you the four rules of friendship.

Who's boss?

An important question to ask yourself is: "in our marriage who's in charge? Who wields the power? Who's the boss?"

If your marriage is going well, the answer is no one. No one is the boss. You are partners -- *equal partners with different roles.* No one is in charge. No one has card blanche. No one has veto power. No one has the right to say, "My way or the highway!" That works in a dictatorship, not in a marriage.

Equal partners with different roles mean, that you may delegate an area to one spouse – for instance, domestics to the wife and finances to the husband – but that is a joint decision. You decided things would work best with a division of labor. You agreed to let one spouse take the lead in that area. Nevertheless, you are equal partners.

The 1st rule of friendship is that friends don't boss friends around.

It Happens to Nice People

I've heard it too often to downplay. Men and women boss their spouse around as if they were a servant. They say it with the assumption of *I know better* or *I'm in charge*. The results aren't surprising. If you don't act like a friend, your spouse isn't going to feel that you're a friend.

As *chassan* and *kallah*, each dreamed it was going to be amazing. First, we're going to agree on everything. We both love cherry soda. We both love blue paint. We both love Colgate toothpaste. It's going to be unbelievable. My wife is going to be waiting on my every desire. My husband is going to intuit all of my emotional needs. It's going to be fantastic.

Then they got married and found out it's not quite that way. They discovered that there are many issues that need to be negotiated. It could be thing as small as painting the wall blue or yellow, whether we keep sugared cereal in house, or do we drive over the speed limit, but it's also more than that. The inability to negotiate the issues of marriage *as friends*, without giving commands, is a classic mistake. And it happens all the time – even to the nicest people.

Hashem put two parts of one *neshamah* into two separate bodies. Each body has its own desires, interests and agendas. A part of each of them is always screaming out, "It's my needs!" "If I don't take charge, my needs won't get met." At the same time, there's another part of them screeching, "It's not me and you -- it's us. We're one unit. We are bonded."

And even more—when it's clear to one that their spouse is failing. "He's always late." "If I don't constantly remind her, she'll wreck our finances." And for the good of the marriage, one spouse takes control. And with the best intentions they wreck their marriage. In their attempt to right the course they cause disunion and strife. The secret to a successful marriage is working together as friends and lovers.

What should she do?

Let's go back to the young man sitting on the couch, while the kids were wrecking the apartment. His wife found herself in a difficult situation, she's working away in the kitchen, the kids are running wild and he's not doing a thing. What should she have done?

"Do you mean I can't ever express myself? Even when my husband is acting like a creep?!"

There's something called communication, which we'll discuss a little bit later on, but she did not communicate. She dictated. She lectured. She acted like a boss. And when you act like a boss, you step out of the role of friend. You might take care of the issue at hand, but you will pay the price as your marriage will suffer. You have needs, and it's unwise and unfair for you to not be able to express those needs but doing it in a way that doesn't damage your relationship requires understanding how to communicate without stepping out of your role.

Sometimes in the thick and thin of things it's not so easy to see that you are stepping out of your role.

The Pretty Secretary

Imagine a couple have been married for about 10 years. One evening at home after work the husband says to his wife: "Dear, you know that secretary in my office," "You know, the young, pretty one?"

"Uh, yeah." She responds.

"Well, I hope you don't mind but we've kind of become friends. It's not that I'm not interested in her or anything, but sometimes during lunch, we take walks together. During our breaks, we spend time together. Just friends, nothing serious. We do see each other on weekends and stuff like that, and we sometimes send cards to each other, but nothing romantic. Just as friends. And dear, the reason I'm bringing this up is because as you know, I'm travelling to Las Vegas for a week next month and I asked her to come with me. That's okay, right? You understand, dear, don't you?"

I sure hope she isn't understanding. Her husband is stepping out of bounds. Way over the line. There are rules in a relationship and certain behaviors are unacceptable. One of them is a romantic interest outside the marriage. That's obvious, but there are other situations which are not so obvious.

Ham Sandwich and Smoking a Cigar

Imagine it's *Yom Kippur* and in the middle of the day a woman comes home from *shul* and finds her husband sitting on the couch eating a ham sandwich and smoking a cigar. She does what any self-respecting woman would do:

"PUT THAT DOWN RIGHT NOW!

It's *Yom Kippur*! WHAT'S WRONG WITH YOU?"

She gives it to him good.

I don't have to tell you that what he's doing is wrong. For a man to be eating a ham sandwich and smoking a cigar on Yom

Kippur—is way, way off. And clearly, she has every right to be aghast, shocked, and certainly upset. However, what she did wasn't right either, because she stepped outside the bounds of marriage.

You may say: *What do you mean—it's Yom Kippur! —He's violating one of the most basic halachas. Doesn't she have a right to demand him to stop?* The answer is she has every right to demand for him to stop if she were his:

- Rabbi,
- mentor
- or mother.

But that's not what she is. She is his life's partner. She is a friend. Equal partner in this thing called marriage. But not in charge of him. Not his boss. Not his Rov.

She might have a choice to make. She may come to the recognition that this partnership is not what she contracted for. "This isn't the marriage I intended. This isn't the vision I had in mind." And she may have to end the partnership. But one thing is certain: as long as she's in the partnership, she has no right to

- demand,
- command.
- dictate

They're equal partners with different roles. They're best friends who love each other.

Way too often a husband or a wife take on the role of Rebbi, mentor or teacher. They feel some moral obligation to make sure their spouse is *frummer,* or dresses better, or learns more, or eats a particular way or whatever. And as Rebbi, mentor or teacher they may be doing a fine job, but as a life partner they are wrecking their marriage.

But shouldn't I help my husband who is being mechalel Shabbos, who is smoking on Yom Kippur?

The answer is yes *if he asks for your help*. But if he doesn't, you're stepping out of the bounds of being a friend. You're stepping into a different role. If you want a different job, apply for that job. You certainly have every right to talk to him about it, to discuss it, even to plead about it. And it would certainly be wise to go with him to someone to discuss it.

But aren't there things worth putting your foot down?

There are many things worth putting your foot down about and there are many relationships where that's called for. A teacher and student. A boss and employee. A judge and a defendant. But not in marriage. Marriage is a relationship of best friends who love each other.

Friends discuss things. Friends negotiate matters. Friends reach compromises. But best friends who love each other don't threaten, intimidate, or bully one another. And "putting your foot down" violates the terms of agreement in marriage. By doing so, one partner has transformed the relationship to boss and employee or judge and defendant. And while it is true that he or she might win this battle they will lose the war—and war it will be.

Are there exceptions? Yes. If something's legitimately dangerous. If you are on the highway and he's driving 95 miles an hour, you have a right to shout emphatically, "Stop it!" Or if someone is physically or mentally abusive, yes. Other than things like that, everything in a marriage should be negotiated *as friends*. If you find your spouse doing something you cannot live with, go for help and discuss it with someone older and wiser, but the choice should never be taking on the role of boss.

And if you want a happy marriage you have to also repress another desire.

Not a Teacher

When we were first married, my wife and I made up to learn *Mesillas Yesharim*. It seemed like a fine idea. The first time we learnt together it went well –at least I though it did. The second time it didn't go so well. After that my wife said that she'd rather not learn anymore. I didn't understand. "Was it something I did? Something I said?"

"No," she said, "I don't know, it's like I feel like I'm in school and you're a teacher."

To this day, I'm not comfortable when my wife attends my *shiurim*. That's not our relationship. That's not the role I have with her. We are *reyim ahuvim*, friends who love each other. We are not teacher and student.

She's wearing skirts about the knees—how do I tell her?

A young man called with a question. He was married about six months and in general he was happy, but there was an issue that was deeply troubling him. His wife was wearing skirts that just barely covered her knee. While she was standing it was OK, but when she sat down, part of her knee would show. His question was what is the best way to tell her that he would like her to wear longer skirts.

I said to him, "What school did your wife go to?" He named one of the popular *Bais Yaakovs*. I said, "I'm confident that after 12 years of hearing about skirt lengths and sleeve lengths that your wife has a good idea of where the halacha stands. So why do you think she isn't doing that?"

"Um… I'm not sure." He said

"I think I know why. It has nothing to do with ignorance. It has everything to do with being accepted by her friends. To a woman the way she dresses represents who she is. It is a way of defining herself and identifying with a particular group. Much like gang members wear certain colors to define their allegiance, how a woman dresses speak volumes to who she considers her peer group and whose opinions she is concerned with. When you go to a wedding and you notice each woman who meets your wife comments on her outfit, and she comments back—it's because clothing is very is important to a woman. For most women one of the highest compliments is when someone she respects says, "She really knows how to dress! But there are many different ways to dress. If this is the way the people in her group dress and she doesn't dress that way—she's just not in—she's either too frum, too straight, too plain, but one thing for sure—she doesn't fit in.

If you were to point out to her that her skirts aren't long enough. I highly doubt she would change. In fact, I don't think that she would hear much about the length of her skirts at all. She would however hear a much louder message, "I don't approve of you. You aren't good enough."

"Rabbi," he said, "are you saying I should just say nothing?"

"Exactly". I responded. "If don't say anything, and build your marriage, hopefully it will get to the point that she feels cherished. She will begin feeling more self-assured, and it could well be that will be enough for her to win the battle and dress more appropriately. It could also be that she won't change at all, but one thing for certain, mentioning anything now will only make it harder for her. And much harder for you as well. Because this will be a sore spot between you. She will constantly feel that you don't approve of her, and it's going to be a point of friction between you for years to come.

The point is that when you criticize your wife you aren't acting as a friend—you are acting as a spiritual guide and teacher. And it's not your role. And even if you do it politely and nicely, the message is the same.

Many times couples get into trouble because they violate this rule of friendship. So let me say it clearly:

You are not responsible for the spiritual level of your spouse.

Your job is *your* spiritual level. Your job is to grow. You have many areas to grow in: *middos*, *davening*, learning, *bitachon* and more. You should be very focused on growing in those areas. But it's your *middos*, your *davening*, your learning, your *Bitachon that you need to focus on—not your spouse's*.

Marriage is a relationship of *reyim ahuvim*, best friends who love each other. There are a lot of obstacles to maneuver, a lot of issues to negotiate. It's requires a very delicate balance. But friends work it out *as friends*. Not as dictators. That is the first rule of friendship: friends don't boss friends.

On to the 2nd rule.

"How do you paint a radiator?"

When my oldest son became a *bar mitzvah* I took him to see my Rebbi, the Rosh Yeshivah zt'l. My son grew up in Rochester, NY, and going to see his father's Rebbi, a *gadol BiYisrael*, was a big occasion. When we walked into the office, the Rosh Yeshivah saw us started laughing and said: "Hah, hah, hah -- how do you paint a radiator? How do you paint a radiator? How do you paint a radiator?"

My son was a perplexed. However, I knew exactly what the Rosh Yeshivah was referring to.

When I was newly married, my wife and I visited the Rosh Yeshivah, zt'l. The Rebbitzen, z'l asked me to help her with something so I stepped into the kitchen, leaving my wife with the Rosh HaYeshiva. He asked my wife how the apartment was. She explained it needed painting and we decided to do it ourselves. (Meaning *I* was going to paint the apartment.) I asked one of my friends to help. One day we showed up with paint cans and rollers—no problem—we got this. Well, there was a problem. I thought he knew how to paint. And he thought I knew how to paint. It turned out neither of us knew how to paint.

We started off well enough. We painted one wall, finished it and went to a second wall, finished it. Then we got to the radiator. It was an old cast iron radiator that had layers and layers of peeling paint. I turned to my friend, and said: "How do you paint a radiator?"

"I don't know," he said. "How do you paint a radiator?"

We both stood there looking at each other.

When my wife told this story to the Rosh Yeshivah, he started laughing. The image of two yeshivah *bachurim* standing there dumbfounded, with paint dripping off them, saying to each other, "How do you paint a radiator?" was funny. When I walked back into the room, the Rosh Yeshivah said, "Hah, hah, hah -- how do you paint a radiator?"

A few days later, I went to the office to ask the Rosh Yeshivah something. The moment he saw me he said, "Hah, hah, hah -- how do you paint a radiator?" A few weeks after that, he did it again. Soon, it became an ongoing refrain. It was the way he greeted me – so much so that years later when I brought my son in, the first thing that the Rosh Yeshivah said was "Hah, hah, hah -- how do you paint a radiator?"

Here's the question. Why would an *adam gadol*, a *tzaddik* who had worked on his *middos* all his life, act with such frivolity?

The Rosh Yeshivah was emphasizing, something that he taught us over and over again-- the need to have a sense of humor. You have to learn to laugh. You have to look at the lighter side. The Rosh Yeshivah was teaching us that having a sense of humor isn't frivolous. It's part of being a successful human being.

In the heavy traffic of life things are going to happen. If you want a good marriage, you have maintain a sense of humor. And one of the safest focuses of your humor –is you. If you learn to gently make fun of your mistakes or foibles, no one gets hurt— things take on a lighter air—and you as well as the people around you will benefit. The point is that you have to have fun in your marriage. You have to be and remain friends. Friends means having a fun attitude and doing things you enjoy together. Fun isn't flippant. Fun isn't optional. It's vital to the success of a marriage -- to success in life.

The 2nd rule is that *friends have fun together.*

Friendship in the marriage requires focus, attention and spending time doing things together that you enjoy, things that are fun -- even if they're not so romantic.

The 3rd Rule of Friendship
Friends Support Each Other

What happens if someone verbally attacks your spouse? Your role as a friend is to defend your spouse. That may sound obvious, but your role is to defend your spouse *even if the person levying the criticism is your mother, father, brother, sister, aunt or uncle.* Your job is to defend your spouse because that's what friends do.

Because you're not just friends you are best friends. And a best friend comes first.

Marriage Comes First

"Therefore, a man leaves his father and his mother and clings to his wife." Bereishis 2:14

Your marriage comes before any other relationship. It comes before your neighbors and friends. It comes before your cousins, and nephews. It comes before your uncles, and aunts. It comes before your brothers and sisters. It comes before your BFF since you were two years old. And it comes before your father or mother. Your first responsibility is to your spouse.

If you find a relative intruding on your marriage, you say to them, "I greatly appreciate all that you've done and I can never repay that debt, but my spouse comes first." Even if they don't agree. Even if they become furious. Even if they threaten to never talk to you again, and to never forgive –your spouse comes first.

But how can I just ignore my mother? How can I stand up to my father? You try to be as soft as you can. You speak as nicely and politely and as often as you can. But push comes to shove your spouse comes first. When you got married that was the agreement. You are leaving family of origin and creating a new family. Your responsibility is now to your spouse before any other human being on the planet.

And while but most people get that, there is another part to this that isn't so simple.

As a best friend, you are responsible to defend your spouse even when your spouse is *wrong*. Even when your spouse is the cause of the problem. Your role is to support your spouse because you are best friends, who love each other.

But there is one more step:

Yaakov and Sheva are at his parent's house and Yaakov's mother says something critical to Sheva. It's not the first time this has happened, and Yaakov delicately tries to sidestep the conversation. It doesn't work. His mother continues. He tries again to gently move to a different topic. To no avail. He tries to bring up another topic. It doesn't help. Things start getting heated. Seeing no other option, Yaakov defends his wife, asking his mother to please not speak to her that way.

He tried his best to avoid it, and it was mighty uncomfortable, but there was no other choice. He did the right thing.

When they come home, he says, "You know, Sheva, I defended you because my job is to defend my spouse, but I want you to know, my mother is right."

He just undid everything he did right.

But it's true. She really was wrong. She really spoke out of turn. That may be true, but that's not your job. That may be your job if you were her mentor or Rebbi, but as a friend, your job is to be supportive.

But who's going to teach her? Not you.

But how's he going to learn? Not from you.

Mark Twain has a line about success in life: "All you need is ignorance and confidence." Most people walk into marriage very ignorant and very confident. In their confidence they are very ignorant of the damage that they are doing to their relationship. If your spouse does something wrong, your job is *not* to teach them, not to help.

But don't friends help each other? If your spouse asks you for help, maybe. Maybe. But unless your spouse explicitly asks, "What do you think about my behavior?" don't even think of volunteering. Even if they do ask, the wisest course would be to keep your thoughts to yourself and your mouth shut.

But that's so dishonest.

For *shalom bayis* it's permitted to lie.

People hate criticism. Men. Women. Kids. Adults. It doesn't matter. No one likes unsolicited advice. No one likes disapproval -- even if it's subtle and worded carefully. And one of the quirks of human nature is that the more wrong I am, the less I want to hear it. And if you let me know I'm wrong, I can't help but feel you're not my friend. You're not my support. You're not on my side.

Oh come on what is my spouse some made out of tissue paper? Does he have a damaged ego? Is she incapable of recognizing she did something wrong? The answer is your spouse is human, just like you. And if you're brutally honest, you'll see that the moment you're on the receiving end that's exactly how you react.

No! Not me. When I'm wrong, I want to know about it. I want to own up to my mistakes.

I have only one answer: try it. Watch what happens when you've done something that makes you look bad in front of others and someone calls you out on it. Ask yourself how you feel towards that person? I doubt it will be all gushy and loving. And even if it didn't bother you,, then you would be the 1 out of a billion people who feel that way—and I haven't met anyone like that yet.

Your job is to be there for you spouse. Not to correct them. Not to show them the error of their ways. Not to help them become better by molding them. Your job is to be a friend.

In fact, here is a formula for a happy marriage: Be deaf, dumb, blind and stupid to your spouse's flaws. You don't see them. You aren't aware of them. You don't even know they exist. If rather you choose to be alert, acute, attuned and focused on your spouse's flaws you are going to pay the price.

The third rule of friendship is that friends support each other. They support each other in public and they support each other in the privacy of their home.

If your friends say your spouse is wrong, it's you and your spouse against your friends. If your family says your spouse is wrong, it's you and your spouse against your family. If the world says your spouse is wrong. It's you and your spouse against the world. (Assuming we aren't dealing with something dangerous or abusive. In which case you need to bring the issue to a Rov or skilled marriage counselor.)

Which brings us to the 4th rule of friendship:

Friends are Tolerant and Forgiving

Many times, a young woman during her high school or seminary years is tolerant, forgiving and accepting. She easily overlooks things that her friends do wrong. Then she gets married and suddenly she becomes highly intolerant. What happened? She seems to have good *middos*.

I don't know the answer, but the fourth rule of friendship is that friends are tolerant and forgiving. If your wife messed up and bounced a check again, you have every right to demand that she stop doing it. But, a successful marriage isn't about rights and demands. It's about friends working together through the issues of life.

But, Rabbi, it's money and it's serious and she bounced another check. I told her so many times!

I'm sure you did. And in a court of law, you'd have a good case. But as a friend, you're tolerant. As a friend, you're forgiving. As a friend, you're nice. (And for the record: I'm willing to guess that she has a few things she finds difficult about you as well.) If you forget that you are friends, your marriage is going to fray.

Learning to live together requires a tremendous amount of growth. Marriage is far more demanding than any other relationship. You may have had many very good friends whose faults you overlooked, but that's because they had their life and you had yours. Your lives weren't joined. For the first time you have to learn to balance out your own strengths and weaknesses against another person's constellation of personality traits. And it may mimic a process you went through when you were younger.

People waste so much time energy and effort blaming themselves for things they're not responsible for.

And many of us while growing up had to learn to make peace with ourselves and accept that I didn't make me, and I didn't choose my strengths nor my flaws. If I was born with a fierce temper that's not something, I decided to put within me. I am responsible to work on my anger, but I didn't make my anger. I am responsible to work on being generous, but I didn't create my natural stinginess. I have to work on not being lazy, but I didn't chose that personality trait. And therefore, that flaw isn't a source of shame. It's my challenge, my area of growth. But it doesn't make me defective and doesn't make me unworthy. I was put into this body, I have a lot to accomplish and I am a work in progress.

Often, it's the same type of tolerance you have to learn to apply in marriage, forgiving your spouse for being who they are. The minute that you decide that there is something in your spouse you can't accept — "I can't accept laziness. "I can't accept a woman who can't keep a house— you are no longer acting like a friend. You are stepping outside the bounds of your marriage. (And you're not being fair-I sure hope you don't hold yourself to the standard of perfection.)

"But I'm right. Isn't it a woman's role to keep the house? Isn't she responsible to have things neat and proper?"

You may be right, you may be wrong, but you just became a boss, a dictator, the person in charge -- and that isn't part of any marriage agreement. *Reyim ahuvim* means friends — friends who are equal partners with different roles, friends who work together and are accepting and tolerant.

"Friend! What friend? Do you know how many times he left his socks on the floor? Do you know how many dishes he leaves everywhere? Friends don't act that way, do they?" Perhaps not, but friends are tolerant anyway.

It's fine to sit down with your husband and explain how you feel when the apartment looks messy. There is nothing wrong with sharing with him it means to you if it looked nicer, but the minute you become intolerant, you've stepped outside the bounds of marriage, you've stopped being a friend. And the same way you had to learn to accept your own shortcomings, you have to accept your spouses. You have to be a friend. And friends who love each other learn to be tolerant, forgiving and look the other way.

Let's Review

1. Friends don't boss around friends
   The first rule of friendship is that friends don't boss friends around. Husband and wife are life partners -- equal partners with different roles, but neither is boss. Even if you're right, even if everyone would agree with you, it's not your job to be your spouse's boss.

2. Friends support friends
   The second rule of friendship is that friends support each other against the world. Even if you know your spouse is wrong, your job is to be their defender.

3. **Friends have fun**
   The third rule of friendship is that friends have fun together. You have to spend time we each other in an enjoyable way. And you have to be protective of that time, going out and doing things that friends do.

4. **Friends are tolerant and forgiving**
   The fourth rule of friendship is that friends forgive each other. This is arguably the hardest because when something really bothers us -- whether it's a spouse who is too sloppy or too neat, or too whatever – it's much more difficult to overlook it in a relationship that's 24/7/ 365.

Every marriage has issues—and they aren't going away. Nevertheless, in a relationship of "friends who love each other" you are able to overlook them. And even more because you are a friend you support your spouse—even if you think she's wrong. You have fun together and keep the air light and you learn to laugh. When your spouse does something that hurts you, you are able to forgive—because friends are forgiving.

Being *reyim ahuvim*, best friends who love each other, requires work and constant vigilance.

The Rebbetzin Protects the Rosh Yeshivah

In his later years, the Rosh Yeshivah, zt'l, wasn't well. Between the Yeshiva and communal responsibilities, he was carrying a very heavy load and the Rebbetzen did all she could to protect his health. She would often keep people out because the Rosh Yeshivah didn't have the strength.

Rav Shmuel Kamenetzky, Shlita, once called the Rosh Yeshivah about a major issue, and the Rebbetzin said, "I'm sorry, but he's resting." Rav Shmuel explained that it was very important. It was an issue on behalf of the *klal* (community). "It's urgent," Rav Shmuel said.

"No, I'm sorry," the Rebbetzin said. "The Rosh Yeshiva is resting. I can't interrupt him."

Rav Shmuel Kamenetzky was one of the *gedolei hador*, but that didn't matter. Her husband's health came first. Her primary focus in life was her husband – and that included protecting him at all costs. That's a marriage. That's the nature of the relationship -- *reyim ahuvim*, best friends who love each other.

No one just falls in love—and no one just stays in love. It is a choice. A choice that requires focus, effort and a plan. Part of which is the ongoing use of the tools that bond. Romance has to be a priority throughout your marriage, to keep the spark alive. Physical contact as well requires intentional and deliberate use. It fosters a connection but can easily be overlooked. Intimacy is a powerful bonding tool, but it too must be used and used properly with the focus being to bring you together to be one. Attraction and appreciation also need to be part of the mix. The last tool, friendship, though, is vital for learning to live together and it's the one that gets you through the thick and thin of life.

There is however, something else that is equally vital for learning to live together.

Chapter 15

Why Couples Fight

Dovid and Shira

Dovid and Shira are a fine young couple. They've been married about two years, they've had their ups and downs, but on the whole things are going pretty well. It's Tuesday night, their date night, sometime in February, they've made up to meet in the city, and Shira is standing outside in the cold, shivering. She looks at her watch. It's 8:10. She looks irritated. A few minutes pass and she looks aggravated. A few more minutes pass. It's now 8:19 and she looks downright angry.

Where is he? He's almost twenty minutes late!

A minute or two later, Dovid pulls up in the car. She gets in, and in a not so pleasant a tone says:

"IT'S FREEZING OUT THERE."

"Sorry, Dear, I tried to rush"

"I CAN'T BELIEVE YOU ARE SO LATE! DO YOU KNOW HOW LONG I WAS STANDING THERE?"

"Look, I'm sorry. I tried my best. I had to finish my work.

"YOUR WORK! VERY NICE. "DO YOU KNOW HOW COLD IT IS? DON'T YOU CARE!?

"Shira, why are you getting all bent out of shape, dear? I'm sorry, but, I told you how important it was."

"YOU ALWAYS DO THIS. ALWAYS!"

I'm sorry, but my boss asked me for that report, and I couldn't leave till I completed it."

"Exactly. Your work comes first" YOU COME FIRST. IT'S ALL ABOUT YOU. ITS ALWAYS YOU AND YOU ONLY.

"I DON'T THINK THAT'S FAIR." he responds.

"NOT FAIR. NOT FAIR. I'LL TELL YOU WHAT'S NOT FAIR. It's not fair that I married a cruel, heartless creep who doesn't give a darn about me or anything that I care about."

Fights

Almost every *chassan* and *kallah* know how great their marriage is going to be. Life is going to be perfect. The relationship will be beautiful. Then they get into their first argument. It's a shock. If they lack self-awareness, the arguments continue and can become self-sustaining cycles of acrimony.

"Rabbi," they tell me, "why do we get into so many arguments – and over such petty issues? With others I'm so nice, but with my own spouse I'm so insensitive. Why can't we just get along?"

It's very important to understand *why* couples who love each other -- couples who may even have a good marriage – argue so much?

The first step is recognizing that marriage is closest relationship any two human beings will ever have. When two people are so emotionally connected, they're extremely vulnerable. And they each have needs, expectations and desires, and often they aren't going to be met. And so, it's inevitable that they are going to hurt each other. And not just hurt. Hurt deeply. Like a stab in the heart. *It's not just anybody who did that. It's my spouse, my best friend, my confidant, my lover.* The pain is so acute because of who it came from.

And I'm sorry to be the bearer of bad news but many couples find that :

- The person who will hurt you more deeply that you have even been hurt—is your spouse.
- The person who will get you more angry than you've ever been in your life—is your spouse.
- The person you will hate more than you have ever hated anyone in your life—is your spouse.

(And this doesn't mean you don't have or can't have a good marriage).

It's unlikely that you've ever felt the intensity of emotions that you'll feel with your spouse. Both the highs and the lows. That's the intimacy of marriage. As a result of the closeness, the hurt penetrates so deeply and causes so much pain.

And that's why even great marriages require a time for adjustment, and all marriages require constant work. And it doesn't mean that your husband is cruel, or that your wife flies on a broom at night. It's just that in the heavy traffic of life, it's inevitable that two people so close will say or do things that hurt each other.

But the more you understand the dynamics of a dispute, and why couples fight, the more you can do to avoid them, and when they do happen the more quickly you can repair the rift.

The Endless Mirror

When I was very young, I was fascinated by the two large mirrors in my parents' bedroom. One mirror was mounted on the wall, and opposite it was the other mirror mounted on on top of the dresser. Because they faced each other when I would look at myself my image would bounce off one mirror and then onto the other mirror. I would stand there transfixed as I watched my image bounce back again and again seemingly forever. There were hundreds of me. No matter how much I would try to find the last me, I never could, because each image bounced back on and on.

The Mirror of the relationship

We react almost unconsciously towards certain cues. A baby's innocent smile, a screeching noise, the sound of a gunshot each elicits a response. We may not even be aware of it, but they cause a physiological and emotional reaction and we act and feel differently because of the experience. And not just outside cues, our own actions, and even our facial expressions impact our emotional state. Studies show that smiling has a direct impact on your mood. No matter how happy or sullen you are the simple act of smiling tends to lift your mood. And as it lifts your mood, it lifts others as well. Try smiling at a person and watch their demeanor. If you do a do a good job at a genuine smile, they will almost have to resist smiling back. As your expression can elicit a positive response so too the opposite. When you scowl at someone, they almost have to resist the urge to scowl back. A frown begets a frown, disapproval begets disapproval, and anger begets anger.

As water reflects an image, to too the heart of man.
–Mishlei 27:19

This is the first step in understanding any fight. It's never one sided. One party did something and that was reflected back, that reflection was reflected back and then echoed back. It may happen at lightning speed, but it involves many reflections back and forth. And like the two mirrors facing each other the reflections bounce back and forth almost endlessly. But with one distinction.

As a young child I looked into the two mirrors facing each other and I saw an accurate reflection of me bouncing back and forth. That's not what happens when a couple get into a fight. Each person has their own biases, emotions, and sensitivities, and interpret things in their own way. Particularly when things get emotionally charged each person's perception is very different. So, it's more like a fun mirror in the carnival, with each reflection slightly distorting the one before it and when the image bounces back and forth, it becomes altered and transformed. Within the blink of an eye things devolve till it we can't even agree on what was said, who said it, and even whether it was said or not. With both sides shrugging their shoulders in wonderment: What happened and how did we get here?

To better understand how fights happen in a marriage, we need to slow the process, and x-ray down into the dynamics. When we do, we'll see that there are three stages to a fight.

It all starts when one spouse does something that hurts the other. It might be an oversight, or an annoying behavior, or something said in a callous manner. The single most important concept in making sense out of any argument is to recognize, that unless you married an utter creep, or a sociopath, it wasn't done maliciously and certainly wasn't done consciously to hurt you—but hurt it did. You are in pain. If it stopped there this chapter would be over and marriage would be a lot simpler. The problem is it doesn't stop there.

Very quickly that pain is expressed, and rarely is it expressed as, "Ouch. That hurt". Rather it's communicated as an angry response. "YOU ARE SO INCONSIDERATE!" "THAT WAS NASTY!" "WHY DO YOU ALWAYS!". And this is where the trouble starts. A legitimate expression of pain is something that in almost any marriage would be met with kindness. The offending spouse would recognize that they did something wrong and either make amends, or at least express regret. But an expression of pain is rarely the response to being hurt. Far more typical is an angry response as in "WHY DID YOU DO THAT? THAT WAS SO INCONSIDERATE." And unwittingly the injured party goes on the attack. This is stage one.

And this begins the cycle. The offending spouse didn't realize they did something to cause pain—if they did—they never would have done it. And then they are met with anger and high emotion and it catches them by surprise. I can't tell you how many times a husband or wife say things like: "I don't know what I said, everything was great and then suddenly out of left field, BLAMO he's all upset ranting and raving..." This fight starts when the victim expresses pain as anger, and now the offending party (who in their mind did nothing wrong,) finds *themselves* under attack.

My Rebbe the Rosh HaYeshiva Zt'l when trying to help a couple in conflict would often ask: "Who threw the first arrow?" Meaning where did the fight start. He might have come late. She might have bounced another check. But who was it that changed the *climate of the relationship* by shooting hurtful words charged with emotion?

Because once things become emotionally charged reason goes out the window and things very quickly escalate. When the spouse who did the offending act, finds themselves attacked. They feel criticized—and for no reason. And now we move on to stage two.

The *Orchas Tzadikim* (*Shaar* 12) explains that when you verbally attack me, it is a given that I will retaliate. It isn't much different than if you were physically assaulting me. I perceive your words as an attack against the essence of me, and it is almost within the category of **self-defense** for me to strike back at you. Every fiber of my being screams out to defend myself against the onslaught of your words.

In almost any relationship that's how fights start. Two friends share many good feelings, spend much time together, greatly enjoy each other's company and suddenly they aren't speaking to each other. What happens is the offending party didn't realize they hurt their friend. The friend, though, sure did. And because he or she was in pain, that pain was translated into anger and the words that came out were anything but sweet. But here is the key: The offending party didn't intend the offense and may not even be aware of it. They now find themselves attacked—and for no reason. Naturally, they will respond. Now the party that was offended gets a round of venom. Which triggers the cycle of harsh words hurled back. The anger bounces back and forth, back and forth, back and forth like an endless mirror.

Sadly, in marriage this happens all the time. Let's say it was the husband who did "something" and the wife who was hurt. She felt pained and not that she's vindictive, but her best friend and lover just stabbed her, and she reacted, and naturally she struck back- she lashed out at him. In his mind he did nothing wrong. (otherwise he never would have done it.) And certainly, nothing egregious enough to warrant that kind of anger! Out of the blue she said nasty, hurtful words. "Ow! Why did she do that!?" I didn't do a thing to get her—and she hauls off and attacks me! For no reason." Now he is in pain. And not that he is meanspirited, but he has been assaulted without cause or provocation. And by the person closest to him. The one he loves and trusts. Naturally when he is attacked, he will answer back with words now *intended* to hurt.

And now the cycle moves into stage three:

She, now on the receiving end of these strong words knows she did nothing wrong. She's the victim. "Not only doesn't he care about how much he hurt me, instead of apologizing he attacks me—and for no reason. He's so MEAN!" And she fires back. He, now attacked more vehemently, knows he did nothing to deserve this and can't help but respond in kind. And like two mirrors reflecting the image, the cycle goes on and on.

But there's one more step to understanding why couples fight.

Nisayon vs. Philosophical Questions

What is the difference between a *nisayon* and a philosophical question?

A philosophical question is when you break your leg and I turn my eyes to heaven and say: "Hashem, I don't understand. He's such a nice guy. Why should he suffer?

A *nisayon* is when I stub my toe. "OUCH!" "WHY ME?"

It's easy to be a philosopher when the pain isn't yours. You can sit back and calmly say to Hashem that you don't understand it. But when you're the one in pain, it's very different. No longer are you cool, calm and collected—suddenly you're in agony. The reason a *nisayon* is exactly that—a test, is because pain blinds. A person in pain isn't thinking clearly. And a person in pain feels their pain in very loud and clear tones.

It's human nature to be sensitive to our own pain but detached to someone else's pain. And even if we try our best, your pain will never feel the same to me as mine will. That makes sense. What's strange is that if you said words to me, and they hurt me deeply, I might then turn around say the exact same thing to you—and not even recognize that you would be hurt by those very words that caused me so much pain. We are MIND BLIND to the pain of others. This plays out in all relationships but especially in in marriage.

The spouse who said hurtful words may be aware they said words that are hurtful, but it doesn't hurt *them*. It's philosophical. However, when they are on the receiving end, it's no longer philosophical. They feel the barbs. They feel the pain -- very acutely. It's a *nisayon*.

The offending party says to themselves, *Yes, I said some not nice words. I'm not saying they were great. I'm not saying I'm a tzaddik, but, they were just words.* The victim says to themselves, *"Ow! Your words tore into my heart."*

I've talked to many divorced couples. Over and over again, she accuses him of being abusive and he accuses her of being controlling. Or the opposite. He's controlling and she's abusive. Either way, it's never, "It just didn't work out."

Each party has a long laundry list of complaints about the other. That's what happens when a marriage spirals out of control. Each side acutely feels the hurt of the other's words, yet hardly recognize the pain their own words are causing.

And the rule of thumb in any conflict, but especially in marriage is that both parties feel they are innocent. Each one is aggrieved; each one is wronged and each one is the victim.

A couple never comes into my office and says, "Rabbi, it's not my wife's fault; it's all mine," and then the woman says, "No rabbi, it's all my fault." What they do say is, "ITS HIS FAULT!" "NO. IT'S HER FAULT!" And even if someone recognizes their contribution to the problem, the line is, "Rabbi, listen, I'm not saying I'm a *tzaddik*. It's 40% my fault," what he's really saying is, "That 40% means little things. The type of things that aren't a big deal. The real problem is her." It's always the other one's fault.

And that's why in every failed marriage both view themselves as the one unjustly treated. Each side with a long litany of complaints and grievances detailing how "bad" their spouse is. Neither side mentions their part in inflicting damage. It's not that either one is lying. They just can't see the pain they caused through their words—but they sure do feel the pain inflicted on them. Even if one party was truly at fault, it set in motion a back-and-forth where hurtful words are hurled at each other like arrows, and they bounce and bounce and bounce and bounce. And each spouse becomes the target of hate, malice and personal attack.

What do Couple Fight About?

This leads us to a critical question: What do couples fight about? What issues cause the quarrels? Is it the children, the in-laws, religion, money, physical intimacy, that the toothpaste should be squeezed from the bottom to the top, that the toilet seat is always left up? That toilet paper should face the wall? What issues are responsible for conflicts in a marriage?

The answer is -- *no issue.*

It's Never the Issue, It's Always the Pain

Couples don't fight about issues. They fight about hurt feelings. It's not about the money, the in-laws, or religion. It's not about whether he was late or sloppy or she bounced a check. It's about how I felt when you said. It's about the pain it caused me. It wasn't the 20 minues that Shira waited in the cold that bothered her. It was that she felt abandoned. "You're supposed to be my friend, the person I rely on, and you left me waiting in the cold. And when I told how much it bothered me, you didn't even care!" The pain starts the conflict. We human beings don't take pain easily. You hurt me, and I just want to dish it right back.

If you want to make your life so much easier, this is the key take away:

It's not the issue that causes the fight. It's the feeling of being hurt. And as long as you stay focused on resolving "the issue", you'll never cure the problem. The issue didn't cause the conflict and so solving the issue won't make the conflict go away.

It's the emotion behind it. It's the sense that my spouse doesn't care about me.

"She's so disrespectful".

"He doesn't love me."

The second most important words in marriage

Do you remember we discussed the most important phrase in your marriage? Now we are ready for the second most important phrase.

The most important phrase is "That's Strange". If Shira had said:

"THAT'S STRANGE!" He's normally so considerate. I know he really cares. Why would he leave me here waiting in the cold?

The evening might have ended differently.

Or if Dovid had said, "That's strange!" She's normally not so emotional. I wonder why she's so upset?"

Things would have proceeded differently.

But they each reacted to the "the issue", so they completely missed what was going on and things went from bad to worse. They each reacted to the outer condition, and didn't focus on what's going on in the inner world of their spouse so they both kept missing the point, until there weren't even speaking to each other. And very quickly it became:

"YOU ALWAYS DO THIS!"

"NO. I'M DON'T."

YES. YOU DO.

"NO. I'M DON'T."

YOU JUST DON'T CARE.

"YES. I DO."

"I MARRIED A HEARTLESS CREEP."

As long as you focus on the words your spouse is saying, and not why they are saying them, the cycle goes on and on and on and on.

"OUCH."

Which brings us to the second most important phrase in your marriage: "OUCH".

When you say "OUCH," your spouse is going to get the message they hurt you. Because the offense wasn't intended, if you let him know that he hurt you, if he's even half a *mentch*, he'll apologize, and figure out what to do in the future to avoid it.

"OUCH." expresses a valid emotion. It's what you're feeling, and you are putting it out in the open. You've done your part. Hopefully your spouse will react appropriately. If not, you've done your job. With that approach, most fights won't even begin. The trouble would end there.

But if instead of "OUCH" you react with anger, you are inciting your spouse to counter in a way that's going to make things much harder for you as a couple. You might feel you have every right to be angry. But anger is a charged emotion—it takes everything up an emotional notch. And worse, anger carries with it a verdict. A verdict of the other person being inconsiderate, hurtful, mean, obnoxious or whatever flavor or nuance you color it with-but guilty. And since he didn't mean it that way, he is now being falsely accused of whatever crime you've painted. And naturally, he's going to defend himself.

But if you train yourself to say "OUCH," then stop, the cycle never begins. In place of things spiraling out of control, you can deal rationally with the real issue—the feeling of being hurt. You've opened up the dialogue and started the first step in the repair.

And so if either Shira or Dovid had said, "OUCH." the results also might have been very different.

When Shira was left standing in the cold: she felt unloved. That is a legitimate and real emotion. And she has every right to express that to her husband, and in a healthy marriage that type of emotion can be dealt with appropriately. Had she said, "Ouch. I'm hurt", she would have given Dovid, the opportunity to cure the wound. The problem is that she didn't react that way. She allowed her hurt to translate into anger and expressed it in attacking words.

(Ladies, the single most powerful tool you have is tears. When a wife is crying—without blaming, accusing, or complaining, just legitimately expressing hurt—there are very few men who wouldn't feel terrible and try to make amends.)

From Pain to Anger

The fight begins when the victim reacts not with an honest expression of pain but with anger. When *"I feel pain"* gets translated into *"I'm fed up and I'm not going to take it anymore!"* The trouble starts. Anger adds blame, turns the victim into the aggressor and changes the dynamic. It begs for that mirror to shine back with exactly that same reaction. One reaction begets another. That starts the spiral. Before either side knows it, the fight is on. After a while, they don't even know why or what they are fighting about. They long ago, forgot the issue, but now super-charged emotions are engaged and sense, generosity and caring are out the window.

And for that reason the second most important phrase in marriage is "OUCH." When you are hurt, as unfortunately you will be, if you express it as a legitimate pain you will find your spouse reacting much more appropriately.

But, sad to say, even if you both learn not to translate emotions into anger, there are still going to be disappointments, hurt feelings, birthdays forgotten, annoying habits that build up and invariably both of you are going to hurt and be hurt. Despite that you can have a very successful marriage – with a few bumps along the way—provided you know how to repair the rifts that are inevitable. The real problems in marriage begin when a couple get into a spat and they aren't able to get out. Where they aren't able to make up and get back to a much different place then things become far more serious. And while learning to limit the damage is important, being able to repair the damage is a skill that is vital for a healthy marriage.

The first step in repairing rifts is understanding the art of the apology.

The Art of the Apology
How to Apologize

It's not easy to apologize. It means taking responsibility. It means owning up to my error. It means admitting that I was wrong. And that's not easy to do.

Amongst the most difficult words to say are the words "I was wrong."

"I'm sorry" isn't that tough.

"You were right", isn't so hard.

"It won't happen again," is easy.

The words we have so much trouble with are: "I was wrong."

When I try to say it, my teeth seem to chatter; my bones shake, my knees knock against each other—anything, anything but don't make me utter that despicable phrase.

But that phrase is vital—for both of you to learn. In marriage, in parenting, in life. Owning up to your side of what went wrong. Not shifting the blame and passing the buck. Just openly and honestly admitting I messed up—I was wrong, is one of the keys to all successful relationships.

But if in life, the words "I was wrong" are difficult to say, in marriage they are doubly hard. "Why do you think I said those things? It wasn't without cause. It wasn't without reason. The only reason I said it was because…" And before you apologize you are likely going to feel that it's not fair—"why should I apologize? After what she said. After what he did. I should apologize!?"

And it has to be that way. No matter who shot the first arrow. No matter who created the mess. Both of you fought that fight. That means both of you said things that you shouldn't have said. And both of you share responsibility for the damage you did to your spouse.

"Yeah, but it's her fault."

"He started it."

"I only started it because she…"

"Well if he didn't… I wouldn't have…."

On and on and on. You can spend your entire life in an endless blame game—and many couples do. Fighting the same fight over and over again. Clashing over nothing and arguing about everything. Dooming their marriage, their families and their lives to a state of endless misery. But it doesn't have to be that way. You can end it. And ending it starts with those most difficult words. "I was wrong. I'm sorry." Even when you don't fully feel it, and especially when you don't really believe it.

How can I apologize?

But how can I apologize when I wasn't wrong? Do you want me to lie? Do you want me to just make a *shmata* out of myself take full responsibility even when I know it wasn't my fault?

When you understand what you are apologizing for, you'll find it a lot easier.

So the million dollar question: What are you apologizing for?

Just as the cause of any fight isn't the issue—it's the hurt feelings. So too, the apology isn't for the *"coming late,"* the *"leaving my socks on the floor"*, the *"insensitive line"*—the apology is for the pain caused. And here is the question: Did you come home this evening with the intent to hurt your husband? Did you walk in the door saying I am looking forward to ripping him to shreds? I kind of doubt it. Rather what happened was: You said something. He said something. You said. He said. And before you knew it you were miles and miles down a road neither of you intended to get on.

So here is the point, while you may feel justified in what said, are you happy that your life's partner, your best friend, the one that you are committed to in thick and thin, is now in pain? *"Well he deserved it! After what he said, he should get twice as much."* I know that you are in pain. I have no doubt about that. The question is are you glad that things have come to this point? Are you happy that you plunged a knife deep into your beloved's heart? Again, I have to imagine the answer is no.

And now you know exactly what you are apologizing for—not the issue. But the pain you caused.

And that is the apology: *"I'm sorry that I hurt you. I feel horrible that I caused you so much pain. You are the best thing that ever happened to me, and the last thing I would want to do is hurt you. Please forgive me."*

And amazingly, once you make up everything changes. The birds start to chirp, love is in the air and peace reigns on this earth. And a couple who an hour ago were at war are now back together in love—a bit bruised for the wear and tear, but nothing that some time and care won't heal.

"But what about *"the issue!"* What about *"his coming late"*? *"Her annoying habit."* What's going to be with that?

The issue is something that you are your spouse can negotiate. One time my way. One time your way. Two reasonable people can find an answer to most any problem that life throws at them. The problem is that both of you were in pain, and when people are in pain, they aren't reasonable. Two unreasonable people can't agree on anything and will fight over everything. Once you both come back to equilibrium you'll see that the issue wasn't intractable. You find a way that both of you can live with. And so, first deal with the wound and later solve the issue. Most of the time if you don't deal with the pain the issue can never be resolved. And once you deal with the pain, the issue wasn't an issue anyway.

And that's the first rule of an apology:

- It's not the issue you are apologizing for, it's the pain your spouse feels.

The hard part is that while both of you share in the blame, one of you has to be man enough to own up to their part and apologize. And that takes raw courage. To put yourself on the line, make yourself vulnerable and step forward is very hard to do. But it's so worth it, because it changes everything, and life becomes bliss again.

An effective apology, however, isn't as simple as just mustering the mettle, the words the approach and the attitude are key.

My Mussar Certificate

For many years a gold framed certificate, sat on a shelf in my study. I was quite proud of it, and so it remained on display. But until I explained it, no one understood why it was there.

Many years ago, I was driving on the highway, and a state trooper signaled for me to pull over. I pulled off to the side of the road. He got out of his car, walked up to my window and waited for me to open it. Then he said, "Do you know why I stopped you?"

"Yes officer, I do." I replied. "I was driving over the speed limit and there is no excuse. I am a law-abiding citizen. I try not speed. But I was speeding. There is no excuse. I apologize."

He looked at me. His jaw dropped. (Keep in mind this was a highway policeman, he probably heard more excuses, than a 6th grade teacher hears when collecting homework), I had just said: "I was wrong. There is no excuse." He walked back to his car. A few minutes later, he returned and instead of a ticket, he handed me a citation for speeding. "Here's a warning," he said to me, "please don't do it again."

I took that citation, put it in a frame and placed it on a shelf in my study where it stood for years. To me, it was an award from the school of *middos*. It took me twenty years of learning *mussar* to be able to say the words. "I was wrong. There is no excuse."

And this is the 2nd rule in the art of the apology:

Don't ruin a good apology with a but...

The first rule is that you are apologizing for the hurt not the issue. The 2nd rule is don't take a good apology and ruin it with the word "but."

Most people ruin their fine apology with that word. "I'm sorry I'm late, *but* my boss needed the report." "I know the house is a mess, *but* my friend needed help." The "but" destroys the apology. The apology says: "I was wrong". The but says, "It was justified".

The problem is that the person on the receiving end of the apology was hurt. And most likely feels that you can't even imagine the pain that they are experiencing (otherwise why would you have done it?)

So while you think the "but" explains why it wasn't so bad, and lessens the offense, all it does it tell the injured party you're not that sorry. The apology says, I wish it never happened. The but says: Under the circumstances it was the right thing to do, and I'll do it again. What happens when you add the "but", is that the offended party now says to themselves, "She's saying what she did was right."

So not only does it ruin the apology it raises the stakes. "She clearly doesn't understand how hurt I was." Now he feels the need to explain to her quite how bad what she did was. So, he ratchets up the emotions on the expression of pain. Letting her know how awful and inexcusable what she did was. She then hears a further escalation of her fault and how terrible she is. (And she wasn't really sure she was that guilty to begin with) She then feels obligated to explain that she really wasn't cruel and heartless, so she amplifies the "but". And the cycle spins downward.

So the second rule of the apology is don't spoil a good apology with a "but". Just say I'm sorry and nothing else. Don't explain, don't make excuses. Apologize and stop.

Which brings us to a very important point. Many times your spouse is upset and you don't know why. Now what? How do you apologize when you don't even know what you did wrong? And you know that if you ask: "What did I do wrong?" The response is going to be: "You're so insensitive that you can't even figure it out! That just proves to me how callous and uncaring you are!"

So what do you do?

Now, you say these words.

"I see that your upset. I've done things wrong in the past. It seems, that I did something wrong here as well. The last thing in the world I want to see is you hurt. Please let me know what it is so I could avoid doing it again."

But, you have to memorize these words and use them exactly like this. (On the receiving end of the apology, please remember that Nevuah ended with the destruction of the 2nd Bais Hamidkdash, and your spouse doesn't share your emotionality and may not be attuned to what you're feeling. That doesn't make them cruel or insensitive and it doesn't mean they don't love you. It just means he has a male psyche she has a female psyche, and you experience things differently so please let them know—gently and kindly.)

But what if your spouse won't let you know? How do you apologize?

#3: Apologize for the Pain Caused

Rule three is: If you don't know what you should apologize for, apologize for the pain.

Remember "it's not the issue, it's the pain." When your spouse says the reason is "x y and z," it's not really about "x y and z." It's not because you came late, bounced a check, or the house is a mess. It's because of the hurt or embarrassment those things caused. It's because your spouse feels pained, neglected and alone.

Once you fully get it that you're apologizing for the pain you'll know exactly what to say:

"Dear, I feel terrible. It's clear that you're hurt and that pains me. The last thing I would want to do is hurt you. Please help me know what I did wrong, so I don't do it the next time."

(As a rule of thumb: The more you understand the pain, the easier it will be for you to apologize and the eaiser it will be for your spouse to graciously accept it. So again, on the receiving end of the apology, please be generous and explain what it is that hurt you.)

But for any apology to work there is one more element needed:

Forgive and forget – Kiss and make up

As difficult as it is to apologize, it's just as difficult to accept an apology. Often, one spouse will genuinely express remorse and ask forgiveness, and even apologize repeatedly and profusely, yet the other spouse won't accept it. What do you do when the offending spouse truly regrets what they did, and they fully express it, yet you still find it incredibly difficult to accept an apology? Intellectually you want to, but emotionally you just can't bring yourself to accept it.

The first thing to do is to talk to yourself. (I'm going to do this in one gender, but it applies equally to both)

I know he's a nice guy. He's always considerate and I know how much he wants me to be happy. He probably didn't mean it. And he may not even be aware of it hurt me. After all he's a guy. Guys are…well guys are…just different. What bothers women doesn't seem to bother them. They have a whole different emotionality. He experiences things differently and he probably wasn't know how hurtful it would be. And more than that, I sure don't want to be here. I want to be close again. I want things to be like they are in the good times.

But you actually have to do the self-talk, for the sake of your marriage and your happiness you have to speak out the words out loud or in your head. Many times, just going through the internal conversation changes things.

But what do you do when even that doesn't work? You want to let it go—but you just can't. Now what?

That's when it's important to understand yourself a little bit better. If you we are brutally honest with yourself, you'll find that a big part of why you can't let it go is because you want to get even. "Do you know what he did to me? Do you know how much pain he caused me? He's not going to get away with this." "She's not going to just say I'm sorry and walk away. That's incredibly unfair. I'm going to set the scales straight. She's going to pay the price."

And even though it's foolish and damaging to you—your goal isn't to get even, you want to be happy and have a wonderful marriage—that sense of injustice will stop you from accepting an apology. And then you guys are stuck. Because no matter how good an apology is, it can only work if its accepted.

That's when you either step up to the plate or you suffer. This is your marriage, and this is your life. You either let go and life is beautiful again, or you continue to languish in misery—the one suffering most being you.

If you find yourself here, I have a perspective that might help.

I have never seen anything like that in my life!

It's interesting to watch the looks that drivers give each other when someone makes a mistake. If you have ever turned a corner too tight and it looked like you were going to hit another car, and at the last minute you veered off avoiding a collision. You might remember the expression of the other driver. Likely it wasn't fear, or even dread. It was an incredulously dismissive look of "What's wrong with you? What planet are you from? Do people like you really exist?"

I find that rather curious, because likely the person giving that look, isn't a perfect driver himself. Probably there were many situation where he was just as at fault—maybe even a half hour ago. But all that is forgotten. The minute you come to close to his car—he gets this look on his face of "How could anyone be so incompetent?"

This type of short-term amnesia plagues us all the time. If I said something inconsiderate, "Come on we all make mistakes. If you said it—"Hey that's rude. What's wrong with you?"

So here is the question: Has it ever happened maybe even once in your life that you weren't the nicest, softest, most sensitive person on the planet? Has it ever, ever occurred that maybe you said things that, while of course you didn't mean them, were insulting to someone? Have you ever hurt someone's feelings? Have you ever had someone cry because of something you did?

It doesn't take much self-awareness to recognize that we all do things like this from time to time. And that's understood, until its my spouse who did it and then – HOW COULD YOU! NO ONE IS EVER SO RUDE AND INCONSIDERATE!

And yet, I'd be willing to bet that there were many times that you did things that hurt or offended your spouse. Maybe you forgot something that was important to them. Maybe you said something that was hurtful. If you think back, I'm sure you'll see that you aren't an angel all dressed up in white, who never slips. When you recognize that you also do things that makes it hard on your spouse—it becomes easier to overlook this lapse.

And even more in this debacle itself, while you are so unforgiving because it's all your spouse's fault, if you were to step outside and look in, you would recognize you had a lot to do with things getting to where they are. It may be true that he started it, but it takes two to tango, and just like it took both of you to get into this mess, it requires both of you to get out of it. His job is to say, I'm sorry. Your job is to let it slide. When you focus your thoughts on this you can start letting go of the pain and move forward.

And now we move on to something practical, I'd like to teach you how to fight.

How to Fight

The first lesson in how fight is: don't do it. There is nothing worth fighting about in a marriage. There are going to be different wants and needs. There are going to be differing opinions. Decisions will have to be made. Compromises too. But the rule is that *nothing* in a marriage is worth fighting over. Fighting is a lose / lose situation.

If you feel something is worth not compromising on be *sho'el eitzah*, ask advice. So often what we think really matters—doesn't, and what we think is really important—isn't. If you can't ask someone older and wiser, then apply the "the five-year rule." Ask yourself will it matter five years from now? The answer usually is: no. *Forget about five years from now –most of the time it doesn't matter the next day!* But whatever you do—don't fight. It gets you nowhere and just damages the relationship.

With that being said, we come to the part that I don't want to write, (and I don't want you to read.)

You will fight.

For most couples: It's inevitable. It's just part of life. Either you or your spouse will say something or do something, or not say something or not do something and before you know you guys are in conflict.

Therefore, I'd like to share with you the RULES OF ENGAGEMENT, so you don't break the marriage… I want to teach you how to fight

Rule one: Stay local, don't go global.

Often when people get upset they say things like:

> "YOU NEVER TAKE OUT THE GARBAGE."
> "YOU'RE ALWAYS LATE."
> "YOU NEVER SAY THE RIGHT THING."
> "YOU'RE ALWAYS EMBARRASSING ME. ALWAYS!"

Those are examples of going global.

Is it true that he *never* takes out the garbage? Is it true that she's *always* late? Is it true he's *always* embarrassing you? No. What she means is that she felt embarrassed when he said that line. And it could be that he did it before, but it certainly isn't always. We go global because when I'm hurt or embarrassed in the *heat of the moment*, I feel my spouse *never* cares. But you end up working against yourself.

When you complain about something, you want your spouse to recognize your perspective—to appreciate what you are experiencing. By saying something that isn't true you're giving your spouse no choice but to defend himself —and be right, because it's not true that he never takes out the garbage. And the response you get is predictable. "What do you mean I never... Just last week I did ...And the week before that ..." And the cycle starts.

What you then hear is "not only doesn't he say he's sorry—he thinks he's right!" Clearly your message isn't getting through, so you up the emotional volume. What he then hears is "She's worse than I thought. She not in touch with reality." So he defends himself even more.

The rule is stay local don't go global. Stick to what happened.

What happened was "When we came late, I was embarrassed." "When you said that line in front of those people, I felt pain." That's staying local. Adding words like "always" or "never" escalates it to the global level. And makes it much more difficult A. For your spouse not to argue. And B. for you guys as a couple to then scale things back down.

By sticking to the issue, keeping to what actually occurred and not expanding it, you limit the damage, and you might actually accomplish something.

#2: Don't throw in the Kitchen Sink

She: "You're always late."

He: "Let's not go there, dear. Do you want me to tell you all of my complaints?"

She: "Why are you always late?"

He: "I said, LET'S NOT GO THERE."

She: "BUT YOU'RE ALWAYS LATE."

He: "OKAY, LET'S DO IT. TO START, HERE'S WHAT I DON'T LIKE…."

The 2nd Rule of Engagement is: Don't throw in the kitchen sink.

Whether the issue is lateness, spending, how to raise the children, respect -- stick to the issue. Don't bring in everything else that's wrong or went wrong since *Maaseh Bereishis*. (time in memorial)

The reason you want to bring up other issues, is because you feel your spouse isn't being fair. *"I also have complaints. There are plenty of things you do that I have to put up with."*

That's probably true. We all have stuff. We all have things that make it hard on our spouse to live with us. The problem is that when you move off the issue at hand your spouse isn't going to say: *"Oh! Your right. I never thought about how it must be for you to put up with me."*

Quite the opposite. Your spouse brought this up because they were pained by what you did. When you respond with other issues. Your spouse is now getting back an entire litany of their faults. The only thing your spouse is going to hear is that you don't accept them. Typically, a woman is going to hear, *he doesn't love me*. A man is going to hear, *she doesn't respect me*. The minute you go from one issue to the whole bag of issues – to everything else your spouse does wrong -- you're going on the offensive and escalating things to much larger proportions.

If you fight, don't throw in the kitchen sink. Limit the complaint.

#3: Character Assassination is murder

"THIS PROVES YOU'RE IRRESPONSIBLE."
"YOU ARE JUST NOT TRUSTWORTHY."
"THIS SHOWS ME AGAIN THAT YOU JUST DON'T CARE."
"YOU'RE LAZY."
"YOU ARE TOTALLY UNRELIABLE."

The third rule of engagement is: character assassination is murder.

When you escalate the issue to now reflect on a person's entire character you are escalating thing so beyond what happened that you are leaving no choice but for your spouse to argue. You are negating the person or proving that they are damaged—which isn't true, and is something your spouse isn't going to take well to.

You need to remember that it's a behavior, not a character flaw.

It's often a chain reaction. One side escalates an issue from the local to the global. Next, someone throws in the kitchen sink… which leads to defining a spouse's character as unworthy. It's taking a feeling and using it as proof of a flaw in your spouse's character. "This just proves to me you're a cold, callous person!" "Once again, you've proven to me that you're unreliable." "Once again, I see that you're lazy."

Because you are going way beyond the problem at hand, you are making it difficult to return to equilibrium. It's the behavior, not the person. The behavior caused the pain. It doesn't reflect on my spouse in general terms. It's not their character. Never assassinate your spouse's character. If you must, point out a behavior, but limit it to that.

#4: Sleep on it

There is one final rule for fighting in marriage. (Besides don't do it.)

When my wife and I were first married, someone offered us advise they *thought* was wise. "Don't go to sleep in an argument," they told us. If you have a disagreement, work it out no matter how much time it takes. Stay up until it's resolved.

The person who said it was sincere, and it could be it works for some people, but I've found that more often it backfires – and backfires dramatically.

For most of us, staying up late makes us tired, cranky and far less tolerant. The issues don't get resolved—they become more entrenched. "Don't go to sleep until you've worked it out" is BAD ADVICE.)If it works for you as a couple—then use it! Just beware that it often produces the opposite effect.) I much sooner recommend that If you find yourselves on one of those spirals that you call a time out. You say to your spouse, "Look, it's clear we're not getting anywhere. All that's happening is we're getting more and more upset. Let's drop it for now and come back to it tomorrow." (This is very different from stonewalling, where one spouse wants to continue the conversation and the other shuts down. I'm suggesting that as a couple, you set a policy that if things get heated and you don't seem to be getting anywhere either one of you can ask to put things on hold with the understanding that you will get back to them the next day.)

Rabbi Yisrael Reisman tells the story of a young couple who had their first fight. It happened one *erev Shabbos*. He did something she found very upsetting, but he didn't know what it was. All day, he asked her what was wrong, but she just fumed. Finally, as they were about to go to bed, he asked her sincerely, "Please tell me what's the matter, dear. What did I do wrong?"

She told him and explained how upsetting it was to her. He didn't react immediately. Instead, he leaned back on his pillow and said, "This is too important to just give a quick answer. Let me have a minute to think about it." She agreed and waited.

A minute went by and he still hadn't answered, but she decided to be patient.

Then a second minute passed. It seemed like hours to her, but she magnanimously decided to give him the time he said he needed.

Then a third minute passed with still no explanation. That was it. She had had enough. She turned to him to really let him have it… and she saw that he had fallen asleep.

The end of the story is that the next day they spent the Shabbos meal at Rabbi Reisman's house and as they told him the story, they were both laughing about it.

You can't run away from an issue, but you can bring it up tomorrow. When you open your eyes in the morning, you might not even remember what you were fighting about, let alone the charged feelings you had. Even if it is a real issue, you'll be much calmer and more capable of working it out.

The bottom line is that a marriage is made up of two very vulnerable, very fragile things called people. And we all have many needs, wants and expectations—not all of which can be met. We also live in our own world—we are mind blind. And so when you live in such close proximity, it's very difficult not to hurt each other. Fighting from time to time is normal. If you follow the RULES OF ENGAGEMENT, it may not eliminate all pain in your marriage, but it will help you create the framework to succeed. The fights will remain at most "time to time." They won't become frequent, they won't spiral out of control, and they won't destroy the fabric of the relationship. They'll be part of the give-and-take in life. Then your work to repair the rift is so much easier. One of you takes the bold step forward and say those difficult words,

"I was wrong. I'm sorry. The other spouse is gracious and accepts you back and life goes on, and you have a beautiful, fulfilling, loving marriage.

Let's put it all together

Be Soft as a Reed

The Gemara (*Taanis* 20a) says, "Always be soft as a reed, never hard as a cedar tree."

This is a principle of life – and especially marriage. A person should always be soft and pliable—not stiff necked and inflexible.

When your heart is soft can feel another person's pain and you can see the error of your ways. When your heart is hard – you stick with your conviction that you are blameless, and all of your relationships suffer, which means you suffer.

It's only a few words in the *Gemara* but they contain a tremendous lesson: "Always be soft as a reed, not hard as a cedar." It applies to men and women. When you react with anger your heart is hard and you're making it very difficult for your spouse to remember that you love them, that you're their best friend. Take a moment, delay the reaction and make yourself "soft as a reed, not a cedar tree." The best way to stop the fight is to nip it in the bud. If you see your spouse react with strong emotions, say the words: "THAT'S STRANGE". Then you can climb into your spouse's world, recognize what they found offensive and you try your best to explain that the last thing in the world you want is to hurt the one you love. If you are on the receiving end of the hurt instead of reacting with anger say: "OUCH, THAT HURT." And give your spouse a chance to understand what's bothering you.

Nevertheless, there are times when fights happen. When they do, remember to limit the damage by using the RULES OF ENGAGEMENT.

1. Don't go global. It's not "you always". It's not "you never". Stick to what actually happened.
2. Don't throw in the kitchen sink. Stick to the issue at hand, don't go dragging up 15 other issues you have with your spouse.
3. Character assassination is murder. What happened doesn't reflect on your spouse as a person. It was one incident out of a multitude.
4. Sometimes, the best thing to do is to sleep on it. Call a time-out, you can resume tomorrow when everyone is calm and well rested.

When things have escalated try scaling them down. It may include saying those oh, so difficult words: "I was wrong." When you do apologize, remember the ART OF THE APOLOGY

1. It's not the issue, it's the pain.
2. Don't ruin a good apology with a but…
3. If you don't know what you should apologize for, apologize for the pain.

And on the flip side if it's your spouse apologizing you have to be being open to accepting it. Your spouse isn't perfect, but neither are you.

Most of all, *daven* to Hashem. With *siyaata dishmaya* you will be able to put these principles into practice, improve your marriage, achieve its full potential and experience harmony, blessing and happiness.

Chapter 16

I Hate Criticism

A WOMAN CAME TO discuss what she described as a major *shalom bayis* issue. She and her husband were so distant, she said, that there were times they didn't talk to each other for three weeks at a time.

"What do you think is the cause of this problem?" I asked her.

"I think it's that I'm much smarter than he is."

"What do you mean?"

"He's not educated. I mean, he's a nice person, but he's ignorant and not polished. I think that deep down that may be the cause of the problem."

I told her that I'd like to meet him, and we set up a time. I was expecting a coarse-speaking, boorish fellow—wearing work overalls and dirty boots. Then, in walks a finely dressed man. He's not only articulate, but he's certainly intelligent. I spoke to him for a while, and I got a very different impression of what was really going on.

I asked to speak to her again. "He seems like a good guy to me. Pretty intelligent. Well spoken. I must be missing something."

Then I said, "If I would ask him what causes him to feel distant from you? What do you think he'd say?"

"Well," she admitted, "to tell you the truth, it could be that I'm a little bit grammar-obsessed. I teach *English arts* and I'm very particular about word usage, pronounciations and grammar. It could be that sometimes I correct the way he speaks.

"Oh," I said. "And do you do this in front of people?"

"Well, we usually have at least one or two of the married kids at the *Shabbos* table."

"And you correct him in front of the married kids?"

"Yeah."

"Do you think he might take offense at that?"

"It could be…."

It turned out that not only does she correct him at the *Shabbos* table, but just about any time he opens his mouth. At the dry cleaners. At the supermarket. At the bank. Anywhere and everywhere. By nature she is highly self-critical. Since she was a little girl, she was constantly berating herself to do better. When she got married, she generously included him in her circle of self. And now no matter what he says, when he says it, or how he says it, she has something to correct.

I tried delicately to explain to her why her husband might be so distant.

"Could it be that he takes these corrections personally, like it's an attack on him as a person?"

"It could be. But that's certainly not my intention."

What she wasn't seeing was his side of their marriage. When she came to me, she framed it as a mystery. "I'm a wonderful *balabusta*. The house is always clean. Meals are always prepared. I do his laundry. I'm an intelligent person and all my friends say how nice I am. All I want is *shalom bayis*. I don't understand, why doesn't he want to speak to me?"

What she wasn't getting was that all day, every day she would punch, jab, and kick at him. What was to her minor "corrections". Were to him constant criticisms. You can be the nicest person in the world, but if your husband feels he's constantly under attack, it's going to be mighty hard for him to want to be around you. No wonder he didn't love her. She's nothing but a constant, throbbing headache.

A rule for life

Here's a life hack: Don't correct people. This is a rule for all relationships not just marriage. If you feel a need to correct people you will find yourself very unpopular, very quickly. When you refute a statement someone made, you may think you are discussing a fact —but to the one who made the statement –it's them you are refuting. The person being corrected will feel they have been personally attacked. It doesn't matter how heedless they were in the formation of their opinion, when a person puts out a statement—they made it. By correcting them, you are putting them down. It is perceived as an attack on the person not on the statement.

It's curious because it sounds so foolish, "Come on. I wasn't attacking you. I was just arguing with the point you made. And it is so difficult for me to hear why you would take offense at something like this until I'm corrected. And then suddenly –boy do I feel it.

But if correcting people is a way to become unpopular, there is something that people do that makes it all but impossible for others to like them.

> **ספר דברים פרק א**
> ג) ויהי בארבעים שנה בעשתי עשר חדש באחד לחדש דבר משה אל בני ישראל ככל אשר צוה ידוד אתו אלהם
>
> **רש"י על דברים פרק א פסוק ג**
> ג) ויהי בארבעים שנה בעשתי עשר חדש באחד לחדש - מלמד שלא הוכיחן אלא סמוך למיתה ממי למד מיעקב שלא הוכיח את בניו אלא סמוך למיתה אמר ראובן בני אני אומר לך מפני מה לא הוכחתיך כל השנים הללו כדי שלא תניחני ותלך ותדבק בעשו אחי ומפני ד' דברים אין מוכיחין את האדם אלא סמוך למיתה כדי שלא יהא מוכיחו וחוזר ומוכיחו ושלא יהא חבירו רואהו ומתבייש ממנו כו' כדאיתא בספרי וכן יהושע לא הוכיח את ישראל אלא סמוך למיתה וכן שמואל שנאמר הנני ענו בי וכן דוד את שלמה בנו:
>
> *"And it was in the fortieth year, in the twelve month, on the first day of the month, when Moshe spoke to the Bnai Yisroel according to everything that HASHEM him to them." — Devarim 1:3*

At the very end of his life Yaakov Avinu gathered his sons around his bed and he gave them rebuke. After telling Reuvain what he had done wrong he said to him.

> "If you are wondering why I didn't admonish you all of these years. It's because I was afraid that if I did, you would leave me and cling to my brother Aysav."
>
> *Rashi Devarim 1:3*

This Rashi is very difficult to understand. Why would Yaakov be afraid that if he criticized Reuvain, that would cause him to leave the path of Torah? First off, it is difficult to imagine a relationship of love, mutual respect, and dedication that was greater than the one that Yaakov and his oldest son Reuvain shared. Aside from the natural sense of attachment of a son to his father, Reuvain accepted his father as his teacher, mentor, and spiritual guide. Surely, that should have allowed Reuvain to know that his father's rebuke was only for his good.

Furthermore, whenever Yaakov spoke to his son, it was with love and sensitivity. If a situation arose where Yaakov felt his son erred, a mature person like Reuvain would willingly accept words of guidance and correct his ways. Why should Yaakov have been afraid?

Two Gun Crowley

It was 1930s, in NYC, and one of the most notorious gangsters was named Two-Gun Crowley. He was also known as "Crowley the Cop Killer." The police commissioner described him as one of the most ruthless, hardened killers who ever walked the streets, "a man who would kill at the drop of a hat."

"Two-Gun" fired his last bullet in a shoot-out with police while holed up in his apartment on Manhattan's West Ninety-First Street. Surrounded by 150 policemen who used everything from tear gas to machine guns mounted on surrounding rooftops, he managed to hold them at bay for over an hour. More than ten thousand onlookers watched from the streets and surrounding apartment buildings as machine-gun fire turned the area into a battlefield.

Finally, after being shot in the chest, he wrote his last will and testament. In a note drenched in his blood it read:

To whom it may concern:

Under my coat lies a lonely heart, but a good heart, a heart that would do no man harm.

And he signed it!

Only hours before he had been sitting in a car in Central Park. A passing police officer asked him for his license and registration, Two-Gun reached into his coat, pulled out a revolver, and shot the cop dead. He then jumped out of the car, grabbed the officer's service revolver, shot the dead policeman once more for good measure, and drove off. He could just as easily have sped off without shooting the policeman. But he didn't —"a good heart, a heart that would do no man harm."

"Our story doesn't end here. Two-Gun survived the shoot-out. After being wounded he passed out. The police broke through the roof of the apartment and found him unconscious. They arrested him and brought him to the hospital. He recovered from his injuries and stood trial. He was found guilty of murder and was sentenced to death. On his way to the electric chair, he was overheard saying, 'This is what I get for trying to defend myself.'"

What makes this story significant is that Two-Gun Crowley wasn't a deranged psychopath. He was an intelligent sane person. His self-assessment seems to be the standard among criminals. In How to Win Friends, Dale Carnegie writes that he had an ongoing correspondence with the warden of Sing Sing prison, who explained that not one of his inmates was guilty. Every one of them had some reason why he had to be quick on the trigger, or why he had to live a life of crime.

Even more, the viewpoint of most criminals seems to be that: "Everyone would steal. The only reason other people don't is because they're scared, or they just aren't as bold. But believe me, if they were as sharp as me, they would be out there stealing all day long."

This perspective isn't limited to criminals. It's the mindset of everyone. No one thinks of themselves as evil or bad, or even that they do things that are wrong. There is always a reason or a rationale, for what I have done. "This situation is different. The normal rules don't apply to me. Anyone who was in my place would have done the same."

We have an uncanny ability to create entire worldviews, sometimes very whimsical ones, to justify what we have done. Rare is the man who can look you in the eye and say, "I was wrong." Most often what we hear are stories, stories that start with excuses and end with justifications, but always consistent with one theme —I wasn't wrong. I was justified and correct in what I did.' And even if we hear that rare: I was wrong, very soon thereafter comes that caveat, 'But….'

This isn't a quirk or insignificant oddity. It has to do with the nature of man, and the reason HASHEM created us.

We were put on this earth to grow and accomplish, and to be challenged by life. We were given a role to play for a few short years, and when we are done are job on this earth we leave and we will be forever what we shaped ourselves into. We were given the opportunity to shape ourselves, either to be phenomenally great, shining like the sun at midday, or small, insignificant and diminutive or somewhere in between. Every situation in life is a choice we either transcend the trappings and temptations of life, or we crumple up giving in to the passing whims. Who we are for eternity is based on the choices we make.

If man is given credit for his choices, he has to be able to choose either side. Then by choosing one he can be called the one who made himself into what he is. That requires a level playing field with both options viable.

When HASHEM made man, He took a pure brilliant nishama and placed it into a body. The I that thinks, and feels, remembers and desires is made up of both. But here lies the problem. Holy

How do tempt a nishama to sin? It came from the most sublime parts of the universe. It is so perfect it simply won't do something wrong. It would never do something selfish or cruel or mean. It would rebel and scream, 'How could you do that? That's nasty.

You're hurting another human being! What right do you have to put your self-interests before another person's?

And the nishama recognizes that anything that I do changes me. It fully understands that every action, every thought every word I speak creates an indelible imprint on me. I will be forever what I make myself into. Every mitzvah helps me grow, every sin damages me. So even if you put me into a body with drives and appetites, I won't choose something that is destructive to me.' Granted, I would have the *physical ability* to do things that were wrong, but I wouldn't do them.

I don't drink bleach. I won't put my hand in a fire. Even if you offer me a king's ransom, I won't do it. It's self-inflicted damage and it's stupid. So even if the body pulls me towards things, I would never do them, because I recognize that they cause me permanent harm. So how would man have free will?

To allow for free will HASHEM put another feature into man called imagination.

Imagine that

If you remember reading a novel as a child, likely found yourself transported to a time and place you had never been. You might have discovered your long-lost brother, who was a mastermind criminal. Or you found yourself falsely accused, languishing in prison. Or you made a comeback from cancer and went on to compete in the Olympics. But if it was well-written, the experience was vivid and real, and it was *you* –living that story.

It was you living in 17th century, a pirate sailing the seven seas. There you were, out on the ocean with the buck and the sway of the waves, fighting off your enemy as he tried to board your ship. The sun glinting in your eyes, you pulled your sword from its scabbard, prepared for the battle. The enemy boarded your vessel; you dug your feet into the deck, tightening your fist on your sword, ready to pounce. And suddenly, your mother called you to dinner. Gone was the pirate ship, gone was the scabbard and sword, and rudely you were pulled back to reality.

That is an example of imagination at work. Imagination is a powerful tool that HASHEM put into a person for a number of reasons. One of its functions is to make a scene, a time, or an event real. It can bring me to a different time, to a land I never saw, to an experience that I never had, and yet it is me right there. I feel it. I experience it. And in my mind's eye, those events are actually happening to me. I may even have physiological reactions; my heart rate will quicken, my blood pressure will increase, and my palms will begin sweating as I **live** that experience. If you have ever cried when you read a book even though you knew the events in it never happened, that is an example of imagination at work.

Just as it can make fiction seem real, so too it functions in all of our cognitive processes. It paints pictures and tells stories. It can create fantasies and make them seem real. Imagination functions as a balancing agent between our nishama and our wants and desires. And it allows for free will.

Now when man is tempted, he isn't limited to whether its right or wrong, he can conjure up a rational that makes it exactly what he wants it to be. Right. Wrong. Good. Evil. The very way he judges that temptation is subjective. If I desire something, no longer is it something that I know is wrong but want to do anyway. I now have this ability to create — almost by instinct — entire rationales that make it permitted:

Now when my nishama cries out that's wrong. There is a counter voice—I'm not so sure about that. When the nishama says the Torah warns against. The voice says—I don't think this is what the Torah meant.

"For me it's OK."

"Other people do far worse."

"HASHEM understands."

A little mental sleight of hand, and now everything is permitted, everything is OK. And because imagination is so powerful, I can actually believe my own story.

Whatever I wish to choose, my nishama can't stop me because in my creativity, whatever I does is right.

Without imagination man couldn't do wrong. His nishama would never allow him to do something wrong. Now man has free will. Not free will to do what's wrong. Free will to take what he wants and make it right. And now man can actually choose his path in life.

And that's why you'll never find someone doing something wrong. He'll have entire theologies and worldviews that justify his behavior. He'll have excuses, rationales and stories. But no one does anything wrong. They can't. They are too great for that. The only way man can do something wrong is by making it right.

Now we can understand the problem with criticism. When you tell me what I did was wrong there is a voice inside me that says. No! It can't be. It's not true. I can't accept what you are saying. And that voice won't let me accept your words. They make me feel dirty, unworthy. Not pure. And, even if I know what you're saying is true, when I hear you say it it's so much more forceful and I can't help but reject it. I just can't hear it.

But one message that I do hear is disapproval.

The damage of criticism

Not disapproval of what I did—disapproval of me. You may not have intended it that way, but that is what I experience. I perceive your words as an attack. There is a powerful sense of dissatisfaction and condemnation that comes across, and I feel struck. The essence of me, who I am, and what I stand for is being assaulted. And every fiber of my being screams out to defend myself. And if I don't fight back, I am forced to at least pull away. The greater you are in my eyes, the greater the damage of your words, and the more they will drive a wedge between us.

Why Yaakov was afraid to criticize Reuvain

This seems to be why Yaakov was so afraid of criticizing Reuvain. Even though it was for Reuvain's benefit, Yaakov was afraid that it would damage the relationship, and perhaps even going so far as to drive Reuvain away. Despite the fact that Reuvain was looking for direction from his loving father, the sense of disapproval would have been so difficult to bear that Reuvain might well have run away to avoid it, even going so far as joining Aysav.

This is a powerful illustration of the damage of rebuke. Even in a relationship based on mutual love and respect, criticism undoes the bond and causes a separation. Here we see it with a great man whose priorities were straight, a man who lived his whole life to serve HASHEM, and recognized his father as the spiritual guide of the generation. Yet words of rebuke could have had the effect of separating and causing even such a man to go off the path.

If for great people, how much more so for us?

If this concept is true for people as great as the Avos, how much more so for us? The reality is that we humans are very sensitive; we hunger for approval and despise rejection. When you criticize me, it may not be your intention, but I feel unwanted and unaccepted. I feel that you don't approve of me, and surely, I am not respected in your eyes. That emotion is very difficult to bear. The easiest course is for me to run away — away from the situation, and away from you. The more I value your opinion, the more hurt I will feel, and the more those words will cause me to want to escape your presence.

Criticism is the universal poisoner of all relationships. As a parent, it is a noxious element that can ruin an otherwise strong relationship. As a sibling it can be the wedge that drives apart a family. And amongst friends, it can be the force that ends an otherwise nurturing relationship.

The strange part is that we have this fantasy that all I have to do is point out what you've done wrong, and immediately you'll stop, and everything will be right again. But it never works. All it does is hurts you, deepens the problem and drives us apart.

3 rules of criticism

For that reason, before you criticize *anyone*, remember the three rules of criticism.

- Rule 1—Don't do it.
- Rule 2 – Don't do it.
- Rule 3- Don't do it.

Don't do it because it hurts. Don't do it because it distances people. Most of all, don't do it because it doesn't work.

Even if your intentions are to help, and even if you only mean these words for the good of the recipient, criticism is a powerful separator that accomplishes no good, merely drives people apart, and should be avoided like the plague.

If there is any place to avoid even the slightest hint of criticism it is in marriage.

My wife was cooking, and she asked one of our girls if the soup tasted right. My daughter said, why don't you ask Abba, he's right there?

My wife said, "I'm not going to ask Abba," "He'll never tell me if he thought the food doesn't taste good."

That's true. When my wife prepares something, I would never tell her it's too salty, overdone or doesn't tastes good. Long ago I learnt that when a husband says he thinks the dish is too salty, slightly burned, tastes off, his wife doesn't hear comments about the food. She hears, "I failed. I didn't succeed. I didn't please him. I'm not good enough." He might as well say the words: youre fat and ugly. He certainly didn't mean anything hurtful, but that's likely how she'll hear it.

And so if you would like to have a happy marriage, avoid any hint, suggestion, insinuation, allusion, reference, trace or nuance, of criticism. (In any shade, flavor or tint). Criticism is a destructive force to be avoided like Covid 19.

A Single's Perspective

One Friday night I was speaking about *shalom bayis* and a young man, who I never met, followed me out of shul. "I don't get it," he says, "you talk about each trying to be *mevater*, to compromise. Sometimes my way and sometimes her way. Why don't you tell people to be totally *mevater*? Always give in totally. Isn't it obvious that if you give in all the time you'll always have *shalam bayis*?"

"You're single, right?" I said to him.

"Yes. But how did you know?"

"Because," I said, "once you're married, you'll realize that no human being can always just give. I have needs. I have ways of doing things. I may be generous and considerate, but at the end of the day, I'm a person. And so is your spouse. It may be seem nice in theory to always give in, but it's not fair to yourself and it won't work.

Which brings us to one of the great challenges in any marriage: what issues do you bring up and which do you overlook.

As a rule of thumb anything that you could possibly overlook you should overlook. Remember that for every issue that bothers you, I guarantee your spouse has at least one (or many more) that bother them. The more that you are able to forgo, the less the climate will be of demands, the more it will be of giving.

But there will be issues that bother you to the core. You try to ignore them, you try your best to overlook them, but they keep coming up. And you feel you need to express them to your spouse. How do you do that in a way addresses the issue and doesn't damage the relationship? How do you communicate effectively?

Effective communication

Let's start with what effective communicating is not.

It is not:

- Carping
- Complaining
- Fault finding
- Moaning
- Venting
- Expressing
- Kvetching

Those are words that hurt. Words that damage. They damage any relationship, so much more so a marriage.

Communicating is expressing a legitimate need or concern. You wife didn't do this. Your husband did that. I need this. I feel this needs to be taken care of. You have feelings, sensitivities and needs. And as an equal partner in this marriage you need to be able to explain to your partner what it is that you feel isn't being met.

If you're not sure whether you are going to express a criticism or a legitimate expression of a need ask yourself: What do I want this conversation to accomplish? What results am I looking for?

If your goal is to help your spouse grow into a better person, teach them, help them improve, set the record straight, or even up the score, Don't do it. If you do, you will pay the price. You may feel better in the moment, but it won't be for long. For some strange reason your otherwise loving, reasonable spouse will stop being loving and reasonable and will turn bitter and resentful. Almost like you attacked them—which you did.

I wish each person had a sign on them that read: Careful underneath this skin lies a delicate, sensitive heart. Please use words that are soft and sweet otherwise you may damage it.

Should I muzzle myself?

I was dealing with a couple who were having serious problems in their marriage, and we worked out a plan to change the way they related to each other. Then the wife said to me: I feel I can't say anything to him.

"What do you mean?"

"I mean, he goes crazy. Every time I bring up a topic, he just gets angry. Do you mean I just have to muzzle myself? In my own marriage I'm not allowed to express myself?"

"I said; it depends on what you are going to be saying. What type of things do you bring up?"

"I mean every time I criticize him."

If I haven't been clear enough, let me say it: if the issue you want to bring up is criticism—don't do it. It's not helpful. It won't work. It surely, won't bring you closer. All it will do is hurt your spouse and drive you guys apart. It's not what you want.

What is effective communication?

When we discuss communication, it is about a legitimate need, concern or feeling that you feel needs to be addressed. Effective communication is conveying your message in a way that allows your spouse to hear it. You want to express your sentiment in a way that allows your spouse to understand your perspective and doesn't shut them down.

You feel hurt. Or sad. Or unloved. And it's clear your spouse doesn't realize it. You want to share that feeling. You want them to feel what you feel. You want them to be able to climb into your reality and experience it as you do. And you want to make it as easy as possible for your spouse to do that. Anything that creates an obstacle, causes unneeded pain, leaves them feeling small or pushes them away makes it more difficult for them to hear the message and makes that communication less effective.

Here are the 4 rules of effective communication:

Rule 1. Never in the heat of the moment

Your husband said X. Your wife did Y. And you are fuming. Livid is a better way of saying it. How many times have I asked her not to do that? How often did we discuss this already?

If your goal is to get your spouse to recognize your reality this is about the worst time to discuss it. Let's face it, you aren't exactly cool, calm, and collected. In fact, you are pretty heated. And your words are going to reflect what you're feeling. Any time you bring charged emotions into a conversation you are risking shutting down your spouse.

All we have to do is ask what is it going to be like on the receiving end? What is your spouse going to hear? What message are they going to get? In the heat of the moment, your words are going to come out fast and furious, strong and stinging. No matter how carefully you try to say them you have feelings and those feeling are going to come out. What your spouse is going to hear is strong accusations, and naturally they are going to defend themselves.

But it's even worse.

The best way to get really angry

The *Orchas Tzadikim* explains that the best way to get really angry is to speak when you are a little angry. You start out, a bit annoyed, just a little bit ticked and then you express it. As you do you appreciate more and more just how bad it was. And as you go on things build and build. And while you may have started out just mildly upset by the end you are going to be really mad.

So the first rule in communication is not in the heat of the moment. Not when your upset. Not when you first find out and are hurt. Wait for a better time, when things are calm, and then you can gently explain what you want to say.

But no matter how calm you are and no matter how much you gently explain what you're feeling there is another implicit message that always comes across. You messed up. You failed. You aren't competent or worthy or good enough or whatever, but you are lacking. That tone carries an accusation and you start to play the Blame and Shame game—which most of us don't play too well. (At least not on the receiving end.)

To prevent this all you have to do is ask yourself what is my goal? Do I want to put my spouse down? Do I want to blame them? Am I looking to shame them?

Hopefully the answer is no. I want to express a legitimate concern. I was hurt. I was let down. I feel unloved. Those are reasonable feeling and if you express them that way, you will have a much better chance of your message getting across the great divide. Which brings us to the 2nd rule:

Rule 2. Use I statements
It's all about me
If there is any place in your marriage to put yourself first, it's here.

"I feel hurt."

"I feel let down."

"I'm upset."

Those are accurate expressions of what's going on. The problem is that often we get sloppy in our messaging and while we mean I was hurt. It comes out as:

"You hurt me."

"You let me down"

"You're the reason I'm upset."

And while the implication may be the same, the results tend to be very different. A "You" message makes it so much more difficult for your spouse to hear it.

Once the focus is "You" your spouse is going hear "Blame and Shame"

"Here we go again."

"I messed up again."

"Nothing I do is ever good enough."

Almost by definition a sentence that begins with "you" is a complaint or a criticism. "*You* were late." "*You* bounced a check." "*You* don't care." *You* points a finger at your spouse.

A sentence that begins with "I" is communicating. It's not accusatory. "*I* felt embarrassed." "*I* felt stressed."

You can even soften things up more by saying:

"It hurts *me* when *I'm* always late."

"It bothers *me* when *I* see the house is a mess."

Isn't that the same thing as blaming? Not at all. An "I statement" takes focus off of your spouse and puts it squarely on you.

If you are really good at this, you can even apologize – "I'm sorry that I'm so sensitive about being late, but I get embarrassed." You're not kvetching, complaining, or carping. You're bringing up a real issue in a manner that hopefully won't force a self-perpetuating, spiraling-out-of-control fight. When I point a finger at you, I'm saying you are the cause of my pain. No one reacts well to that. We are acutely aware when someone points a finger at us.

Stick to "I statements", and you make it much easier for your spouse to actually receive your message.

Even if you avoid the "You" part, the next obstacle that will prevent your message from getting through is the larger message—a lack of approval. We're all bright enough to realize what happened:

I caused you pain

I hurt you

Meaning:

I messed up

I failed you

By nature, we crave acceptance and approval. Especially by someone who looms so large in our life. When you point out something I did that hurt you, no matter how diplomatic you are I can't help but feel I let you down. I failed you. You were expecting better, and I didn't live up to your expectations. And you aren't pleased with me. But this is the key—it's not what I did, it's me that you're not pleased with. And that is a very hard message for a spouse to hear.

I hope that is the furthest thing from what you mean to say, but that is the message that your spouse will hear. So to avoid this we come to rule 3.

#3: Compliments First

Rule three: Any expression of displeasure has to be preceded by at least one sincere, real compliment. (Preferably a lot more than one).

Before you explain to your wife what bothers you, or what she did that hurt you, first explain how much you appreciate her -- how she always takes care of the house and the kids and how happy you are that you found her. After at least one sincere, real compliment, you can add the line, "There's only one little thing. I feel hurt when I open the bank statement and we have an overdraft charge. Maybe I'm too sensitive. I know money's not everything, but I feel hurt."

When you express it that way it's legitimate. You're bringing up a real issue and not acting angrily or offensively. You're not pointing the finger. You're not begging for an angry reaction. And you are sending a larger message, that I accept you, I respect you. I love you. We have something that I feels needs attention, but you're good—we're good.

It doesn't work

A young man once said to me, "Rabbi, I tried your method, and it doesn't work. "She still ends up just as hurt."

I asked him what he meant.

He explained. "Since I heard you speak about this, any time I have something negative to say, I precede it with a compliment. And right way she says: "What did I do wrong now?' Sorry, Rabbi, your trick just doesn't work.

He defined it well. If the only time you say nice things to your spouse is when you have a complaint, it won't go over very well. And if you use this as a trick, or a gimmick to get away with criticizing your spouse, it's not going to work. If you have an occasional real complaint and you start with a compliment it makes it much easier to listen to. If the only time your spouse hears a compliment is when you are about to critique her, we have a problem.

Complimenting your spouse is part of a successful marriage. You should do it all the time. Don't save your compliments only for moments of criticism. Complimenting, praising and expressing appreciation should be a part of the normal give-and-take in your marriage.

So the rule is compliment all the time, but especially before you bring up a sensitive issue, precede it with a sincere compliment.

But, no matter what you do, please don't violate rule 4.

Start Soft

I used to smoke cigars. It was many years ago, I was younger, and smoking wasn't as taboo as it is now. At the time I was a Rebbi in Rochester, my parents, a'h, lived in Queens and often I would drive in with my wife and kids. I would start out with a big, long cigar and hours later when we arrived my kids would say: "Abba what happened to your big cigar? It's so small. I really enjoyed those cigars. but I stopped. Cold Turkey. And haven't smoked a cigar since. Because one day my wife said to me in her soft, sweet voice: "Please stop smoking. Do it for me, please."

Oooooooh! What a low blow!

Had she said, one "It's not good for your health". Or, "It's bad for the kids to see," Or, "Stop it right now." I'd probably still be smoking today. Yet, it's been almost three decades since I puffed on a cigar. Why? Because she did that underhanded, sneaky thing that women sometimes do, she said softly, "Do it for me, dear, please." (A lot of guys are going to be angry with me for letting their wives into the great secret of how to get their husbands to do things for them.)

And this is probably the most important rule for communication: *start soft.*

Likely the message that you are going to deliver has an edge to it. No matter how you careful you are in saying it, you're telling your spouse you're upset with something they did. And those are tough words to hear. If you start out soft it's not a confrontation. It's not a scolding, you just want to share your feelings. Starting soft, allows you to remember that you guys are best friends, you would do anything for each other, and it makes it much easier for your spouse to be open to what you are sharing.

Putting it together

Let's put it together. What should our Drill Sargent from Chapter 13 have done? She certainly should have asked for help at the time. That normal, that's expected and assuming she asked respectfully, he's a mentch, he would have gotten up and helped. But she would still have another issue to deal with: she was hurt. How can he just sit there? Doesn't he care? That should be dealt with afterwards when things were calm, then she could have addressed the hurt feelings. She could have sat him down and said, "Dovid, I feel so secure that you're always there for us—for me, for the kids. And it means the world to me. I know how hard you work. I see when you come home at the end of the day that you're zonked. I want you to know that I really appreciate everything you do for us. I also want to share with you that sometimes I feel overwhelmed. Like the other night when you came home, and I was in the kitchen. The kids were wrecking the place and I felt the whole burden was on me.

Wow! What a difference those words would have made. He would have to be a pretty big creep not to react well to that approach.

Here's a mnemonic to remember this:

To communicate effectively remember to be N. I. C. E.

> *N. Never in the heat of the moment*
> *I. I Statements only*
> *C. Compliments First*
> *E. Effective communication Starts Soft*

Communication is essential in marriage. Unfortunately, there will be disappointments, let downs and hurt feelings. And there will be times when you will need to convey that. We're only human, and there will be times when things just come out. Your upset. There's a lot going on and before you even think you say something—in the heat of the moment, you start off strong with words that blame. That's part of life. No one's perfect, and no marriage is perfect. But it's important to understand how effective communication works so that when you do have the presence of mind you can use it.

If you follow these rules, hopefully you will be able to share your perspective in a way that your spouse can hear. If you don't, you may find a very peculiar reaction.

Porcupines trying to get through a cold winter

Imagine a family of porcupines, it's winter so they all huddle up together to keep warm. Mom, dad, and babies. And it would all be cute and cozy except that porcupines have needles. Many needles. About 30,000 very sharp needles! And each porcupine can't help but poke the one next to them, so the family huddle doesn't work out so well.

Sometimes couples wonder why they have a tough time getting along. They want the same things in life, they love each other, yet stuff keeps coming up and things spiral out of control. The desire to be close isn't enough. You have to make sure that you aren't sticking barbs out that makes it difficult on your spouse. Knowing what to say and how to say it can do a lot to help take the barb off.

As a relationship needs careful nurturing you also have to be careful not to damage it. You can be a great guy, do all the right things, but just criticize your spouse and you'll find your marriage will deteriorate very rapidly. And it doesn't have to happen too often to do a lot of damage. It creates an overtone of disapproval and it's not easy to forget. You may say: "What's the big deal?" I was only saying it for her good. But to your spouse they are words that damage. Do it a few times too many, and you might just find that you're your spouse becomes a very different person than the one you married. Do it a few more times after that and you might find yourself in a place you don't want to be. Learning to overlook things isn't easy, but it's a life skill that is needed in all relationships but especially in the closest of all relationships. And if you do need to say something please remember inside that other person is a soft, vulnerable heart.

Chapter 17

Closing Thoughts

A Final Recap

The first thing that a husband and wife need to know is that marriage is the most beautiful, meaningful fulfilling relationship in the world. It is the completion of both people—but it takes work to make it work—a lot of work.

The main force driving is the knowledge that HASHEM doesn't make mistakes. HASHEM chose the ideal partner for me. It may take a bit to grow into things, but together you grow.

On a day to day basis what holds the marriage together is love—love is the glue of marriage. But love doesn't mean "Romantic love" as potrayed by popular culture. Love means caring, feeling responsible wanting the best for this person. Learning to love another doesn't just happen.

HASHEM gave us tools that bond. They have to be used properly throughout a marriage. As Rav Pam, zt'l used to say "The courtship has to continue." They have to continue nurturing it. They have to continue being there for each other, and they have to spend time together as a couple. Spend a lot of time speaking. As the Chazon Ish tells us, communication is essential. It's more natural to a woman than to a man, but both have to participate.

Arguably the most difficult part of creating a vibrant loving marriage—is learning to live together. Learning to live with another person sounds a whole lot easier than it is. We each have our indosyncies and ways of doing things, and making room for another person to have a way that is different than mine and is still legitimate doesn't come naturally.

You have to avoid the negative as well. Beware of the love busters, the things that take the air out of the balloon: criticism, disrespect, selfish demands, annoying habits and angry outbursts. And while you understand that you have to change those things that bother your spouse, you also have to understand that it's unlikely your spouse is going to change them anytime soon. Just as you have flaws that bother your spouse even though they don't bother you, so too your spouse has flaws. You can communicate, you can let him or her know, but at a certain point you have to accept them for who they are.

Remember that there are vast differences between you and your spouse. That means that as a husband you have to validate your wife. You have to listen to her. You have to pay careful attention to her emotions. She's not criticizing you when she's complaining and venting. She's not blaming you for the fact that her boss is too tough or the situation is rough. It's not a condemnation of you. She's just trying to share.

As a wife, you have to recognize that your husband doesn't need fixing -- and if he does, you'd better not be the one to do it. Just as love is the most important thing to you, respect is the most important thing to him. Love is very important to him, but if he doesn't feel respected his feelings of love aren't going to blossom. They going to be strained.

Learn that you're different. Don't be dismissive and don't assume that only you know the right way. Instead, train your tongue to say, "That's strange. Why did my spouse react that way?" Then you won't fall prey to what so many of us do: become judgmental. You'll find that spouses have pictures of each other that no one else shares. She doesn't see the real him. She sees what she expects to see.

At the same time, learn to be appreciative of your spouse. Recognize all that he or she does. Is appreciation natural? No, it takes training. We have to train ourselves to recognize the advantages of our spouses. *Baruch* Hashem, He gave you the right person. "But he's not perfect!" That's right. And neither are you. He meets your needs and you meet his needs. Train yourself to see his positive attributes, and not his flaws, which are the more natural thing to see.

Probably more than anything, you have to understand the nature of the relationship of marriage. Marriage means that you are best friends forever, *reyim ahuvim*, friends who love one another. Friends are tolerant and accepting. Friends overlook flaws. Friends enjoy life together. Friends don't boss each other around or criticize each other. Friends don't act like intolerant people.

The relationship requires protecting. It's going to have tough moments. G-d willing, you'll have a lot of beautiful times together, but there are going to be times when you're hurt and angry. You will probably fight. In your heart, you're going to desire to get even. Resisting that is one of the great challenges of life.

Marriage isn't easy. But Hashem gave us this laboratory for growth called life. He gave us many opportunities to be challenged, and one of the great test of life is to be successfully married. It requires changing and growing. It sometimes requires holding your tongue and overlooking things. Many times, it requires saying the words, "I was wrong. I'm sorry."

Rabbi Akiva Eiger

In an *igeress,* Rabbi Akiva Eiger writes something amazing. After his wife passed away someone suggested a prospective match. Here's a loose translation of how he responded:

> *How can I answer you? All my senses are confused. I can't concentrate on anything. How can I forget the love of my wife, the wife of my youth, my pure dove, who* Hashem *blessed me with? We produced wonderful children together. She raised them to Torah,* yerei shomayim. *She supported my every effort. She cared for my health and wellness. Who shall I share my worries with and receive comfort? Who will look after and care for me?*

Absorb that for a moment before reading the next thing he wrote.

> *As you can tell, I'm a broken man in a dark world. I have lost all pleasure. I accept* Hashem's *decree, but I cannot answer any questions now. The tears make me unable to read. I did everything in my power to care for my wife and keep her alive. Now I am too weak and in grave danger. I am unable to eat. I can barely keep anything down. I can't sleep. I can't daven without distraction. I can barely learn.*

Those are the words of one of the greatest human beings of his generation, one of the greatest *talmidei chachamim* on any recent generation. Rabbi Akiva Eiger! He says he can't make *berachos* properly. He can't learn. He is broken – because his wife is gone.

When you find great people that's the type of marriage you find. When you peer into the lives of *gedolim* you see the love. It's not publicly displayed; there are no public displays of emotion.

But when you dig deeper you see the attachment, the bond, the love – and you understand what a marriage really is.

Hashem made for you a match in heaven. It's the most beautiful relationship in existence. When a husband and wife are together, it's beautiful, enriching and empowering. Each one cherishes the other. Each one is there for the other. It's the closest relationship that exists. But it requires work and change.

Never stop *davening*. May Hashem help you have a beautiful, successful marriage. May He grant you only *nachas, mazal* and *berachah*. May you find, from now on, tremendous Divine Assistance.

SPONSORSHIPS

Town & Country
PEDIATRICS AND FAMILY MEDICINE, PC

www.doctorsct.net

Dr. Ephraim Bartfeld • Dr. Jacqueline Lustig • and Associates

| 380 Main St.
Watertown, CT
06795 | Mon-Thur 8am-8pm
Fri 8am-4pm
Sun 8am-2pm | 205 Columbia Blvd.
Waterbury, CT
06710 |

Tel: (860) 274-8891

In great gratitude with anavah for the hatzlachot of Tiferes Bnei Torah and Shmuz, I am profoundly dedicating the wisdom from this book to all those that truly seek Hashem's face or direction as it relates to the machinations of a fruitful union. This sefer gives us hope and inspiration when it comes to the area of shidduchim. We know that in the beginning Hashem's intention for the creation of the first power couple Adam and Eve, was "it is not good for man to be alone", as our great Sages, Rabbi Akiva said as much in (Sotah 17b), keying off of the Hebrew words for husband (איש) and wife (אשה), which combine to form the words, "fire" (אש) and "G-d" (י-ה).

"Husband and wife, if they are meritorious, the divine presence (Shechinah) dwells among them. If they are not, a fire consumes them." The Holy Zohar (I 91a) teaches us that marriage isn't just a guy and a girl brought together by happenstance, but rather "a husband and wife are one soul, separated only through their descent to this world. When they are married, they are reunited again."

In conclusion, we also pray to share from the zechus of all the good works and happy marriages that Rabbi Shafier has been part of over the years.

Peter Oseghale & Family

לזכר נשמת חיים בן ר' טובי-ה גדלי-ה

חו-ה פייגה בת ר' שמעי-ה

To my wife Pam (Tirzah bas Chana)
My partner, my rudder, my friend, my love. For all you've done for me, and for everything you do for our family.
Thank you for writing to me

Refuah Shleima for my bride of over 54 years, Leslie A. Lowenstein (Liba Chana bat Mindl)

In gratitude for Tiferes Bnai Torah and Shmuz

In loving memory of:
R' Chaim Baruch ben Binyamin
Esther Hinda bas Michael
Avraham ben Baruch
Leah bas Shimon
Shmuel ben Shimon
Miriam Chava bas Chaim Baruch
Basha Devorah bas Chaim Yaakov
By Carolyn & Barry Stein & Family

Mazal Tov and Hatzlacha Raba to Rabbi Shafier and to the entire Shmuz organization. May you continue to bring such helpful tools Klal Yisrael!
Shimon and Atara Lobel

ECG RESOURCES

WEALTH
MANAGEMENT
EXECUTIVE
SEARCH

This book is dedicated by Herschel Chomsky in memory of my dear beloved parents Rabbi Aaron and Rebbetzin Lillian Chomsky

---

To have the zechus of all the happy marriages Rabbi Shafier is a part of.

To my אשת חיל, Yonat,

May Hashem guide us to follow the advice in this book, that we may be זוכה to many more years of שלום בית, health and happiness, and נחת from our children.

Your loving husband,
Laizer

לע"נ הב' יוסף ע"ה בן יצחק פרץ נ"י
כ"ה תמוז תשס"ד לפ"ק
לע"נ דוד בן עקיבא צבי ע"ה
י"ד מרחשון תשע"ט לפ"ק
לע"נ משה דוב בן אלעזר ע"ה
י"ז אב תשע"ט לפ"ק

(לא הניחו אחריהם זרע של קיימא)

In Memory of Gedalya ben Yehuda,
May his soul have an aliya.

This book is dedicated by Rafael Elazar in honor of my mother, מלכה, Margarita Elazar, the most generous person that I know in the world.

In memory of Klonimus Kalman ben Moshe Aharon
and Leah bas Yechiel Michel   לעלוי נשמת קלונימוס קלמן בן משה אהרן ולאה בת יחיאל מיכל

May Hashem bless our children to find their soulmates.
Shawn and Shoshana Couzens

Dedicated by Larry and Jackie Shafron
Dallas, TX

לע"נ

חיים יום טוב בן משולם

רבקה פעריל בת מרדכי

דב בן דב

Dedicated by Robert Lazarus in memory of Aharon ben Yosef Dov

---

Dedicated by Abe Gluck

This book is dedicated by Avi and Rivky Pruzansky לע"נ ר' אהרן יעקב בן חיים נחמן Rosenberg

Made in the USA
Middletown, DE
12 March 2021